BIBLICAL
PERSONALITIES
AND
ARCHAEOLOGY

BIBLICAL PERSONALITIES AND ARCHAEOLOGY

Leah Bronner

KETER PUBLISHING HOUSE JERUSALEM LTD.

Contents

v

Preface

Every year brings new discoveries from the lands of the Bible, thanks to the work of archaeologists. Whereas the archaeologist gives the facts only, it is the task of the Biblical scholar to interpret the archaeological finds in their relation to Biblical studies. While there are already many excellent books on archaeology and the Bible, new discoveries call for a closer investigation. Discoveries made a few decades ago can be interpreted afresh in the light of the new data that have been forthcoming.

This book tries to give the teacher, student, and interested layman an idea of what the new facts have revealed. It follows the sequence of Biblical history, and concentrates on some of the most important personalities who have left their imprint on the saga of Israel. It is based on a study of the publications of archaeologists, and the personal impressions the author received from her frequent visits to digs in the Holy Land, and archaeological collections to be found both there and in other parts of the world.

The notes are intended to guide the reader to the more specialized literature on the subject.

The author expresses her sincere thanks to archaeologists and museum personnel everywhere in the world for their unselfish efforts to promote our knowledge of ancient times. As a result of their patient work the Bible has acquired a new relevance for the present age.

CHAPTER ONE

Introduction

Archaeology has a great fascination for most people. It is thrilling to dig and see the spade unearth the secrets of the past. Biblical archaeology has fired the imagination of men and women throughout the ages, and they have flocked to the Holy Land to discover the sites where the heroes of the Bible lived their lives. Even in modern times the stream of pilgrims has not abated. Jews, Christians, and Moslems continue to visit the land of the Bible in ever growing numbers. This interest in the Bible is understandable as it is the bedrock of Western civilization. One of the surprises of modern archaeological discoveries has been that the peripheral lands of Meso-

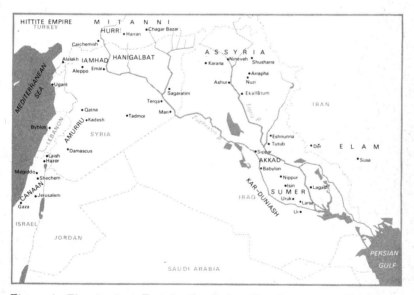

Figure 1. The Ancient East in the 2nd millennium B.C.E. Borders of modern states are in gray.

1

potamia, Egypt, Syria, and Anatolia have greatly added to Biblical knowledge. From each of these neighboring countries have come written documents and monuments of great importance for the understanding of the life, literature, and history of the peoples who once dwelt in Palestine. I shall endeavor to illustrate in this book how history, as treated in the Bible, has been greatly enlarged by the past century of archaeological investigation.

First, let us ask ourselves — what is the aim and what are the methods of archaeology in general, and Biblical archaeology in particular? The term archaeology is derived from the two Greek words *archaios,* meaning ancient, and *logos,* meaning knowledge. Archaeology is the study of past civilizations through their material remains. To begin with, archaeology is not an end in itself, not just an abstract study. It is the method of finding out about the past of the human race in all its material aspects and the study of the products of this past — the way people lived, the way they worshiped, the way they built, their art, their trade, their travels. All these aspects are of course also studied by historians. But it must be pointed out that historians are primarily concerned with written records, while archaeologists deal with the solid material remains of civilizations. It studies very closely the objects man used and made, his dwelling places and defense structures, his tools and weapons, the remains of his food, his own bones and burial places. From these he deduces how he lived. Archaeologists work like detectives and treat the artifacts they find as clues to the lives of the people who made and used them. Archaeologists may make exciting new discoveries such as Egyptian tombs filled with gold, as was the case with the Tutankhamon discovery by Carter in 1922. But a few grains of hardened corn from a buried cave in Palestine may reveal more about the life of men in that country than all the treasures of the pyramids.

Archaeology today is a well-developed science. The archaeologist needs the help of many kinds of scientists to carry on his work. Geologists tell him about the earth structure at different periods. Botanists trace ancient plant life for him. Zoologists identify animals. Petrologists and mineralogists supply information about stones and other minerals used for implements and weapons. Chemists and physicists help discover what things were made of and contribute new methods of dating and preserving archaeological finds and discoveries.

Archaeology is also considered a branch of anthropology, and other branches of this science also help the archaeologist. Physical anthropologists identify the faces of early men from parts of their skeletons. Cultural, or social, anthropologists help figure out the religious beliefs, social organization, and other customs of ancient peoples.

Biblical archaeology is a special branch of general archaeology. The Biblical archaeologist may or may not himself dig, but he studies closely the discoveries resulting from the numerous excavations taking place which touch on the Bible, and he endeavors to glean from them every fact that throws a direct or indirect light on Scripture. The Biblical archaeologist must be fully at home with stratigraphy and typology, upon which the methodology of modern archaeology rests and of which more will be said later in this chapter. Yet his chief concern is not with techniques or pots or weapons in themselves. His central and absorbing interest is the understanding and exposition of the Scriptures. For there are two sides to archaeology — digging and deciphering. The Biblical archaeologist may excavate, but his major concern is to study the results of excavations and help interpret them and see what light they can shed on his understanding of the Bible.

The exciting story of Biblical archaeology has been narrated in many books. Yet it will not be out of place to name a few of the epoch-making discoveries in the history of this discipline. One may begin with the discovery of the Rosetta stone in Egypt by Napoleon's men. The engineer Bouchard and his companions who discovered the stone immediately sensed that they had hit upon something of great moment. They proved correct. The Rosetta stone, which has three different scripts inscribed on it, namely hieroglyphic, demotic, and Greek, was the epoch-making find which made Egyptian records available to Western man. It was the Greek inscription which made possible the decipherment of the hieroglyphic characters, the old picture writing which was used from the earliest times for nearly all state and ceremonial documents that were intended to be seen by the public, and the demotic characters, a cursive and abbreviated form of the hieratic script which was a later development of the hieroglyphs. It came into use in the 7th century B.C.E. and was the prevailing script in the Ptolemaic period. The hieroglyphic text consists of 14 lines only, and these correspond to the last 28 lines of the Greek text. The demotic text consists of 32 lines, the first 14 being imperfect at the beginnings; the Greek text consists of 54 lines, the last 26 being imperfect at the ends. It was Champollion who correctly deciphered the writing on this stone and thus supplied the master key to unlock the secrets of the records of ancient Egypt. The Rosetta stone is one of the prized possessions of the British Museum.

The next landmark in the field of Biblical archaeology was the dis-

Figure 2.   Excerpts from the Sumerian king list (column1) dating to the 2nd millennium B.C.E. It resembles the Biblical "Book of Generations of Adam" (Genesis 5) and the tradition of the Flood (Genesis 6).

covery of the Behistun rock in Iran. The Englishman Rawlinson risked life itself in order to scale the rock and transcribe part of the inscription. International political friction forced Rawlinson to leave the country before he finished his work. Eventually he returned and this time he was able to transcribe and decipher the inscription on the Behistun rock. The writing on the stone described in three languages — Old Persian, Elamite and Babylonian — the triumph of Darius the Great over all enemies in revolt against him; Rawlinson's work proved to be the master key which revealed the secrets of the Assyrian and Babylonian literatures, which have an important bearing on Biblical events.

These discoveries were eventually followed by numerous others in different countries of the Near East. In 1887 the Amarna tablets were found accidentally by a woman digging in the southern part of Egypt. They are the only cuneiform tablets found on Egyptian soil. The year 1902 witnessed the discovery of the code of Hammurapi. Since then many other sizeable collections of laws have been discovered in the Ancient Near East. We shall discuss these in a later chapter.[1] The Ugaritic texts were discovered in 1929, and they broadened our understanding of the gods and religion of Canaan before the coming of the Israelites. These were followed by discoveries at Nuzi, Mari, and the Dead Sea. Some of these finds were the result of planned excavations while others, as in the case of the Dead Sea Scrolls, were the result of sheer chance. It was the decipherment of the various ancient languages that gave Biblical archaeology a new significance and led to an intensified search for more written material.

In the first stages of archaeological research, the excavators were merely looking for museum pieces, especially sculptures and reliefs. Chiera, in his interesting book *They Wrote on Clay,* tells us that whenever he led visitors through the Oriental Institute of Chicago, which houses a large quantity of relics of the Assyrian world, he found that they were always dazzled by the huge bulls, the massive stone reliefs that he had brought back from the palaces of the Assyrian kings. When they turned to enter the room containing the ancient clay tablets, most of them seemed uninterested and anxious to move on to more spectacular finds. Chiera always tried to impress upon the visitors to the archaeological museum that the most interesting material was to be found in the writing room where the cuneiform tablets are stored. He felt that here lay the key with which to unravel the riddles of past civilizations. These writings open up the secrets of the diaries of the past. Museum pieces of towering sizes and precious metals indeed dazzle the layman, but the archaeologist knows that it is the dull-looking clay tablets that communicate the most exciting information about how the people in the ancient world lived and what they thought about God, man, and history.

Methods of excavation have improved greatly in the last few decades. It was H. Schliemann who looked for Homeric Troy and discovered the true nature and importance of mounds. Throughout the Near East one sees curious earthen formations in the general shape of a rounded hill or truncated cone. These are the remains of ruined cities called in Hebrew *tel* and in Arabic *tell*. The archaeologist excavates these mounds and makes a careful study of each stratum. This is known as stratigraphy. Typology is the science which concerns itself with the study of artifacts, especially the pottery found on each level of the mound. These finds enable excavators to relate stratum to pottery and thus arrive at the date of the specific level. In other words, typology and stratigraphy are the alphabet of archaeology.

It was Flinders Petrie who demonstrated the importance of typology especially for digging in the Land of Israel. In countries like Egypt and Assyria, where one finds the ruins of magnificent palaces and tombs which are adorned with reliefs and inscriptions, the chronological problem is less acute. For these inscriptions indicate to which period of history these finds belong. But in a poor country like Palestine, where palaces were indeed rare and even inscriptions very few, it is the science of typology and stratigraphy that enables the dating of ruins.

The science of Palestinian archaeology was born with the arrival of Flinders Petrie in that country in 1890. He began to dig at a mound called by the Arabs Tell el-Hesy, where there was an abundance of ancient pottery, a site which he felt was therefore worth a dozen other places put together. Although Petrie mistakenly thought it was the ancient site of Lachish, it now seems likely that it was the Biblical Eglon. He was the first to stress that the importance of excavation in Palestine cannot be measured in terms of museum pieces. The great discovery was the demonstration by Petrie that the history of ancient Palestine was written in the forms and shapes of broken fragments of pottery. It was he who established the need for scrupulous and accurate recording of every scrap of evidence found on a dig. His publication of the results of his digging at Tell el-Hesy has five large plates of drawings of pottery, each piece carefully marked with the depth at which it was found. The observation that certain types of pottery belong to certain layers of occupation, and the dating of these strata by the presence of objects whose age was known, cleared the way for determining the chronology of ancient Palestine. Flinders Petrie made the famous statement: "Once settle the pottery of a country, and the key is in our hands for all future explorations. A simple glance at a mound of ruins, even without dismounting, will show as much to anyone who knows the styles of pottery, as weeks of work may reveal to a beginner."[2]

This trustworthy standard has been checked, revised, and improved since Petrie by leading archaeologists such as W.F. Albright, K. Kenyon, R. Amiran, and many others. In Amiran's book, entitled *The Ancient Pottery of the Holy Land*, she writes: "In 1890 Petrie conducted the first excavation of a tell in this country, after accumulating much knowledge and experience in ten years of digging in Egypt. While working at Tell el-Hesy, Petrie recognized the chronological value of potsherds in stratigraphical excavation and established a basic scale of dated shards. Every field or desk-work undertaken since then has contributed to the steady progress being made in the study of pottery and other aspects of archaeology as well."[3] It was Petrie's discovery of the value of pottery as an index to chronology, the essential alphabet of archaeology, which more than anything else justly earned for him the title given to him by the great American archaeologist Albright — "The Revered Nestor of Archaeologists."

Pottery is a very sensitive product of human inventive power. Though the potter's craft serves the needs of everyday life, it reflects all the changes which political events and artistic trends bring about in the progress of humanity. A brief glance at a chart indicating the different shapes of pottery from earliest times until, let us say, the Hellenistic period illustrates even to the untrained eye of the layman how quickly pottery styles change.[4] Thus, these artifacts play a most important role in sequence dating.

Today archaeology has become an exceedingly careful and meticulous study. The science of Palestinian topography was begun by E. Robinson who undertook his epoch-making trips to the Land of the Bible (1837, 1852), in the course of which he improved existing maps and located hundreds of modern sites there. However, since his days the science has been greatly improved and perfected and the serious student can find numerous excellent books to guide him in this field.[5] The archaeologist now is expected to undertake his work with an adequate staff; it is no longer a random treasure-hunt. The excavating team is provided with all necessary equipment such as surveying instruments, photographic apparatus, drawing tools, hoes, sieves, and other necessary material. Many photographs are taken to show the exact appearance of the ruins as they are cleared, and especially to record the relation of objects to one another as well as to the entire dig. The drawings and photographs that are prepared by the excavating team enable scholars who have not participated in the excavation to understand and identify it and then to get down to the difficult task of interpreting the finds.

As soon as a discovery is made the task of interpretation arises. It is the duty of the Biblical scholar to study the finds and endeavor to explain their significance for Biblical studies. Needless to say, there will always be differences of opinion concerning the material discovered. It is accordingly undesirable to be too dogmatic about archaeology. As in other spheres of study, whether it be history or literature, there are large gaps in the material available, with the result that divergent opinions are often held by experts. This is more true in the field of archaeology than in other disciplines, for the material available for study is often fragmentary. The scholars study the internal evidence of the Bible and the external evidence of archaeology. Both are interpreted and re-interpreted. However, different scholars still arrive at different opinions concerning problems which are of central importance to the study of Scripture. As an example, we might cite the different views that have been advanced for the date of the Patriarchs. There is still no unanimity on the date of this period.

With the assistance of the above-described methods, archaeology is able to reconstruct the ancient world. For archaeology aims at recreating the material world of the Biblical heroes. To cite an example from II Kings: We are told there that the Shunammite woman prepared for Elisha a little room where he could lodge when he visited that part of the country. It is written: "Let us make a little chamber, I pray thee, and let us set for him there a bed and a table, and a stool, and a candlestick; and it shall be, when he cometh to us that he shall turn in thither."[6] It is the task of archaeology to try to reconstruct what such a chamber and its furnishings looked like. This gives us the nature of the physical environment in which the people of the Bible worked, walked, lived, and thought.

Archaeology is also interested in the political, cultural, and religious history of the times, because these events influenced the thinking of the people. Being a science that deals with the material remains of civilization, it brings back the objects of religious worship, such as altars, idols, lamps, and temples. But it cannot bring back the life of the soul, or all the spiritual values associated with it. However, if you can reconstruct the physical environment, the spiritual teachings become more acceptable and feasible. Thus, archaeology can bring back the world of Abraham, Isaac, and Jacob. It cannot bring back the moment God spoke to Abraham. This was, and will always be, a matter of faith. But archaeology gives us greater confidence in the encounter of God with man, because now at least we can visualize that world because of recent archaeological discoveries.

Let us cite a few concrete examples to illustrate what archaeology has done. The Bible tells us that the Assyrians captured Samaria.[7] Cuneiform texts tell us the same thing.[8] Again, the Bible declared that when Sennacherib tried to conquer Jerusalem, God protected the city and the invading army was destroyed through Divine intervention.[9] From Sennacherib's own account we know that he attacked Jerusalem. In the Taylor Prism he claimed that he locked up Hezekiah, the Jew, "as a caged bird in his royal city Jerusalem." [10] Though the text continues to describe all that Hezekiah had to pay to the king, it never claimed that he conquered the city of Jerusalem. Thus, one can state that these texts corroborate the Bible.

Another direct contact between the Bible and archaeological finds is the Moabite stone. The inscription on this stone refers to the triumph of Mesha, the son of Chemosh, king of Moab, whose father reigned over that country for 30 years. He tells us he threw off the yoke of Israel and honored his god by building an altar to him. Part of the inscription on the stone reads as follows: "As for Omri, King of Israel, he humbled Moab for many years. For Chemosh was angry at his land. And his son followed him and said, 'I will humble Moab.' In time he spoke thus but I triumphed over him and over his house, while Israel has perished forever. Now Omri had occupied the land of Medeba and Israel had dwelt there in his time and half the time of his son [Ahab], forty years; but Chemosh dwelt there in my time." [11] This account seems to imply that Mesha broke free from Israel before Ahab's death. It thus appears to clash with II Kings i:1, where it is written: "Then Moab rebelled against Israel after the death of Ahab." [12] There is no contradiction, however, for during the last years of Ahab's life he was hardpressed by the Syrian wars and probably lost control over Moab. From Mesha's point of view his freedom dated from then, but as far as Israel was concerned Moab could not be regarded as free until after the abortive campaign conducted by Ahab's son Joram described in II Kings iii.

On the other hand, the Assyrian king Shalmaneser, on his Black Obelisk, presents a picture of Jehu paying him homage and bringing him presents. That episode is not to be found in the Bible.[13] Are we to conclude then that the Bible is not true? Of course not. The correct interpretation is that the Biblical historian did not find it important for his purpose to mention this incident. He was not concerned primarily with history *per se,* but with ethical and religious truths. Those incidents that he felt would underline these were included; and those that would not were omitted.

The ancient writer of Jewish history, whose work was preserved by the People of Israel and enshrined in the Bible, was interested chiefly in spiritual and ethical attitudes. What interested him was a religious evaluation of the activities of the kings. Thus, of every king it is written whether he did good in the eyes of the Lord or whether he did evil in the eyes of the Lord. Then he adds that "the rest of the doings of this or that king are to be found in the records of the kings of Israel or Judah." Political and secular matters did not concern him. The salient fact is that it was not the royal political and military archives that survived but religious history, and it became eternal. We would not even know that royal archives of this nature ever existed, had it not been mentioned incidentally by the spiritual history which ignored most of their content. The historian was a religious historian, whose aim was to demonstrate that evil led to national destruction and righteousness to God's help. The Talmud stresses that only "those prophecies that had a moral message for coming generations were written down."[14] Therefore, events like the one with Jehu, as represented on the Black Obelisk, or even the Battle of Karkar and many others, are not mentioned, for they are not important for the ethical and religious history of mankind.

Often when writing on this subject one finds the layman asking — does archaeology prove or disprove the Bible? Any intelligent student of archaeology knows that is impossible to answer such a question with an outright "yes" or "no." One must be careful when answering such a question. One must clearly define the problem before endeavoring to reply to it. In the sense that the Biblical languages, the life and customs of its people, its history and its conceptions have been illuminated by archaeological discoveries, the scholar believes that such a question can be answered in the affirmative. Biblical literature no longer stems from the chaos of history as though it were a fossil; there is now contemporary evidence to demonstrate its authenticity. The scholar knows that the primary purpose of Biblical archaeology is not to prove but to discover. The vast majority of the digs neither prove nor disprove. They fill in the background and provide the setting for the story. The ultimate aim of the Biblical archaeologist is Truth. Indeed, archaeology has illumined the dark past and has realized the word of the Psalmist that "truth has sprung forth from the earth" to illustrate the living world of the Bible.[15]

NOTES

[1]   Pritchard, J.B. *Ancient Near Eastern Texts (ANET)*, pp. 159ff. The

more correct form for the spelling of Hammurabi is Hammurapi. It is now believed that it comes not from the root *rab* ("mighty"), but from *rafa,* which means "to heal."

[2]   Wright, G.E. *Biblical Archaeology,* 1957, p. 24.

[3]   Amiran, R. *Ancient Pottery of the Holy Land,* 1969, p. 13.

[4]   Consult the chart in Chiera's *They Wrote on Clay,* 1939, pp. 34—35 and in the *Encyclopaedia Judaica,* Vol. I, pp. 221—271.

[5]   Smith, G. *Historical Geography of the Holy Land,* 1894. Glueck, N. *Rivers in the Desert,* 1959; *The Other Side of the Jordan,* 1945.

[6]   II Ki. iv:10.

[7]   II Ki. xvii:3ff.

[8]   Barnett, R.D. *Illustrations of Old Testament History,* 1968, Nimrud Prism iv, 25—41, p. 52.

[9]   II Ki. xix:35; Is.xxxvii:36.

[10]   *ANET,* p. 288.

[11]   *ANET,* p. 320.

[12]   II Ki. iii:5.

[13]   The Black Obelisk is permanently housed in the British Museum. See Chapter Six for more details on the importance of this obelisk.

[14]   *Megillah,* 14a. It is written: "Only the prophecy which contained a lesson for future generations was written down, and that which did not contain such a lesson was not written."

[15]   Ps. lxxxv:12.

CHAPTER TWO

Abraham and His Age

The patriarchal narratives have been greatly illuminated by dramatic
archaeological discoveries. These finds have necessitated a veritable re-
evaluation of the significance of the Bible in general and the patriarchal
age in particular. Until the 18th century, the Bible was universally
accepted as a trustworthy record of antiquity. But when the age of reason
dawned, and in turn gave way to the 19th century philosophy of evolution
and scientific materialism, the Bible, in common with all other records of
antiquity, was considerably discounted as a reliable basis for the reconstruction of ancient history. The epic struggles of the Patriarchs, Abraham,
Isaac, Jacob, and others, were regarded as myth and legend.

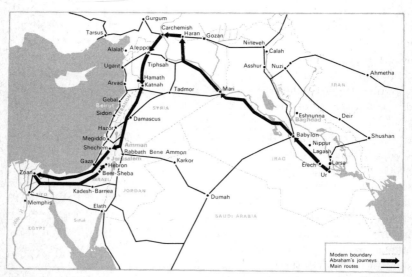

Figure 3. Map showing route of Abraham's wanderings and other main
routes of the Ancient East.

The above attitude toward Biblical personalities was epitomized by Wellhausen. Under the influence of his school of Biblical criticism, it was very common among scholars in the first part of the present century to deny the historicity of the Hebrew Patriarchs. Various theories were advanced to dissolve these Biblical characters into mythical and legendary creations. They were sometimes even viewed as lunar or astral figures, ancient Canaanite divinities, mythical heroes or personifications of clans and tribes, or as fictitious characters in a cycle of legends.[1]

This negative attitude to the Bible is still found, for example, in the writings of the philosopher Bertrand Russell. In his *History of Western Philosophy* he wrote: "The early history of the Israelites cannot be confirmed from any source outside of the Old Testament, and it is impossible to know at what point it ceases to be purely legendary. David and Solomon may be accepted as Kings who probably had a real existence, but at the earliest point at which we come to something certainly historical there are already two kingdoms of Israel and Judah."[2]

The general view accepted among most scholars today, except for some diehards, is that the patriarchal narratives record events that actually took place. They no longer regard the stories as being only symbolic, but as being based on true fact. In other words, prior to those sensational archaeological discoveries, scholars maintained that the patriarchal stories were invented by people who lived in a later age. They claimed that these narratives were retrojections of men who lived in the period of the monarchy. But were the Biblical description of the lives of the Patriarchs a later invention, there would be the greatest difficulty in finding an adequate explanation of its origin — since it does not agree at all with conditions in any part of Palestine from 1200–900 B.C.E., to say nothing of a later period. "Wellhausen and his followers did not even recognize the difficulty, because of their ignorance of modern Palestine and adjoining lands."[3]

Now in the light of the new information gleaned from archaeological sources, scholars accept that they are the reflections of the life of real people who existed in a particular time in history. The contention of many scholars is that the patriarchal narratives took place during the 2nd millennium, that is, anywhere between 2000 and 1500 B.C.E.[4] Thus, the great service archaeological research is performing is to demonstrate that the picture of the Patriarchs as presented in Genesis fits the frame of life in the Middle Bronze Age, that the momentous role they play in the religious story of mankind dovetails into the larger drama of secular history. Today archaeology compels a more general respect for the historical quality of the patriarchal stories.

Figure 4.   Reconstruction of the tower of Babel. After E. Unger.

The Bible describes the journeys of Abraham in some detail. Leaving Ur, he first traveled northwest to the town of Haran, where he lived for a number of years before setting out again to journey to Palestine. What has archaeology to tell us about these routes crossed and the cities inhabited by Abraham? The Genesis stories about Abraham and his descendants are painted in a black and white, simple canvas with no perspective in depth. These stories depict certain individuals and their families who walk through the world almost as if they were alone in it. These stories had a goal. They did not aim to teach history or literature, but religion. They wished to show that God took a family and through them tried to human- ize mankind. This of course is no defect; indeed it is the sole merit of the narratives. Fortunately for the historian and archaeologist, these narratives mention names of people and places, routes and customs, which have enabled scholars to reconstruct the world of Abraham and his descendants.

The most startling evidence about the nature of the patriarchal material has come from excavations of three cities of the Ancient Near East — Ur, Nuzi, and Mari.

The city of Ur was excavated by Woolley, and he revealed its important treasures to the world.[5] He discovered in the cemetery of Ur graves that contained golden daggers, spears, jewelry, and other items which bore witness to the high level of their arts and crafts. The mosaic standard of Ur, with its "war" panel and "peace" panel, is one of the masterpieces of ancient art.

The ziggurat, a temple-tower, was a dominant feature of the ancient city of Ur. It was built from baked clay bricks bonded with bitumen mortar and formed three terraces, each of diminishing size and of a different color. The color blue predominated, and it was crowned by a small temple of gold and silver. Access was by stairways and the upper terraces were decorated with trees and plants. The "hanging gardens" at Babylon may refer to a similar ornamentation of the temple-tower there. The Biblical story of the Tower of Babel[6] must derive from such a "ziggurat" or "skyscraper" edifice.

Thus, the Mesopotamian civilization whence Abraham hailed was cosmopolitan, progressive, and sophisticated. It was most probably the Ur of Hammurapi's time. A common heritage of law and government, which was stabilized by the use of the same script and international language, served to safeguard social gains and facilitate relations among various states of the land. The art of writing was universal — not only as the medium of law, administration, and business, but also as a vehicle for literary and scientific enterprise. In addition to law, outstanding advances were being made in linguistics, history, and business, and in art and architecture. In short, the Ur of Hammurapi and his neighbors was the most advanced land in the world — a vigorous force at home and a magnet to other countries near and far.

Yet it was this glorious center of culture that Abraham chose to leave in order to turn towards an unknown destination. What motivated him to this course of action? According to Genesis it was the call from the Deity. The same tradition tells us about his connection with Ur and that he abandoned it for a spiritual quest. The Bible seems specially concerned to stress that Abraham came from Ur. Thus, it is written: "Terah took Abram his son and Lot the son of Haran, his grandson, and Sarai his daughter-in-law, his son Abram's wife, and they went forth together into the land of Canaan."[7] "And he said to him: 'I am the Lord who brought you out from Ur of the Chaldees, to give you this land to occupy' "[8] " 'Thou art the Lord, the God who chose Abram and brought him out of Ur of the Chaldees and named him Abraham.' "[9] It is traditionally stressed that even though the Patriarchs later seemed to consider northwest Mesopotamia, more precisely the region of Haran, as the cradle of the family, the point of departure remains Ur of the Chaldees.[10] Thus, Abraham emigrated from this famous city of Ur when it was in the heyday of its power and prestige.

The patriarchal narratives show that excellent connections of travel existed between Egypt, Canaan, and Mesopotamia in the Fertile Crescent, as this area is called in our days. Archaeological evidence corroborates these facts. The story discovered about Sinuhe, the Egyptian, illustrates this most graphically. Sinuhe was a high official in the Egyptian government who had to flee his native land for political reasons. After numerous adventures and hardships he reached the country of the east, Syria. Here he met an Amorite chieftain, of the same type as Laban. This sheikh was delighted to see him and made him a member of the tribe by giving him his eldest daughter in marriage. Sinuhe does, however, tell us that in later life he experienced nostalgia for his home country. He made his peace with Pharaoh and returned to the land of Egypt.[11]

A relief from a tomb in Beni Hasan, Egypt, likewise demonstrates the ease of communication that prevailed between the two countries. This relief shows 37 Semites entering the land of Egypt at a time of famine.[12] These two episodes remind us of the fact that Abraham, likewise, in time of hunger turned his gaze to the rich and fertile valley of the Nile. Once again, owing to modern discoveries, we see how well the Biblical and archaeological dates dovetail. Both illustrate the comings and goings between Egypt and Canaan.

Likewise, the descriptions of the wanderings of Abraham in the land of Canaan have a flavor of authenticity. Abraham is never associated with the northern part of Palestine. He is depicted as roaming in the central mountain range in Palestine from the area of Shechem, south to the Negev. In the mountain country, the Patriarchs were associated with such places as Mamre (Hebron), Bethel, Shechem, and Dothan. Abraham also has links with Jerusalem. It is now known from archaeology that these places existed in the 2nd millennium B.C.E. If these stories had been late creations, this authentic record of occupation in the land could not have been preserved. In later periods of history, the focus of activity is set in different parts of the land.[13]

The city of Nuzi was excavated by Chiera[14] and has yielded a wealth of information about the customs of the days of Abraham and his descendants. The archives at Nuzi are significant for the study of the patriarchal period because the most important political and religious center of the Hurrian people in addition to Nuzi was the city of Haran. The picture of life and customs as it emerges from the Nuzi text would apply equally to life at Haran.

All students of the Bible know that Haran is the most prominent place connected with the origins of Abraham and his family. Here Terah, the father of the Patriarch, and his family settled when they came from Ur. It was in this ancient city of Haran that the Bible tells us that Abraham received the call and set out for the land of Canaan.[15] His relatives stayed on at Haran for many generations. It was to this area that Abraham later sent for a wife for his son Isaac. It was in the vicinity of this city that Jacob spent many years of his life, married, and raised children. The reconstructon of life at Nuzi and Mari was thus bound to illuminate the stories in Genesis. It has done so to a startling degree.

The palace of King Zimri-Lim at Mari was excavated by Parrot and has yielded a rich treasure of information about this period. These excavations have unearthed the diaries of the past, which speak and reveal the secrets of antiquity.[16]

The fact that we now have not only the internal evidence of the Bible but also the external evidence of Ur, Nuzi, and Mari lends authenticity to Biblical history and is of new significance for the critical scholar. Now he has a wealth of external information with which to compare and contrast the Biblical material. The stories no longer protrude as fossils from antiquity but are seen and understood in their proper setting and place in the annals of mankind.

The names of the Patriarchs Abraham and Jacob have, with slight variations in spelling, been discovered at Mari. In the Balikh Valley, south of Haran, the names of certain Patriarchs mentioned in the Bible were

Figure 5. Wall painting in the tomb of Khnum-Hotep III at Beni Hasan, c. 1890 B.C.E. It depicts a caravan of Semitic nomads entering Egypt.

preserved in the designation of sites such as Serug, Peleg, Terah; while Nahor appears in the Mari tablets. It is clear that in the 2nd millennium B.C.E., the names Abraham, Isaac, Jacob, Laban, and Joseph were in common usage. This of course is not to claim that we have identified the Biblical characters. It does nevertheless prove that these people of the Bible lived and belonged to a definite period in history. For these names are never again encountered in the Bible.[17]

The most fascinating information, shedding light on the lives of the Patriarchs, comes from the archives of Nuzi, which describe the customs of those far-off days.[18] For instance, in Genesis,[19] Abraham complained to God that he had no son. The man who is to be his heir is one Eliezer, who apparently was "the elder of his house that ruled over all he had."[20] Thereupon God answered him saying: "This servant shall not inherit thee, but one that shall go out of thy inward parts. He shall inherit thee." The Nuzi tablets explain this in a most original manner. It appeared to be a custom in Nuzi for a couple who were childless to adopt someone as their son. This adopted son was to take care of them in life and death. In return for his service, he inherited the property of the couple. However, the agreement was annulled if a true son was born. Apparently Eliezer was the adopted son of Abraham, but with the birth of Isaac his status was changed, and he was no longer considered the heir.

Marriage in Nuzi appeared to be contracted not only for companionship but also and primarily for assuring progeny. When a woman failed to bear children her husband was supplied with a handmaid. In the light of this the story of Abraham and Sarah, which is found only in the patriarchal narratives and nowhere else in the Bible, becomes intelligible. At times they appeared indeed strange to the Bible student. Sarah, Abraham's wife, once said to him: "Behold now, the Lord has kept me from bearing. Go I pray thee unto my handmaid. Perhaps I shall be built from her."[21] We know now that this was in keeping with the customs of the times. However, when Sarah demanded that Abraham eject Hagar and her son after the birth of Isaac, we find Abraham hesitating. In Nuzi law the wife was expressly forbidden to expel the handmaid's offspring. It is written in one of the texts: "Gilimninu shall not send the handmaids' offspring away."[22] The special emphasis in these sources indicates that this injustice toward the servant girl was often perpetrated.

The Code of Hammurapi states that the son of a concubine, when recognized by the father, is permitted to share in the inheritance.[23] Sarah wanted to take no chances on the inheritance being divided between Isaac and Ishmael, stating: "Drive out this handmaid and her son, for the son of this handmaid shall not inherit along with my son, Isaac."[24]

Figure 6. Two paragraphs from the Code of Hammurapi in cuneiform writing. It deals with the punishment of a man who covets someone else's property.

Abraham only consented to Sarah's demand after a special revelation commanding him: "Everything thy wife Sarah says, hearken to her voice." However, the narrative continues to explain Abraham's action in the Bible. Firstly, God assured him that he would take care of the handmaid and her son, and they would not be left to an uncertain fate in the desert. Likewise, God promised him that through Isaac his line would be continued. God is concerned with Abraham's posterity, with the fulfillment of the divine plan in history. A story that originated in an Ancient Near Eastern social and legal custom is transformed in the Bible into a situation involving moral dilemmas and God's long-range purpose.

Another interesting story in the life of Abraham, which often worried Bible students, was his attempt to ward off personal danger in Egypt by stating that his wife Sarah was his sister.[25] This wife-sister motif occurs only in the Book of Genesis, where it is repeated three times.[26] Recent research once again of the Nuzi archives sheds fascinating new light on this problem. There was an institution, peculiar to Hurrian society, which may be described as "wife-sistership." In other words "sistership" in Nuzi did not necessarily have anything to do with blood ties, for it could indicate a purely legal status. In Hurrian society the bonds of marriage were strongest and most solemn when the wife had simultaneously the juridical status of sister, regardless of actual blood ties. The practice apparently gave the woman, the adopted sister, greater protection and higher social status. In the light of this evidence, it must be assumed that Sarah and Rebecca were both holders of this wife-sister privilege, peculiar to the society where they lived. The patriarchal stories have faithfully recorded this unique institution, and there is thus no attempt at deception.[27]

Marriage practices at Nuzi are paralleled in the Bible stories about Jacob and his wives. In Nuzi a man worked for a period of time for the father of a girl before he could obtain her as his wife. This immediately recalls the stories of Jacob, Rachel, and Leah.

It seems that Laban at first had no male heir, so he adopted Jacob as his son and gave him his daughters, Leah and Rachel, for wives. It was also stipulated by custom that Jacob could not take other wives [28] and Laban accordingly gave each daughter a handmaid.[29] The rule was that, if Laban begot a son in the future, that son was to share in the inheritance and receive the family gods or *teraphim*.

The story of Rachel's theft of her father's *teraphim* is all the more interesting because of the information obtained from Nuzi. This act on Rachel's part disturbed many scholars. Why did Rachel steal her father's gods? The ancient Midrash[30] claimed that she wanted to wean him away from worshiping idols. No one could however explain satisfactorily why she took them and did not destroy them if they were an abomination to her. The Nuzi texts offer a new explanation for her behavior. They appeared to indicate that the person who owned the *teraphim* not only was assured of a successful life but was to become the possessor of the family inheritance. Little wonder that Laban was so upset by the loss of his *teraphim* and accosted Jacob: "Wherefore hast thou stolen my gods?"[31]

The blessings of Biblical characters as, for example, those of the Patriarchs, were taken very seriously in the Bible. Even after Esau's blessing had been extorted from Isaac by Jacob under false pretences, Isaac, though distressed, could not go back on his promise. He said that whoever it was who got the blessing even he shall remain blessed.[32] It was usually impending death which provided the occasion for the bestowing of blessings such as we see in the case of Isaac and Jacob.[33] This respect for deathbed wills was recognized and highly respected in Nuzi as well. In the Nuzi texts a case is quoted where a man Tarmiya won his lawsuit against his brothers who contested his right to take a certain woman by citing the last words of his dying father. Tarmiya reported to the court that his father, sick and dying, had said: "I give Zululishtan to thee as a wife."[34] The oral testament was accepted as valid legal evidence.

The Patriarchs are portrayed as semi-nomads living in tents, wandering up and down Palestine and its borderlands in search of seasonal pasture for their flocks; and on occasion making longer journeys to Egypt or Mesopotamia. They were not true Bedouins, for they never pressed deep into the desert. On the other hand, except for Lot, they did not settle in towns nor did they farm, except possibly in a limited way. They owned no land save for the modest plot purchased for burying their dead.

It is interesting at this juncture to recall Abraham's purchase of the Cave of Machpelah.[35] This passage used to be assigned by critical scholars to a very late date. Yet, as Bright shows, the story of the purchase makes sense only when it is realized that the transaction took place under Hittite law, which linked feudal obligation to ownership of real property rather than to the person.[36] The haggling between Abraham and Ephron reveals such use of legal terminology that is characteristic of Near Eastern court records and gives the tale a truly authentic coloring.[37] The whole episode is very important in terms of the history of the divine promise and fulfillment. The possession of the land was, after all, not the same thing as ownership. The latter had been endowed and was irrevocable. But possession was still far beyond the horizon. The Patriarch Abraham so far has only been a wanderer. It is true that chapter xiv shows him as a prosperous settler who can mobilize on short notice a sizeable army from among his retainers and put an invading horde to rout: "When Abram heard that his kinsman had been taken prisoner, he mustered his retainers, men born in his household, three hundred and eighteen of them . . . he pursued them . . . and brought back all the flocks and herds, and also Lot."[38] He refused to take any of the booty. It is now recognized that this entire narrative is based upon sound fact, but it lies beyond our scope to deal with it in the text. The interested reader should read Speiser, Bright, Albright, and Sarna on its significance.[39] The story still only shows Abraham as an alien in the land. Therefore, the cave purchase is so important. It is the first instance where Abraham actually acquired possession and ownership of a piece of land in Canaan, the first acquisition in Israel's history.

Scholars maintained that the use of the words "camel" and "Philistines" in the Genesis narratives were anachronistic. However, some writers maintain that this is no longer acceptable in the light of the new evidence at hand. While it is true that use of the camel as a regular beast of burden became customary only by the 12th century B.C.E., there can be no doubt that the camel was an important means of transport during the patriarchal period. Thus, an 18th century B.C.E. cuneiform tablet from Alalakh, in northern Syria, contained a list of fodder for domesticated animals in which the camel was specifically mentioned.

When Parrot was excavating Mari, he discovered camel bones in the rooms of a house belonging to the pre-Sargonic era. A relief from Byblos, in Phoenicia, dating back to the 18th century B.C.E., depicted a camel in a kneeling position. Finally, a recently discovered cylinder seal from northern Mesopotamia, dating from the patriarchal era, showed riders seated upon camels.[40]

The same may be said, to a less demonstrable extent, about the allegation that the appearance of Philistines in the patriarchal narratives is also anachronistic. While it is true that a significantly large body of Philistines settled in Palestine in 1187 B.C.E., after being defeated by Ramses III, there are good reasons for believing that Philistines were present in Canaan at a considerably earlier period. However, if the term "Philistines" is extended to include Minoan and other Aegean peoples, they are mentioned in an 18th century B.C.E. Mari tablet, which recorded that a king of Hazor in Palestine sent gifts to Crete. Furthermore, Middle Minoan pottery has been recovered from the seaport of Ugarit, from Hazor, and in Egypt from Abydos and Memphis. A long series of migrations had brought the inhabitants of Caphtor and others to Palestine well in advance of 1600 B.C.E. — so that by the Amarna period the Philistine settlement in Canaan experienced no linguistic difficulties whatever in dealing with the native inhabitants.[41]

The story of the binding of Isaac is perhaps the most soul-shattering event in the life of Abraham. Abraham had waited patiently for an heir. Often it appeared as if the promise of progeny would never be fulfilled. But Abraham continued to believe and hope and the gift of a son was finally granted. But then he is commanded to sacrifice this son to his God. The story has been given various interpretations by Kierkegaard, Reik, Maybaum, and many others.[42] In the light of archaeology, the only interpretation of interest to us here is that this was a protest against human sacrifice. The story proclaims for all times that the God of Israel rejects human sacrifice and demands ethical and moral behavior. This event was but the first of many which Abraham and his descendants were to enact which would eventually change the whole course of human destiny.[43]

Before leaving Abraham, it would be fitting to discuss the creation and flood stories. Many scholars believe that the Patriarchs who hailed from Mesopotamia brought the traditions of the creation and its stories to the land of Canaan. Woolley claimed to have found the relics of the deluge mentioned in the Gilgamesh Epic at Ur.[44]

The Biblical drama in the Book of Genesis begins by describing with true majesty the creation of the world, of man, and his increase on the

Figure 7. Clay plaque from Hafafa (Mesopotamia) showing a god stabbing a monster with twelve horns flanking her head — probably Marduk and Tiamat. Beginning of the 2nd millennium B.C.E.

Figure 8a,b. Silver cup (a) from a tomb of the Middle Bronze I in Samaria Mountains. Its incised decoration (b) was interpreted by Y. Yadin to be a mythological scene from the Enûma elish, portraying the splitting of the body of Tiamat by Marduk.

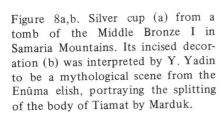

face of the earth, also the judgement of the flood, and the rise of the nations. The first eleven chapters intend briefly to deal with the origin and rise of mankind. It is only in chapter xii, as indicated above, that the story of Abraham and Israel begins. All religions have a cosmogony which is an explanation of how the world and man came into existence. Most of these stories not only describe the origin of the world, but begin by depicting how the gods emerged out of pre-existent chaos, that is, theogony. The Babylonians had many creation stories, the most famous one being known as the Enûma elish, meaning "when on high" after its opening words. The narrative was written down on seven tablets and discovered by Layard and Rassam among a library of clay tablets in the palaces of Sennacherib and Ashurbanipal.[45] It was George Smith, of the British Museum, who had drawn the attention of the world to the flood stories, which also awakened interest in the creation narratives.

The Enûma elish begins with a picture of the earliest imaginable period of primordial time, when only the divine pair Apsu, the fresh water, and Tiamat, the salt water, were in existence. It commences thus:

> When on high the heaven had not been named,
> Firm ground below had not been called by name,
> Naught but primordial Apsu, their begetter,
> And Mummu Tiamat, she who bore them all,
> Their waters commingling as a single body;
> No reed hut had been matted, no marsh land had appeared,
> When no gods whatever had been brought into being,
> Uncalled by name, their destinies undetermined
> Then it was that the gods were formed within them.[46]

It immediately becomes apparent that here as in all polytheistic mythologies creation is always expressed in terms of procreation. Apparently paganism was unable to conceive of any primal creative force other than in terms of sex. More will be said about this later.

The Enûma elish continues to describe that Apsu became annoyed with the younger gods, who were creating a great amount of noise which he could not tolerate. He says:

> By day I find no relief, nor repose at night.
> I will destroy, I will wreck their ways,
> That quiet may restore. Let us have rest.

Tiamat vehemently opposed the plan of her husband, crying out in painful rage:

> What? Should we destroy that which we have built?
> Their ways indeed are most troublesome, but let us
>   attend kindly.[47]

When the young gods learned of Apsu's plan they joined together under the leadership of the god Ea, the wise earth and water god, and planned to destroy Apsu.

> Ea, all-wise, saw through their scheme.
> A master design against it he devised and set up,
> Made artful his spell against it, surpassing and holy.
> He recited it and made it subsist in the deep . . .
> Having fettered Apsu, he slew him.
> Mummu he bound and left behind lock.[48]

This act of violence against her husband enraged Tiamat, the mother, and she determined revenge by a well-planned attack on the younger gods. A large section of the dramatic poem deals with her preparation for war against these deities. In this moment of supreme crisis, a happy thought occurred to the young gods and they appointed the brave and valiant Marduk to take up their cause and destroy Tiamat and her allies. The conflict between Marduk and Tiamat is vividly portrayed.

> While the gods of battle sharpen their weapons
> Then joined issue Tiamat and Marduk, wisest of gods.
> They strove in single combat, locked in battle.[49]

Tiamat's cruel destruction is delineated in great and gory detail. This dramatic triumph of the young hero Marduk over Tiamat and her band of helpers is a prelude to the process of creation. When Marduk had vanquished the host of Tiamat, he turned to the rebellious goddess herself, split her carcass into two halves. The one which he fixed on high was to form a firmament supporting the waters above, and the other he made into the foundation of the earth below. In this grotesque manner the narrative continues to describe the formation of the sun, moon, plants, animals and man. Marduk creates man from the blood of the rebellious god and ally of Tiamat, Kingu. Marduk states:

I will establish a savage, "man" shall be his name.
Verily, savage man I will create.
He shall be charged with the service of the gods
That they might be at ease.[50]

The Enûma elish concludes with Marduk dividing the gods and assigning to each one of them duties to perform in heaven and on earth. This is followed by an epilogue urging the people to study the names of the gods, to hold them in remembrance, and to rejoice in Marduk that it may be well with them.

Another important version of the creation of man and a flood narrative have been made available by the discovery of the Athrahasis epic. This poem contains elements which were already known from the eleventh tablet of Gilgamesh on the one hand and the Enûma elish, on the other, although it was written much earlier than the latter. The Athrahasis epic deals with mankind's sins and their consequent punishment through all kinds of catastrophes, including plagues and a deluge. It is interesting that in this epic man is created to enable the gods to rest.[51]

Other creation fragments with various versions of creation have been found, the most important of which recounts that the gods formed mankind with the blood of certain other gods. In other accounts flesh and blood of a slain god are said to have been mixed with clay to form man.[52]

We have described the Enûma elish in some detail because it must be remembered that the Mesopotamian and Hebrew cosmogonies, each in its own way, express through symbolism the world views and values that animated the civilization that each represents. The opening chapters of the Bible reveal the main pillars upon which the Israelite outlook rested. Whether the Hebrew Genesis account was meant to be science or not is beyond the scope of this discussion. The reader is directed to read Epstein, Hertz, and others for an analysis from this angle.[53] But it was certainly meant to convey a statement of faith. As was mentioned previously, the Patriarchs hailing from Mesopotamia must have been familiar with these Babylonian creation stories, but in the light of their religious experience they took on new spiritual significance for the Israelites. They became, as Kaufmann claims, a polemic against paganism.[54] This God has no myth; there are no stories about any events in His life. He performs no magical acts. The opening chapters of Genesis are but an introduction to the central motif of the Bible, namely, the Exodus from Egypt, and God's acts in history. The Genesis creation narrative is primarily the record of the event which inaugurated the Biblical historical process, and which ensures that there is a divine purpose behind creation that works itself out on the

Figure 9. The Gilgamesh Epic, Tablet XI, dating c. 2000-1800 B.C.E. It gives the Babylonian version of the flood, in cuneiform script.

human scene. The characteristic trends of Mesopotamian society and religion assert themselves in an equally powerful manner in the Enûma elish. It outlines the philosophy of that pagan world.

It is therefore enlightening for the Biblical student to study the points of resemblance and of difference between the Biblical and Babylonian accounts. It is commonly recognized that there are some interesting parallels between the version of creation given in the Babylonian literature, particularly the Enûma elish, and that given in Genesis. Although these similarities are genuine they are too often exaggerated, and erroneous conclusions have frequently been drawn from them. Some resemblances immediately come to light, as for instance the divine origin of the visible world. Both accounts know a time when the earth was waste and void. In both there is an etymological equivalence in the names used to denote the dark watery chaos, which was later separated into heaven and earth. In the Enûma elish it is a proper noun, the mythical personality Tiamat. In Genesis it is *tehom,* a common noun with no mythological connotations, but describing the vast watery mass from which the waters above the firmament were separated on the second day and out of which dry land emerged on the third day.[55] Likewise the word *hivdil,* frequently used in Genesis, reminds us of the splitting of the body of Tiamat by Marduk.[56]

In the Babylonian sources creation is the outcome of a struggle, and some savants wish to connect this with several passages in the Hebrew Bible where references are made to the monsters such as *rahab, leviathan, tannin.* [57]

There is also a Babylonian story which tells about the forming of several beings out of clay, and this has been compared to Genesis, where the creation of man is described as follows: "Then the Lord God formed man from the dust of the ground and breathed into his nostrils the breath of life. Thus the man became a living creature."[58]

On the other hand, there are striking differences between these two accounts of creation. The Babylonian stories are polytheistic; the Biblical account is monotheistic. The former are suffused with a magical spirit. They speak not only of successive generations of gods and goddesses proceeding from Apsu and Tiamat, with all of them in need of physical nourishment, since all consist of matter as well as spirit, but they speak also of different creators. According to the Enûma elish, Apsu and Tiamat are the ancestors of all the Babylonian and Assyrian divinities. These deities in turn personify different cosmic spaces and forces in nature. Apsu and Tiamat are not simply the parents of divine beings having nothing to do with the work of creation; by giving birth to these gods they have a direct share in the actual creation of the universe. The earliest stages of creation are thus ascribed to sexual congress. Apsu and Tiamat represent respectively male and female powers which, through the "commingling of their waters," gave birth to the first generation of gods. The sex element accordingly existed already before the cosmos came into being. All the gods were apparently themselves creatures of sex.

On the other hand, Genesis refers only to one Creator and Maintainer of all things, one God who created and transcends all cosmic matter. There is no trace of a theogony. No events in His personal life are recorded. He has no physical qualities or needs. He is uniquely alone, without a partner or female counterpart. He begets no children.[59]

This myth of the birth of the gods, and their physical relation to the world is found in all civilizations except the Hebrew one. Perhaps the Biblical verse "God created man in his own image; in the image of God he created them; male and female he created them"[60] may be intended as a protest against such a pagan notion.

In the Biblical conception of creation there is no room for an identification between creator and creation. The God of creation is externally existent, removed from all corporeality, and creation comes about through the simple divine word: "Let there be!" The Babylonian sources are ridden with a latent pantheism. The visible world is created out of the body of Tiamat, a divine being — and mankind out of the blood of Kingu.

From what has been said about the nature of Apsu and Tiamat, it is apparent that for the Babylonians matter was eternal. The Babylonians could conceive of a time when there was neither heaven nor earth, a time when only Apsu and Tiamat existed, but apparently they could not conceive of a time when there was nothing whatever except a transcendental deity; they postulated the existence of divine beings in a manner which is completely different from the Greek distinction between the material and the spiritual. Genesis describes a creation out of nothing, *creatio ex nihilo,* that is to say. It asserts that by the sovereign will and power of God, matter was brought into existence from vacuous nothing at the creation of the universe.[61]

In the Babylonian epic mankind is created to serve and feed the gods. "The service of the gods was his 'portion'."[62] In Genesis, man is created for his own sake, to rule the earth and develop his own potential. "Be fruitful and increase, fill the earth, and subdue it, rule over the fish in the sea, the birds of heaven, and every living thing that moves upon the earth."[63]

Thus, a close reading of these creation stories indicates that the points of resemblance concern matters of detail, and the points of difference matters of principle. A study of the two accounts will convince the reader that whereas the ancient cosmogonies are rather crude and primitive, the Genesis version is simple and sublime.[64]

To conclude: A comparison of the Babylonian creation with the first chapter of Genesis makes the sublime character of the latter stand out in bold relief. Enûma elish refers to a multitude of divinities emanating from the elementary world-matter; the universe has its origin in the generation of numerous gods and goddesses personifying cosmic spaces or forces in nature ... the world is not created in the Biblical sense of the term, but fashioned after the manner of human craftsmen; as for man, he is created with the blood of a deity that might well be called a devil among the gods, and the sphere of activity assigned to man is the service of the gods. In Genesis i:1 — ii:3, on the other hand, there stands at the very beginning one God, who is not co-united and co-existent with an eternal world matter, and who does not first develop Himself into a series of separate deities, but who creates matter out of nothing and exists independently of all cosmic matter and remains one God to the end. Here the world is created by the sovereign word of God, without recourse to all sorts of external agencies. God speaks, and it is done; He commands and it stands fast. Add to this the doctrine that man was created in the image of a holy and righteous God, to be the lord of the earth, and we have a number of differences between the Enûma elish and Genesis that make all similarities shrink into insignificance.[65] Biblical record, with its lofty conception of God, bears a dignity unparalleled in any other ancient account.

The discovery of a flood story in ancient cuneiform manuscripts is to the credit of George Smith, who copied cuneiform tablets at the British Museum. George Smith made his discovery known, and it caused great excitement at that time. The London *Daily Telegraph,* sensing the news value of the sensational discovery of a flood story, immediately proposed the re-opening of the excavations at Nineveh at the expense of the newspaper. Smith discovered more parts of the flood epic which later came to be known as the eleventh tablet of the Gilgamesh Epic. The episode of the flood represents only one scene in the Epic of Gilgamesh, the one in which the hero of the flood, Utnapishtim, recounts the story of how he escaped the general destruction of mankind by flood. The great gods of the ancient city Shuruppak resolved to destroy mankind by flood. The god Ea disclosed the divine decree to Utnapishtim, and gave him the following advice:

> Man of Shuruppak, son of Ubar-Tutu,
> Tear down this house, build a ship.
> Give up possessions, seek thou life.
> Forswear wordly goods and keep the soul alive.
> Aboard the ship take thou the seed of all living things
> This ship that thou shalt build. [66]

After a conversation between Ea and Utnapishtim, there follows the depiction of the building of the ship. The flood comes upon the earth; all men are destroyed. Only Utnapishtim is saved. However, when the flood is over and he emerges from his ship, all the gods come and stand around his sacrifices and beg for food. Utnapishtim is saved, but he is not human any longer. He and his wife are made into gods. "Hitherto Utnapishtim has been human. Henceforth Utnapishtim and his wife shall be like unto us gods. Utnapishtim shall reside far away at the fount of the rivers."[67]

It is no wonder that this ancient tale has been of interest to students of the Bible. The Babylonian gods resolve to destroy mankind by floods; the Lord repents that He has made man, and decides to destroy him. The god Ea discloses the advice to one man that he should build a ship; the Lord divulges his plan of destruction to Noah and orders him to make an ark. Both accounts give specifications for the building of a boat; both tell of the loading of the vessels; and both record the duration of the flood. Utnapishtim's ship comes to rest on Mount Nisir; Noah's ark settles on Mt. Ararat. Human sinfulness is the reason for the flood, which itself is an immense catastrophe in the valley of the Euphrates and Tigris rivers. Both stories have descriptions of the building of the arks. Both mention the use of birds by the crew of the ark, and sacrifices after leaving the ark. While these are points of agreement, the religious concept underlying the Hebrew account are strikingly different from those found in the Babylonian version.

In the Babylonian version we have polytheism, in the Bible monotheism. There is no moral reason for the salvation of Utnapishtim. He is saved by divine caprice. Noah is spared because of his own moral and ethical qualities. "Noah was in his generation a man righteous and wholehearted; Noah walked with God."[68] The moral factor features prominently in the Biblical version, and a new promise is held out to mankind. The traditions of the flood in the Ancient East, like those of creation, were no doubt known to the founding fathers of Israel, but the manner in which they understood and passed them down to their descendants was quite different.

Before concluding this subject, it should be mentioned that the Gilgamesh Epic as a whole is a great piece of literature. It contains all the popular themes of a great work of art, such as love, combat, friendship, adventure, valor, loyalty, and above all man's eternal search for immortality. Gilgamesh had one friend, Enkidu. When his friend died, Gilgamesh began to search for eternal life. His friend's demise had brought home to him the reality of death. As Gilgamesh bitterly weeps for his friend, he reflects: "When I die, shall I not be like Enkidu?"[69] Gilgamesh, prompted by grief and fear, undertakes a long journey to the place where Utnapishtim, the hero of the flood, lives, in order to ask him about death and life. In fact Utnapishtim indicates to him where to find a plant which he calls "Man becomes young in old age." However, on the homeward journey Gilgamesh stops for the night, and while he is bathing in a cool pool of water a serpent snuffs the fragrance of the plant and carries it off.

Frustrated in his search, Gilgamesh returns home. He now knows that "When the gods created mankind, death for mankind they set aside."[70]

There are two types of archaeological material bearing on the Bible, direct and indirect. The evidence of archaeology is indirect in the case of the Patriarchs. It must be stressed that in spite of all the light it has cast on the patriarchal age, archaeology has not proved that the stories of the Patriarchs happened just as the Bible tells them. In the nature of the case, it cannot do so, and we cannot expect it to. At the same time, and this must be said with equal emphasis, no evidence has come to light contradicting any item in the tradition. It has lent to the picture of Israel's origin, as drawn in Genesis, a touch of reality and has provided the background for understanding it. It is not an overstatement to suggest that there cannot be a true appreciation of the significance of Abraham if we attempt to understand him without the background material we have briefly outlined in this chapter. As we grasp this setting more firmly, we understand more clearly the character of Abraham, the father of a great multitude. As Albright states: "Abraham, Isaac and Jacob no longer seem isolated figures, much less reflections of later history; they now appear as true children of their age, bearing the same names, moving about over the same territory, visiting the same towns, practising the same customs as their contemporaries."[71]

NOTES

[1] Wellhausen, J. *Prologomena to the History of Israel,* English edition, 1961, pp. 318ff.

[2] Russell, B. *History of Western Philosophy,* 1957, p.329.

[3] Albright, W.F. *The Archaeology of Palestine and the Bible,* 1935, pp.130ff.

[4] It must however be pointed out that the opinions as to the exact date for the Patriarchs differ greatly. Albright and De Vaux place Abraham between 1900–1700 B.C.E.; Rowley places him in the 18th–17th centuries; Gordon as late as the Amarna Age, i.e. the 14th century. The uncertainty is due in part to the present inability to give the precise date for Hammurapi, the principal Amorite ruler of Babylon. According to the writer in this book, the Patriarchs probably belong somewhere in the Middle Bronze period (2000–1550 B.C.E.). This is also in keeping with the opinions of Albright, and Wright in the *Westminster Historical Atlas to the Bible;* Hummel H.D., *The O.T. in Modern Research,* 1970, pp.191–194.

5 Woolley, C.L. *Excavations at Ur,* 1954.
6 Gn. xi:4.
7 Gn. xi:31. Ur is also mentioned in Gn. xi:28.
8 Gn. xv:7.
9 Ne. ix:7.
10 It must be pointed out that in the Greek version of the Hebrew Bible, the Septuagint, these verses speak only of "the land of the Chaldees" and do not mention Ur specifically. This may be the result of textual corruption; see also Albright's comment in *The Jews,* by Finkelstein L., 1949, p.55.
11 Pritchard, J.B. *Ancient Near Eastern Texts,* 1955, p. 18. *(ANET)*
12 Pritchard, J.B. *The Ancient Near East in Pictures (ANEP),* 1960, p.3.
13 Parrot, A. *Abraham and His Times,* English translation, 1971, pp.66ff.
14 Excavations at Nuzi are described in *Biblical Archaeologist Reader,* 2, 1964, pp. 21ff. and in *Encyclopaedia Judaica,* Vol. 12, col.1287.
15 Gn. xii:1−4.
16 Sanders, J.A. *Near Eastern Archaeology in the Twentieth Century,* 1970. Article by Malamat, A., "Northern Canaan and the Mari Texts," pp. 164ff; Parrot, A. *Abraham and His Times,* 1971.
17 Bright, J. *History of Israel,* 1964, p. 70.
18 Gordon, C.H. *An Introduction to Old Testament Times,* 1953, pp. 100ff; *Biblical Archaeologist Reader,* 2, 1964, pp. 21ff.
19 Gn. xv:2.
20 Gn. xxiv:2.
21 Gn. xvi:2.
22 Gordon, C.H. *Biblical Archaeologist Reader,* 2, 1964, p.23.
23 *ANET,* Code of Hammurapi, Section 170, p. 173.
24 Gn. xxi:10.
25 Gn. xii:11ff; xxvi:6ff.
26 Gn. xx:1ff; xxvi:6ff; xii:11ff.
27 Speiser, E.A. *Anchor Bible,* 1964, Gn., pp. 91ff; However, Gn. xx:12 still presents a problem.
28 Gn. xxxi:50.
29 Gordon, C.H. *Biblical Archaeologist Reader,* 2, 1964, p. 25.
30 Rashi offers this comment to Gn. xxxi:19. He mentions that Midrash Rabba is his source for the explanation.
31 Gn. xxxi:30. M. Greenberg offers a different explanation in his article, "Another Look at Rachel's Theft of the Teraphim," *Journal of Biblical Literature,* pp. 239ff.
32 Paraphrase of Gn. xxvii:33.
33 Gn. xxvii:2; xlix:33.
34 Gordon, C.H. *Biblical Archaeologist Reader,* 2, 1964, p. 28.
35 Gn. xxiii.

[36]   Bright, J. *History of Israel,* 1964, p. 72.

[37]   Gn. xxiii.

[38]   Gn. xiv:14ff.

[39]   There is still much about this chapter that is open to wide differences of opinion. See Speiser, E.A. *The Anchor Bible,* Gn., pp. 105ff; Sarna, N.M. *Understanding Genesis,* 1967, pp. 110ff.

[40]   Parrot, A. *Abraham and His Times,* 1971, pp. 100—101.
Harrison, R.K. *An Introduction to the Old Testament,* 1970, p. 331; *Views of the Biblical World,* 1959, Vol.1.
Gordon, C.H. *World of the Old Testament,* 1953, p. 124.

[41]   *Ibid.* Harrison, pp.331ff.

[42]   For interesting theological and psychological discussions on the Sacrifice of Isaac, see: Kierkegaard, S. *Fear and Trembling,* pp. 21ff; Reik, T. *Temptation,* 1958, pp. 1ff; Maybaum, I. *The Sacrifice of Isaac,* 1953, pp. 1—24.

[43]   Gn.xxii:2ff. The problem of human sacrifice in the ancient world is a thorny one. There are a few references in the Bible to child sacrifice. Lv.xviii:21, 27; Dt. xii:31; xviii:9ff, mention child sacrifice as one of the abominations of the Canaanites. Other verses in Scripture consistently attribute its presence in Israel to the importation of foreign practice, i.e. II Ki xvi:3, xvii:8, 17; xxi:2,6; Ps. cvi:37ff. See also II Ki. iii:27; Finegan, J. *Light from the Ancient Past,* 1969, p. 148.

[44]   Woolley, C.L. *Excavations at Ur,* 1954.

[45]   Barnett, R.D. *Illustrations of Old Testament History,* 1968, p. 7.

[46]   Pritchard, J.B. *ANET,* p. 61. All quotes from the Enûma elish will come from this translation and therefore we will only indicate this by *ibid.,* tablet and line; See also Frankfort, H.A., Wilson, J.A., Jacobsen, T., and Irwin, W.A. *The Intellectual Adventure of Ancient Man,* 1946, pp.168ff.

[47]   *Ibid.* Tablet I, 46ff.

[48]   *Ibid.* Tablet I, 60ff.

[49]   *Ibid.* Tablet III, 90ff.

[50]   *Ibid.* Tablet VI, 7ff.

[51]   *ANET,* pp. 104ff; Lambert, W.I., and Millard, A.R., *Atraḫasis, The Babylonian Story of the Flood,* 1969.

[52]   Heidel, A. *The Babylonian Genesis,* 1969, pp. 61—81.

[53]   Epstein, I. *The Faith of Judaism,* 1954.
Hertz, J.H. *The Pentateuch and Haftorahs,* 1962, pp.193ff.

[54]   Kaufmann, Y. *The Religion of Israel,* 1960.

[55]   Gn. i:2.

[56]   Gn. i:4ff.

[57]   Is. xxvii:1, li:9—10; Jb. xli:2—13.

[58]   Gn. ii:7; Heidel, p. 66.

[59]   Wright, G.E. *Biblical Archaeology*, 1957, pp. 111ff.
       Kaufmann, Y. *Religion of Israel*, 1960, pp. 60ff.

[60]   Gn. i:27.

[61]   Heidel, 1969, pp.89ff.

[62]   Heidel, 1969, pp.121ff.

[63]   Gn. i:28.

[64]   It is beyond the scope of this chapter to go into the problems of authorship of Genesis. See *Anchor Bible* on Genesis, Segal, Harrison, and others.

[65]   Heidel, pp. 139–140. It is beyond the scope of this study to discuss the two versions of creation in Genesis. For completely opposing views, see Speiser *Genesis*, 1962, pp.9ff; Hertz *The Pentateuch and Haftorahs*, 1962, pp. 6ff. For a unique philosophical approach to these chapters, see Soloveitchik, J.B. *Confrontation* in a *Treasury of Tradition*, edited by Lamm, N., and Wurzburger, W.S., 1967, pp. 55ff.

[66]   *ANET*, p. 93. Utnapishtim is also called Atrahasis, *ANET*, p. 95. The name Atrahasis means 'Exceeding Wise' and is associated with more than one hero of the epic literature of Mesopotamia.

[67]   *ANET*, p.95.

[68]   Gn. vi:9. The eleventh tablet of the Gilgamesh Epic, which has, as shown, a parallel in the Bible, also found its way into Canaan. It should be mentioned that there exists a Sumerian poem of the flood, not embedded in the Gilgamesh saga. The Atrahasis epic mentioned earlier also has a flood story. Thus we note that one and the same oral tradition found several literary elaborations.

[69]   *ANET*, p.88.

[70]   *ANET*, p.95. Utnapishtim is turned into a god and only thus does he achieve eternal life.

[71]   Albright as quoted by Owen, G.F., *Archaeology and the Bible*, 1961, p. 120.

CHAPTER THREE

Moses—The Eisodus and Exodus

The Exodus from Egyptian slavery is the dominant event in Israelite history and faith. This was the unique event in which God revealed Himself as the Sovereign Lord of history and brought Israel into being as a nation – for His own purpose in history. Compared with Egyptian bondage and the deliverance from it, everything else in the history of the Bible is of secondary importance. The memory of that bondage and deliverance is woven into the message of legislator, historian, psalmist, prophet, and priest. A large portion of Jewish life both in Biblical and post-Biblical ages is but an echo and reminder of that great divine event, which marked the birth of Israel as a nation. The mighty acts of God in Egypt and in the Wilderness were a sign, a wonder, giving evidence of a power greater than all the powers of this world. Repeatedly in later generations, the prophets, when exhorting Israel to return to her God, and the psalmists in their meditations, harp back to the Exodus.

What light do archaeological discoveries shed on the Eisodus, the going into Egypt of Joseph and his family, the Sojourn, the Exodus, and Moses? In this chapter we shall endeavor to illustrate that the "finds" have reconstructed the setting for the Biblical stories. It is well known that at one stage some scholars even questioned whether there ever was an Oppression or an Exodus. What has archaeology to tell us about these events? We find that the Egyptian coloring in the story of Joseph and the Sojourn is very vivid, and must have been given to it by those who knew Egypt well. Whereas the historical setting for the patriarchal narratives, that is, the routes, the names, and the customs, fit well into the setting of the Ancient Near East in the Middle Bronze Age, the background for the stories of Joseph and the Exodus and Moses fit well into the Egyptian milieu of approximately 1700 to 1220 B.C.E.

The story of Joseph is one of the most graphic and attractive in the Hebrew Bible: a spoilt boy sold into Egyptian slavery by jealous brothers, he makes good in adversity, and from an unjust imprisonment rises to the highest office of the state.[1] Many thought it peculiar that a foreigner like Joseph should have risen to such a high position of eminence and authority in the land of Egypt. Now we know that Joseph lived at a time when foreigners were ruling Egypt. His rise to power was therefore not unusual and is in harmony with the coloring and setting of Egypt.

The Hyksos who ruled Egypt, probably from about 1720–1570 B.C.E., were of Asian stock. The invasion of Egypt by the Hyksos is described by the historian Manetho in a passage preserved by Josephus. "There was a king of ours whose name was Timaus. Under him it came to us, that there came, after a surprising manner men of ignoble birth out of the eastern parts, and had boldness enough to make an expedition into our country, and with ease subdued it by force, yet without our hazarding a battle with them. So when they had gotten those that governed us under their power, they afterwards burnt down our cities, and demolished the temples of the gods, and used all the inhabitants after a most barbarous manner; . . . At length they made one of themselves king, whose name was Salatis."[2] Manetho continues to narrate that the Hyksos king Salitis ruled from Memphis, and that he also rebuilt as a powerful stronghold a city very favorably situated on the eastern branch of the Nile and called it Avaris. this eventually became the capital of the Hyksos rulers.

Manetho also explains the meaning of the name Hyksos. He states that the word *hyk* means "king" and *sos* means "shepherds." Hence, the term Hyksos can be translated as "king-shepherds." It is probable that this is only a late popular etymology, and that the name actually was derived from Egyptian words meaning "rulers of foreign lands."[3]

The military success of the Hyksos was due largely to the introduction of the horse-drawn chariot and the strong compound Asiatic bow as weapons of war. The massive fortifications of their capital Avaris have been excavated and found to conform to the general pattern of Hyksos defense works and weapons. Even more important for this period of Hyksos rule was the discovery of the stele erected by Ramses I in about 1320 B.C.E. This stele was erected at the order of Ramses I to commemorate the four hundredth anniversary of the founding of Avaris, thus furnishing a date of 1720 B.C.E. for the beginning of formal Hyksos rule.[4] The seat of government during the rule of the Semitic Hyksos invaders was Avaris in the Delta. Thus, we see the authentic atmosphere of the Joseph stories, which indicate that the land of Goshen, where the Hebrews settled, was not very far from the capital. The Hebrews had easy access to the court. Both before and after the Hyksos rule the Egyptian capital was at the city of Thebes. The only exceptions to this rule, as we shall see, were the reigns of the Hyksos, Ikhenaton, and Ramses II.

When the story of Joseph begins to be narrated in the Bible, we are immediately plunged into an Egyptian environment, with all its flavor and color. Manners and customs are mentioned in connection with the life of Joseph that are only understandable in the light of life in Egypt during the Hyksos rule.

The whole incident of Potiphar's wife with Joseph reveals the Egyptian background with all its local coloring. There is an Egyptian story of the two brothers, Anubis and Bota,[5] which provides so many similarities to our story that it may serve to illuminate the whole episode with Joseph. Although such love affairs could occur in any country, the charm of the narrative lies in its Egyptian background and coloring.

In brief, the tale of the two brothers describes how a conscientious young man was falsely accused of a proposal of adultery by the wife of his elder brother after he had rejected her advances. This part of the narrative immediately recalls to the mind of the reader the advances of Potiphar's wife against Joseph, and her false accusations against him.

Another small but authentic detail in the Joseph stories is the price paid for Joseph by the Ishmaelites. It is written: "Meanwhile some Midianite merchants passed by and drew Joseph out of the pit. They sold him for twenty pieces of silver to the Ishmaelites, and they brought Joseph to Egypt. . . . Meanwhile the Midianites had sold Joseph in Egypt to Potiphar, one of Pharaoh's eunuchs the captain of the guard."[6] The price of twenty shekels of silver paid for Joseph in Genesis is the correct average price for a slave in about the 18th century B.C.E. Before then, slaves were cheaper — about ten to fifteen shekels; and later they became steadily dearer. This is then one little detail true to its period in cultural history.[7]

At this juncture in Bible history, there suddenly appear a number of Egyptian names such as Potiphar,[8] Zaphenath-paneah,[9] Asenath,[10] and many others. Even the name of Moses, according to Egyptian sources, means "child," whereas according to Hebrew sources it is explained to mean "to draw out."[11]

Egyptian sources indicate that they regarded dreams as extremely significant. Different methods were developed into an occult science by the wise men of Egypt and recorded in special "dream books." One of these "dream books" is extant in a copy made in the 13th century B.C.E. in the Hieratic Egyptian script. Joseph must have known the Egyptian methods of dream interpretation, and his wisdom helped him to succeed even where the Egyptians failed.[12]

The titles "chief of the butlers" and "chief of the bakers"[13] occur in Egyptian inscriptions. The birthday of Pharaoh is known to have been an occasion for feasting, and possibly for the release of prisoners. The

Ptolemaic records, for instance, indicate that the Pharaohs used to commemorate their birthdays with court celebrations and a general amnesty. This recalls the feast which Pharaoh made for his servants on his birthday as described in the Bible. This was the time when the chief butler and the chief baker were released from prison, the one to life and the other death.[14] The Bible tells us that when Joseph was taken out of the prison and prepared to be brought before Pharaoh, he had to have his head shaved and his clothes changed. The shaving of Joseph is in accordance with the custom of the aristocracy in Egypt, who used to shave their faces, unlike the bearded Semitic Canaanites. This contrast is conspicuous in Egyptian art and reliefs.[15]

In the story of Joseph, we are told that Potiphar made him "overseer over his house," a title which is a direct translation of an office in the houses of great Egyptian nobles. Joseph received a similar title from the Pharaoh in the administration of the realm,[16] and it has recently been shown that the Israelite official title "the one who is over the house," corresponds exactly to the office of prime minister, or vizier, of Egypt, who was the actual ruler of the country, second in power to no one but the Pharaoh.

The Bible reference describes the manner in which the Pharaoh honored Joseph in these words: "He took off his signet-ring and put it on Joseph's finger, he had him dressed in fine linen, and hung a gold chain round his neck. He mounted him in his viceroy's chariot and men cried 'Make way!' before him. Thus Pharaoh made him ruler over all Egypt and said to him, 'I am the Pharaoh. Without your consent no man shall lift hand or foot throughout Egypt.' Pharaoh named him Zaphenath-paneah, and he gave him as wife Asenath the daughter of Potiphera, priest of On. And Joseph's authority extended over the whole of Egypt."[17]

The manner of Joseph's appointment is illustrated by various Egyptian paintings which portray such ceremonies in detail.[18] The reference to "riding in a chariot" is an important piece of local color for the time of the Hyksos rulers, for it was they who introduced the chariot into Egypt and used it for public occasions for the first time in this country.

We know also that magicians were plentiful in Egypt, and that "every Asiatic shepherd is an abomination of the Egyptians."[19] Moreover, seven years' famine were otherwise known in Egypt; Joseph's life span of 110 years was considered the traditional length of a happy, prosperous life in Egyptian inscriptions; and the embalming or mummification of Jacob[20] and Joseph was the customary Egyptian preparation of the body of an important person for burial. Jacob is described as "dying on a bed" in Genesis.[21] It is well known that this was the Egyptian custom of sleeping on a bed. This was foreign to the Semitic tribes of Palestine, who used to sleep on skins spread on the ground. Thus, Sinuhe, the Egyptian, upon his return to his native land boasts: "I slept on a bed. I gave up the sand to them who are in it," that is, the Asiatics. Only in the days of the prophet Amos, who lived during the prosperous period of the 8th century B.C.E., when foreign influences were rampant, do we again hear of the luxury of sleeping on beds.[22] As numerous examples indicate, the Bible has faithfully represented the Egyptian setting with its authentic local color, and numerous manners and customs. It is also worth noting that the names Jacob-el and Joseph-el appear during the Hyksos period. However, it is impossible to identify these Hyksos chiefs with anyone in the Bible.

As mentioned in the previous chapter, and illustrated by the story of Sinuhe[23] and the picture at the Beni-Hasan tomb in Egypt,[24] excellent roads of communication existed in the Fertile Crescent. Thus, the descent of Joseph's brothers in time of famine to buy food in Egypt was not anything out of the ordinary. For we learn from Egyptian texts that it was customary for Pharaoh's frontier policemen to allow Asiatic tribes into the delta to get better pasturage. Thus, one text reads: "We had finished letting the Bedouin tribes of Edom past the fortress."[25] Whenever famine hit the land of Canaan, people turned their gaze to the rich and fertile lands of the Nile Valley for sustenance.

Since the Egyptians were normally hostile to the ambitions of enterprising immigrants, the dramatic rise to power of the Semite Joseph can be explained most satisfactorily in terms of a period of Hyksos rule. Thus, the position of eminence which Joseph attained in Egypt is now well illustrated by inscriptions and reliefs.

How did such a turn of the tide take place in the fortunes of the descendants of Jacob? Eventually there was a clash between the Hyksos overlords in the north and the line of princes at Thebes. The Hyksos were expelled. The expulsion of the Hyksos marked the change from the 17th to the 18th Dynasty. In an inscription written almost a century after their expulsion, the queen Hatshepsut expresses some of the national sense of indignation: "Hear ye, all people and the folk as many as they may be, I have done things to the council of my heart, I have not slept forgetfully, but I have restored that which had been ruined. I have raised up that which has gone to pieces formerly, since the Asiatics were in the midst of Avaris."[26]

Egyptian sources otherwise tended to ignore the Hyksos period, as it was their custom to record only victories and ignore defeats. It was the custom of the Pharaohs, as well as other ancient sources, to turn the tale of a catastrophe into tidings of glorious victory, just as so many have done throughout the centuries up to our own time. However, though the Egyptians tried to eradicate every trace of the Hyksos rule, excavations have brought to light that they were not as primitive as Manetho and Queen Hatshepsut tried to depict them, but that they, too, enhanced the culture of Egypt greatly during the period of their reign there. Numerous objects used by the Hyksos have been discovered, and these include gold jewelry, bronze daggers, and scarabs with names of Hyksos rulers. As already mentioned, they brought the horse and chariot to Egypt, which later greatly increased the prosperity of Egypt.[27]

There was, then, a considerable collection of Semitic peoples in the delta area of Egypt, especially at the time of the Hyksos rulers. When, as mentioned above, the native Egyptians rose in revolt, energetic leaders from Thebes expelled the foreigners a little over a century after their invasion. The large Semitic population of Egypt, however, still remained in the delta area. It must be recalled that this is the area of Goshen, where Pharaoh allowed Joseph's family to settle. We can suppose that the little group of Israelites lived there quite unnoticed, among a mixed collection of people. The reaction of the Egyptians was now to take these peoples under some sort of supervision lest the same sad fate of the Hyksos nightmare befall Egypt again.

The Book of Exodus opens with a picture of oppression for God's people. It was a "king who knew not Joseph" that now arose to oppress the People of Israel. This must have been a king of the new 18th Dynasty, which took over the rule of Egypt after the expulsion of the Hyksos rulers. It is difficult to know how long a period is represented by the story we have in the first chapter of Exodus. It must be a lapse of some four hundred years. This lapse of time is referred to more than once in the Bible. Thus, it is written: "The Israelites had been settled in Egypt for four hundred and thirty years."[28] It is interesting to note that the story of these years is a closed one. The only details about them are offered in Exodus i. This section opens with a summary of the original descent into Egypt.[29] Then there is a vivid description of the great increase in the number of these people couched in typical Biblical language. The canvas is a black and white one where there are no exact dates or names. The aim of the story, it must be remembered, is to describe God's providential guidance of his people. The narrative is "theocentric," and events are viewed under the light of eternity. Details, such as the exact names of impious heathen oppressors, are passed over, and all the emphasis is placed on religious truths with which the story throbs.

Modern excavations have shown that the rulers of the 19th Dynasty were great builders, and that they moved their capital to the eastern delta and rebuilt Avaris in order to be able to keep a control over their Asiatic lands.

This great impetus given to building activity in the eastern delta by both Sethos I and Ramses II, with the consequent need of a large and economic labor force, set the background for the oppression of the Hebrews which culminated in the work of Pithom and Ramses described in Exodus.[30] "So they [that is, the Israelites] were made to work in gangs with officers set over them, to break their spirit with heavy labor." This is how Pharaoh's store cities, Pithom and Ramses, were built.[31]

There has been some debate about the exact position of these two towns mentioned in Scripture. We are now able to arrive at a reasonable identification of the two owing to the work of the French archaeologist Montet.[32] Pithom can be identified with an ancient site in the valley which connects the Nile with Lake Timsah. This site has a fine temple built by the great Ramses II. Ramses was built on the same site as Tanis, or Avaris, which was once the capital of the Hyksos.

In Exodus I some details are given of the conditions of slavery and the background for the Hebrews' brick-making.[33] Now we learn from reliefs of the 19th and 20th Dynasties that brick-making was indeed the occupation of many slaves in Egypt. We discover that straw or stubble was regularly used in Egypt to make bricks, as this reinforced them. In one contemporary papyrus, an official reports of his workmen: "They are making their quota of bricks daily," while another complains, "There are neither men to make bricks nor straw in the neighborhood."[34] Exodus states: "And Pharaoh commanded the same day the taskmasters of the people and their officers saying, 'Ye shall no more give the people straw to make bricks, as hitherto: let them go and gather straw for themselves. . . . there is no straw given unto thy servants and they say to us, make bricks; and behold thy servants are beaten; but the fault is in thy own people.' "[35] Thus, the book of Exodus accurately reflects brick-making usage in ancient Egypt.

Figure 10. Wall painting from the tomb of Rekh-mi-Re' at Thebes, depicting foreigners working at brick-making.

There are, for instance, now to be found texts depicting the escape of slaves from Egypt. Thus, one text reads: "When my letter reaches you, write to me about all that has happened to them [that is, the escaped slaves]. Who found their tracks? Which watch found their tracks? What people are after them? Write to me about all that has happened to them and how many people you sent out after them."[36]

The Book of Exodus speaks about the midwives, who are called Shiphrah and Puah.[37] It is interesting to note that the names of these women have now been found in ancient texts. Shiphrah is mentioned in an 18th century list of slaves and Puah is known from the Ras Shamra texts.[38]

Having shown that the names of people and places mentioned in the first chapter of Exodus are now found in external sources as well, we can now inquire – when did the Exodus take place? If the story of Joseph belongs to the Hyksos period, to what date may we assign Moses and the Exodus? Here we encounter one of the most debated questions in Biblical history. There is no unanimity on the subject.

There are various theories and several candidates for the position of Pharaoh of the Exodus. One theory is based on the verse in I Kings, [39] which states that Solomon began building the temple in the fourth year of his reign and the four hundred and eightieth year after the Exodus from Egypt.[40] The division of the kingdom under Rehoboam and Jeroboam must have taken place about 930 B.C.E. Since Solomon is said to have reigned for forty years in I Kings,[41] his fourth year must have been about 967 or 966 B.C.E. If this was the four hundred and eightieth year after the departure from Egypt, the Exodus must have taken place around 1446 B.C.E.

This date falls within the last few years of the reign of the Pharaoh Thutmose III (1436 B.C.E.). If we accept this, he must have been the Pharaoh of the Exodus. There is evidence to support the view that Thutmose III was the oppressor of the Israelites, since we know that he was a great builder and employed Asiatic captives on his construction projects.[42] Ahmose, who expelled the Hyksos, might have been "the new King over Egypt, who did not know Joseph," mentioned in Exodus i: 8, and Hatshepsut might have been Pharaoh's daughter of Exodus.[43] Making allowance for the traditional forty years in the wilderness, the Israelites would have arrived in Palestine shortly before 1400 B.C.E., and might be identified with the Habiru who were pressing into the land at the time. Furthermore, we know that there was a city at Jericho around 1400 B.C.E. which could have been taken by Joshua. From the excavations at the site now, we do not know if there was a city there a century later, as the famous archaeologist Kenyon has shown in her work *Digging up Jericho.* [44] We will deal with the problem of Jericho and the conquest in the next chapter.

Attractive as the theory outlined above may seem, it must be emphasized that there are serious objections to it. The identification of the Habiru of the Amarna letters with the Biblical Hebrews is today unacceptable to most scholars. The reason for this is that the Habiru make their appearance not only in the Amarna texts, but also in a wide variety of other cuneiform documents in the Sumerian, Akkadian, and Hittite languages from many parts of Western Asia dating between the 20th and 12th centuries B.C.E. The Habiru are also sometimes denoted in texts by the ideograph SA-GAZ.[45] Akkadian texts from Mari describe Habiru soldiers as contingents in various armies, or as forming independent military groups of their own and threatening the security of certain Mesopotamian towns. The Habiru are mentioned in over 30 Nuzian documents, only here they appear not as mercenary contingents but as people hiring themselves out under contract as household servants. It is these Habiru household personnel of Nuzi who most closely resemble the Hebrew bondmen of Exodus.[46] Thus, the Habiru appeared to have formed a sociological element in several societies and in different centuries of the Ancient Near East. They were people who for different reasons lost their sedentary habits and were living somewhere on the fringe of cultivated land. Sometimes they acted as hired laborers, often as hired mercenaries who raided villages and towns for loot. These Habiru mentioned in the Amarna letters and elsewhere in ancient texts cannot be identified with the Hebrews any longer. Perhaps we may say that Simeon and Levi in Genesis [47] acted in a way reminiscent of the Habiru, but there is no reason at all to connect the Hebrews with the Habiru. The name Habiru, or rather the noun *habiri,* occurs centuries before the Patriarchs.

To return to Thutmose III as a possible candidate for Pharaoh of the Oppression: he carried out large building projects and these activities were mainly confined, as far as we know, to upper Egypt. It was not until the 19th Dynasty that Pharaoh resided in the Delta and greatly concerned himself with building operations there. But it was in the Delta that the Israelites are said to have lived and worked. All this makes it unlikely that Thutmose III was connected with the Exodus.

Some savants date the Oppression and the Exodus to the century preceding Ramses II, and connect it with the religious revolution of Amenophis IV, or, as he later was known, Ikhenaton (1383–1365 B.C.E.). This extraordinary personality, whom Breasted has called "the first individual in history," [48] abolished the multitudinous deities of the

Egyptian pantheon, and devoted himself exclusively to the worship of the Sun. These scholars maintain that there was a connection between the faith of the Israelites and the solar monotheism of Ikhenaton, and that the Israelite influence was partly responsible for this subversion of the gross idolatry of Egypt. Ikhenaton was hated by the people as the "heretic king," and his innovations were abandoned under his son-in-law, Tutankhamon. They were eventually altogether uprooted by Haremheb, the last Pharaoh of the 18th Dynasty. When the native religion was restored, these scholars maintain, the Israelites suffered persecution and degradation and the Oppression formed part of the extirpation of Ikhenaton's heresy. [49] More will be said about this solar revolution later in this chapter.

The great majority of scholars however nowadays wish to place the Exodus in the 13th century during the reign of Ramses II (1298-1232), who ruled longer and built more than any Pharaoh before or after him. The basis of this theory is the observation already made that "the Israelites built for Pharaoh store cities, Pithom and Ramses." The name Ramses in this verse could hardly be other than Per-Ramses, which has been identified with Tanis-Qantir. Since Tanis was the Avaris of the Hyksos, which was abandoned and allowed to fall into ruins after their expulsion in 1570 B.C.E., and was only reestablished by Seti I, it is not likely that any large construction activities were being conducted in this vicinity in the years just before 1446 B.C.E. But in the days of Seti I and Ramses II the Israelites could have toiled in construction work at Ramses and also at Pithom. The only other explanation of Exodus I could be that the Israelites labored at these places at some far earlier time, presumably back in the Hyksos period, and the use of the name is an anachronism. Yet one cannot accept this, nor can one expect an Egyptian town to have been named Ramses before that name had been brought into vogue by an august bearer. The first Ramses ruled Egypt for a short time only in 1309. The second was the famous splendor-loving Ramses II who built more than any other Pharaoh. Thus, we must conclude that Ramses II was the Pharaoh under whom the Oppression of the Hebrews reached its climax. This is in accordance with our knowledge of his vast building activities and particularly with the fact that he resided in the Delta and devoted the opening years of his reign largely to building operations at Tanis.

The general impression given by the Exodus is that the Israelites were settled not far from Pharaoh's court. In Psalm lxxviii, they are definitely said to have lived "in the land of Egypt, in the fields of Zoan." The Egyptian Tanis is called Zoan in the Bible. [50] Thus, we have a picture of the Israelites as living in the vicinity of Tanis at a time when Pharaoh's court was there. This could have taken place in the time of Ramses II, but not in the earlier days of either Thutmose III or Amenophis IV (Ikhenaton).

In connection with the presence of the Children of Israel in Egypt, it is also of interest to note that a number of Egyptian texts dating from the 15th to the 12th centuries mention the Apiru, a term which is most certainly the equivalent of the Akkadian Habiru. In some of these texts the Apiru are servants; for example, two inscriptions on tomb illustrations from c. 1400 B.C.E. refer to the Apiru as straining out wine. Two papyrus letters from the time of Ramses II prescribe an issue of grain for the Apiru who were engaged in transporting stone for the great pylon of the king's house. Thus, the use of immigrant slave labor on Egyptian projects is attested to once again, not only for this period in general but also more precisely in the reign of Ramses II.[51]

The other argument in favor of a 13th century Exodus is of a general archaeological nature. In the Hebrew Bible no iron is mentioned in connection with the Israelites before the invasion of Canaan; on the other hand it is said that the Canaanite warriors had iron chariots at their disposal.[52] Now we know that the transition from bronze to iron as the favored metal for implements and weapons is to be dated about the end of the 13th century.[53]

It should also be remembered that when Israel came in contact with the Edomites and the Moabites the latter were already settled in their different countries and governed by kings. According to archaeological evidence this happened at the beginning of the Iron Age, as Glueck and Van Zyl illustrate.[54] Thus, it seems probable that Exodus i:8 is to be explained as referring to the succession of the 18th by the 19th Dynasty in Egypt; that Ramses II was the Pharaoh of the Oppression and that the Exodus took place under his successor Merneptah.

It is from the reign of Merneptah that a stela was discovered which contains the name Israel. This inscription is worthy of special attention since it is the only mention of the name Israel in any Egyptian source. The closing portion of the inscription reads :

The princes are prostrate, saying: Mercy!
Not one raises his head among the Nine Bows.
Desolation is for Tehenu, Hatti is pacified;
Plundered is the Canaan with every evil;
Carried off is Ashkelon; seized upon Gezer;

Figure 11. Stele of the Egyptian king Merneptah dated c. 1220 B.C.E. It is a victory hymn in hieroglyphics, mentioning the name Israel for the first time.

Yanoam is made as that which does not exist;
Israel is laid waste, his seed is not;
Hurru is become a widow for Egypt.[55]

Thus, Israel is here clearly listed among other strong and dangerous peoples in the west of Palestine upon whom Merneptah inflicted a defeat. But while the other names in the Merneptah inscription are written with a sign that they indicate regions, the name Israel is preceded by the sign for "nation." So the incident took place while Israel was not yet settled in Canaan but still roamed in the Sinai Desert. Nevertheless, from this we may assume that by about 1225 B.C.E. Israel had already begun her entry into Canaan. Thus, the inscription provides further evidence that the Exodus took place in the 13th century.

We must assume that Merneptah did not take a personal part in the pursuit of the Israelites but sent part of his chariot corps under the command of his general, who is called Pharaoh in Exodus xiv. Such an assumption is necessary because the mummy of Merneptah does not show signs of drowning. Possibly Merneptah's inscription refers to the happenings described in Exodus xiv, when Pharaoh's officials turned the story of the catastrophe into tidings of glorious victory, just as so many have done throughout the centuries up to our own times.[56]

The route of the Exodus can be established with reasonable accuracy now that Ramses has been identified. Considerations of security dictated a journey toward Succoth, so as to avoid the frontier fortress of Zilu which guarded access to the "way of the land of the Philistines."[57] The crossing of the Red Sea has been beset with misunderstanding owing to an incorrect rendering of the Hebrew name *yam suf* which should be translated "Reed Sea" and not "Red Sea." The actual crossing of the Israelites may have been made somewhat north of the Bitter Lakes, where similar terrain was to be found. In the Sinai Peninsula Moses, according to tradition, received a divine revelation which culminated in the establishing of Israel as the People of the Covenant.

The figure of Moses, the great deliverer, prophet, and lawgiver, towers over the events of the Sojourn, the plagues, the Exodus, the wandering in the desert, and the receiving of the law. What light does archaeology shed on the life of Moses? The story of how the Egyptian princess found him in the ark of papyrus among the flags by the riverside has, it is claimed, many parallels in other ancient sources. It is usually compared to a cuneiform legend in the 19th century B.C.E., which speaks of Sargon, who ruled over Akkad about 2260 B.C.E.:

My humble mother conceived me, in secret she bore me.
She set me in a basket of rushes, and with bitumen she sealed the lid.
She cast me into the river which rose not over me.
The river bore me up and carried me to Akki, the drawer of water.
Akki, the drawer of water, lifted me out as he did his ewer.
Akki, the drawer of water, took me as his son and reared me.[58]

The story of the birth of Moses is described in Exodus in the following manner: "A descendant of Levi married a Levite woman who conceived and bore a son. When she saw what a fine child he was, she hid him for three months, but then she could conceal him no longer. So she got a rush basket, made it watertight with clay and tar, laid him in it, and put it among the reeds by the bank of the Nile. The child's sister took her stand at a distance to see what would happen to him. Pharaoh's daughter came down to bathe in the river, while her ladies-in-waiting walked along the bank. She noticed the basket among the reeds and sent her slave-girl for it. She took it from her and when she opened it, she saw the child. It was crying, and she was filled with pity for it, 'Why,' she said, 'it is a little Hebrew boy.' Thereupon the sister said to Pharaoh's daughter, 'Shall I go and fetch one of the Hebrew women as a wet-nurse to suckle the child for you?' Pharaoh's daughter told her to go; so the girl went and called the baby's mother. Pharaoh's daughter said to her, 'Here is the child, suckle him for me, and I will pay you for it myself.' So the woman took the child and suckled him. When the child was old enough she brought him to Pharaoh's daughter, who adopted him and called him Moses, 'because,' she said, 'I drew him out of the water.' "[59]

Ever since the discovery of the story of Sargon I, it has been customary for scholars to state that this is the source for the story of Moses. Therefore we quoted the versions in full detail, in order to allow the reader to judge and to illustrate that in essence and character, as well as in content and form, the two narratives are completely different. In the case of Sargon, his mother, in contrast to the mother of Moses, exposed the child to drowning because as a priestess she was not allowed to give birth to a child.

Moreover, there is a notable difference in language and local color, as Yahuda points out. In the story of Sargon everything bears the stamp of Babylonia; the ark is the basket-shaped boat *(kuppu)*, the material is derived from the Babylonian reed *(suri)*, and was pitched with the asphalt *(iddu)* commonly used there. In the case of Moses there is no trace of these materials. In his story the background and color is definitely

Egyptian. The word *teba* for ark is in meaning and form Egyptian, as is the material papyrus reed *(gome)*. Thus, it is not the similarities but rather the differences that are striking in the two stories. In fact there is really no need to postulate a common origin for such simple and natural stories. [60]

That Moses was born in Egypt and reared under strong Egyptian influence is independently attested by his clearly Egyptian name, supported by the Egyptian names current among his kinsmen for two centuries. The name itself is apparently nothing more than the Egyptian *mose*, which means "one born" — by analogy a "child." The word is preserved in composites like Ahmose meaning the son of the god Ah, or Thutmose, the son of the god Thot.

It is, in fact, quite probable that Pharaoh's daughter did not give a special name to this unknown infant, a child of an alien race, and she contented herself simply to name him "child." The interpretation given by the Bible, on the other hand, by peculiar coincidence of sound and circumstance in the story, is connected with the Hebrew root *masha* ("to draw out") because Pharaoh's daughter drew the infant out of the water. [61] This pun would come naturally to a Hebrew speaker rather than to an Egyptian. It would favor the view that it was Moses' own mother, rather than the princess, who first named him. Hence, Moses' name may simply be Semitic, assimilated to Egyptian while he was in Egypt. The majority view is, however, that the daughter of Pharaoh called him *mose* ("child"), which passed into Hebrew speech — meaning the one who was drawn out of water.

That Moses should be able to gain ready access to Pharaoh is not very surprising, especially if the Pharaoh of the Exodus was, as we claim, Ramses II. Montet appositely refers to Papyrus Anastasi III, which describes how the "young people of [Pi Ramses] Great Victories . . . stand by their doors . . . on the day of the entry of Wosermaetre-Setepenre [Ramses II] . . . every man being like his fellow in his voicing his petitions [to the king]." [62]

Likewise the account of the plagues, as with the story of Joseph, abounds in authentic local coloring. The miracles consisted of events that were natural to Egypt, the supernatural element consisting in the great augmentation of their normal intensity and their introduction in an unusual sequence. The ten plagues form a symmetrical and regularly unfolding scheme. The first nine plagues consist of three series of three each; blood, frogs, gnats; then fleas, murrain, boils; then hail, locusts, darkness. In each series the first plague is announced to Pharaoh beforehand at the brink of the Nile; the second is proclaimed by Moses at the palace; and the third is sent without warning. The plagues are but miraculously intensified forms of the diseases and other natural occurrences to which Egypt is more or less susceptible.

Between June and August the Nile usually turns to a dull red, owing to the presence of vegetable matter. Generally, after this time, the slime of the river breeds a vast number of frogs, and the air is filled with swarms of flies, which in turn spread disease and eventually infect the animals as well. We can therefore understand that an exceptional defilement would vastly increase the frogs which swarm in its waters, that the huge heaps of dying frogs would inevitably breed great hordes of flies which would in turn spread germs that attacked the animals. The element of miracle in these plagues is usually bound up with their intensity, timing, and duration. The first nine of the plagues bear a direct relation to the natural phenomena in the Nile Valley and indicate a compounding of the natural and super-natural. But the tenth, the death of the first born, belongs wholly to the realm of the supernatural. These natural Egyptian "terrors," occurring in particular severity at one time, indeed appeared to Moses and Israel as witness of the anger of God against the recalcitrant Pharaoh. From the standpoint of religious philosophy, a miracle is still a wonderful thing. But it does not have to be a break in the laws of nature. A miracle may be defined broadly as a unique unexpected event at the right time for the right purpose.

It is worth noticing that there is a connection between the plagues and the Egyptian gods. The plagues challenged the powers of the principal deities that were worshiped by the Egyptians. The river was a god; it became loathsome to its worshipers. The frog was venerated as a sign of fertility, and it was turned into a horror. The cattle, the sacred cow, the sacred ram, the sacred goat were all smitten. The plague of darkness showed the eclipse of Ra, the Sun-god. The tenth plague was especially directed against the firstborn of the king, who was regarded as being divine like his father, the Pharaoh. But if only the king's first child died it could be said it was an accident. Therefore the plague attacked all firstborn. We have here a vivid contrast between the God of Israel, the Master of the Universe, and the impotent idols of Egypt. The plagues vividly illustrate that : "I execute judgement, I the Lord, against all the gods of Egypt."[63]

The modern knowledge of Egypt yields a rich background for the early life of Moses. There is ample evidence of the upbringing and training of foreigners, especially Semites, at the courts of the Pharaohs of Egypt. Thus, the royal upbringing of Moses recorded in Exodus would be nothing exceptional, but is in fact characteristic for the "New Kingdom," the period that followed the expulsion of the Hyksos. Likewise, once we accept the veracity of the fact that Moses did have a court upbringing, which the Egyptian background makes natural and typical, then the assumption becomes obligatory that Moses was subjected to the kind of intellectual training received by young men in the Egyptian scripts, literature, and administrative methods. He would thus be free to use his native tongue and simple linear scripts, living in a social climate where Asiatic modes, words, and literature were fashionable. In fact, Kitchen shows that the ability to write historical narrative, record laws, and compose poetry in one man is not unique. An Egyptian example of this kind of talent seven centuries before Moses is probably furnished by Khety, who was apparently educator, political propagandist, and poet. Likewise we learn that mere workmen at Theban tomb sites and Sinai mines had no inhibitions about using writing for mundane lists and religious memorials.

It is unwarranted and unrealistic to ascribe such inhibitions to the eventual leader of a new nation, especially one conditioned in Egyptian attitudes to the written word, and to adopt a theoretical oral traditionism patently at variance with the usage of the Ancient Near East when properly understood. There is no objective reason why Moses should not have written down laws and given them to his people. Now that the Egyptian background has made it clear that writing was widespread, it is strange that many scholars should claim that Moses could not write. In support of their views, they make reference to the existence of an oral tradition[64] and express the view that writing and editing of documents came at a relatively late date. Against this contention stands the whole evidence of the Ancient Near East. Matters that were considered important, or that should go on permanent record for posterity, were written, inscribed in the land of the contemporary Near East — not left to the care of bards and romancers. Therefore there is no valid reason for depriving Moses of the ability to write laws for his people. The onus of proof rests upon those who argue to the contrary.[65]

It is interesting to note that in the Ancient Near East the oral dissemination of material was of great importance, as the Scandinavian scholars Nielson, Engnell, and others claim,[66] but it was done from written documents. A striking example is found in II Chronicles,[67] in which we see King Jehoshaphat sending out Levites to teach the people orally from a written law. In the transmission of any thing important to posterity, the ancient resorted to the written word rather than the oral. Archaeology has clearly illustrated this preference for the written word in the Fertile Crescent by digging up thousands of clay tablets, inscriptions, and ostraca which vividly depict the manners and customs of the ancient Orient. The contention by Nielsen and his colleagues that writing was the affair of the specialist can no longer be accepted in light of archaeology.[68]

This uniform testimony of Oriental literary practice is substantiated by archaeological discoveries at Mari, Nuzi, Boghazkoy, Amarna, Ras Shamra, and elsewhere. These discoveries furnish us with abundant evidence that matters which were considered important were written or inscribed in permanent form. This should influence scholars to view the literary achievements of Moses in a new light. One could even argue for a degree of popular literacy in ancient Israel from the passage in Judges viii:14, where a young man, called *na- -ar*, who was not a scribe *(sopher)*, was captured by Gideon and after interrogation provided his captors with a list of prominent officials in Succoth. Jewish scholarship has always manifested a coolness toward the documentary hypothesis. Segal and Cassuto claimed that most of the Pentateuch is quite literally Mosaic, only drawing attention to certain problems of glosses and anachronisms.[69] The traditional objections to the entire documentary hypothesis have been presented most cogently again by Harrison in his new book *Introduction to the Old Testament.* Archaeological discoveries have played a major role in undermining the documentary theory.

The great mystery in the development of religion and civilization in the Near East was the emergence of what is called "Monotheism." This mystery continues to taunt and fascinate scholar and layman alike. To understand it is to understand one of the crucial factors in the development of Western civilization. No satisfactory explanation of this all-important phenomenon has as yet been given. Indeed it is doubtful whether any complete explanation of such a complex phenomenon can be given. We will endeavor to restudy and re-evaluate the birth of monotheism in the light of new archaeological evidence that has an important bearing on it, and also on Moses.

Monotheism is one of the most important achievements in the realm of human thought. It may be defined as a deep and mighty spiritual revolution, that begins with a series of affirmations concerning God and ends by transforming the entire structure of human society. This marvellous reorientation of the human soul achieved its triumph among the Children of Israel during the Biblical period. In later centuries, a similar metamorphosis was to transmute the spirit of the Greco-Roman world through the emergence of Christianity; and still later, the lands of Western Asia and Northern Africa were to be similarly affected by the rise of Islam.

Many explanations have been offered to explain the appearance of this sublime concept, ranging from the traditional point of view to the most critical one. The classical point of view, as it appears in the pages of Scripture, claims that God revealed this great idea to His near ones. These truths remained the possession of the descendants of Abraham until the appearance of Moses, through whom the divine Torah was given to the Children of Israel. Following the death of the great lawgiver, the variations in Israel's spiritual life consisted only in periodic oscillations between loyalty and rebellion, faithfulness to Israel's peculiar heritage and surrender to the law of alien gods.

In direct opposition to this traditional point of view, the 19th century school of Biblical criticism postulated a progressive evolution of monotheistic thought that was primarily achieved by slow evolutionary growth from the later prophets till the Babylonian exile. Under the influence of Darwin and Hegel, Wellhausen described the religion of Israel in terms of an evolutionary development from the lower to the higher forms. The lofty idea of God and the strong ethical elements in the Biblical description of Mosaic religion, as well as the notion of the covenant itself, were widely held to be retrojections of later beliefs. However, as already indicated above, the essential pillars of "higher criticism" have been considerable undermined by the progress of Biblical study. As Kaufmann writes : "Biblical scholars, while admitting that the ground has crumbled away under the documentary hypothesis, nevertheless continued to adhere to its conclusions."[70]

In the light of the abundant material recovered from the Ancient Near East, it has become apparent that the documentary theory rested on fallacious grounds. Firstly, unilinear evolution is a fallacy. It is valid only with a small field of reference for a limited segment of time, and not for whole cultures over long periods of time. It is now recognized from geological studies that progress occurs by spasms or leaps, and not by slow, scarcely perceptible procedures of improvement or differentiation as postulated by Darwin and his followers. As regards the optimistic views current at the end of the 19th century concerning the inevitable material, intellectual, and moral progress of the human species, numerous sociological, theological, and other studies have made it abundantly clear that technological development and social uplifting have not been accompanied by a corresponding degree of maturity in the human spirit. Ultimately the outlook for the human race is best expressed in negative and deteriorative rather than positive and progressive terms. It is doubtful whether it is justifiable to apply the metaphors of growth and development that Wellhausen borrowed from biological sources to religious phenomena. Comparative studies in the area of religious development have shown clearly that the "primitive" and "advanced" conceptions of the deity can coexist in the mind of any one individual without being mutually exclusive.[71]

Furthermore, the way in which Wellhausen thought of the growth of the Israelite religion from rudimentary beginnings to advanced monotheism is completely contrary in significant areas to the Old Testament interpretation of its own history. This attitude requires that the Biblical narrative be taken at something like face value, a procedure that is still anathema to many liberal scholars, or at best is regarded as fraught with danger for all save the most wary. At the risk of repudiating the evolutionism of an earlier phase of Old Testament scholarship, however, it should be observed that the Old Testament narrative saw the historical process as anything but an ordered and progressive development, like that contemplated by the critical school of Wellhausen. Instead, the Hebrew Bible writers constantly thought of their history as a dynamic confrontation of humanity by the Divine Word, against a background of revealed monotheism.[72] It is beyond the scope of this book to enumerate all the reasons for scholars repudiating the documentary hypothesis. The interested reader will find the works mentioned above of Cassuto, Segal, Harrison, Kitchen, and many others most informative and thought-provoking. Rowley's new book *The Growth of the Old Testament* gives a good summary of the liberal point of view.[73] As Kitchen so effectively illustrates, the documentary theory was created in a vacuum, where scholars imposed Western literary thought and logic upon an ancient literature without recognizing the basic characteristics of the literature of that world.[74]

Nowhere else in the whole of Ancient Near Eastern history has the literary, religious, and historical development of a nation been subjected to such drastic and wholesale reconstructions at such variance with the existing documentary evidence.[75]

In the light of these facts, many scholars have begun to plead for formulating a method of study in which the genuine and factual will take precedence over the spurious and the imaginary. Even a critical scholar like Gordon has decried the inadequacies of the JEDP documentary hypothesis. Gordon tells us that when he was studying the Babylonian account of the construction of the ark in the eleventh tablet of the Gilgamesh Epic, he suddenly was struck by the similarities in the specifications in this text with those in the Genesis version. He recalled that this section of Genesis is ascribed by critical scholars to document P belonging to the Second Temple period. Thus, he thought, on the basis of this evidence, that the Gilgamesh Epic likewise belongs to P, a suggestion which is absurd. His studies in the field of Ugaritic further strengthened his conviction that the documentary theory is based on erroneous evidence, when, for instance, it claims that doublets, that is, double versions of a story or double names for the deity, are proof of different authorship. He shows that in Ugaritic literature Baal may be called by various names in one and the same poem. It is against this background that we must evaluate the multiplicity of God's name in the Bible. They need not imply different authorship in a chapter of the Bible any more than they do in an Ugaritic myth. Thus, Gordon pleads: Let us keep our eyes open and our minds sharp. Let us make observations and check them against the available facts. But let us not erect vast edifices on shifting sands.[76]

Having stressed the importance of archaeology, and comparing the Bible to Ancient Near Eastern literature, one must survey briefly the monotheistic trends that manifested themselves in the ancient Orient. With the rise of the Pan-Babylonian school, scholars wished to show that Israel arrived at the idea of monotheism from the world of the Assyrians and Babylonians. However, as Meek wrote in his book *Hebrew Origins:* "Monotheism in that world was a monotheism by syncretism, and this was the only kind of monotheism to which these people ever attained."[77] Occasionally, we find a passage in these sources which appears to imply a belief in monotheism. To give but one example: it is written in one inscription, "Trust thou in Nabu, and trust thou in no other gods."[78] Though hymns and prayers to local gods might often be worded as to suggest monotheism, they were merely aimed to flatter the one god, and similar hymns were written in honor of all the gods in the pantheon. It is not evidence of monotheism, for the same worshiper will make the same extravagant addresses to each of the gods in turn.

Turning to Egyptian civilization, it is well known that King Ikhenaton has been regarded as a monotheist because he worshiped only the sun disc Aton. This however is a very thorny and debatable question. It can be argued that only Ikhenaton and his family worshiped the Aton. Ikhenaton's courtiers also worshiped him, but the great majority of the Egyptians were ignorant of or hostile to the new faith.[79] Ikhenaton's revolution was an imperfect "monotheism."[80] There was no ethical quality in Atonism; even the great Hymn expresses nothing more than Aton's general benevolence in creating and sustaining life; the faith, for instance, had no bearing on Ikhenaton's marrying his own daughter. In other words, the faith had no sexual morality or social justice, as found in Biblical sources. It might also be pointed out that the aniconic feature so prominent in the laws of Moses was completely absent here.

Archaeology corroborates the aniconic character of the Mosaic faith, for though concrete visualizations of all gods of the ancient world were unearthed, never was the image of the God of Israel or "YHWH" found.[81] The prohibition of making graven images was thus of very ancient origin.

By force of this prohibition the God of Israel was comprehended without any effigy, as a deity far beyond all human visualization. This is what made the law of Israel fundamentally different from all embryonic forms of monotheism that appeared in various part of the Ancient East.[82] Ikhenaton's marriage to his daughter, and the absence of protest against images in his religious worship, are cogent arguments against Freud's theory that Moses had been influenced by Ikhenaton.[83] In addition it is well to remember that in the hundred years after Ikhenaton's death no trace of his religion had been left in Egyptian culture. Accordingly it is wrong to assume that Aton monotheism influenced Moses, whose career unfolds itself in the next century, during the reign of Ramses II. The activities of Ikhenaton were unknown until 1887. In that year a peasant woman digging in the ruins of Amarna, Egypt, discovered some tablets which brought back the life activities of this ancient Egyptian dreamer. None of the discoveries has given us a fixed starting point for understanding the unfolding of Israelite monotheism. Even Wellhausen, the great pathfinder of the developmental history, often used to admit: "Why Chemosh of Moab never became the God of righteousness and the Creator of Heaven and Earth, is a question to which one can give no satisfactory answer."[84]

The archaeological discoveries in the Fertile Crescent have shed fascinating light on paganism. The Bible depicts pagans almost as worshiping sticks and stones, i.e. as fetishists. In the light of recent Near Eastern discoveries, we know that this was not only the worship of inanimate objects, but involved the deification of the natural phenomenon. The deification of nature gave rise to the worship of natural gods, personal gods, whose lives were bound up in the unfolding of nature. Observing natural events, such as lightning or thunder, dawn or dusk, the pagan created stories about the life of the gods. Such stories about what happened to the gods constitute mythology. Myths tell of the birth of gods and goddesses, their growth, marriage, wars, death, and resurrection. But every pagan religion has its theogony, an account of the birth of the gods. They were born or created out of some primeval substance which precedes them in time and transcends them in power. This is the great symbol of the essence of paganism: the gods are not ultimately sovereign; they emerge out of a pre-existent realm and are subject to a transcendent order.[85] We referred to this in Chapter Two when we compared and contrasted the Genesis and Babylonian accounts of the creation.

Deification of nature entails the imposition of natural or super-natural compulsion upon the gods. They are subject to "biological" conditions: they must eat and drink; they grow old, become sick, and die.

Sexual impulses rule them. In short, these pagan gods are subject to decrees of fate — the Greek *moira,* the Latin *fatum.* Paganism does not accord ultimate freedom to its gods.

Monotheism alone explained the world in different terms. The Israelite religious idea was that the will of God is transcendent and sovereign over all. It liberates the Godhead from mythological and magical subjection. The Israelite religion has no theogony; its God did not emerge from a pre-existent substance, nor is He subject to or dependent upon anything outside or above Himself. He is ageless and has no sexual qualities. The Israelite religion has no male and female deities, no engendering of or by the Deity. Its God does not die and is not resurrected. All that is contained in the universe is created by His word, "He spoke — and it was."[86]

In the description of the burning bush we really find, according to Kaufmann, a summary of the differences between paganism and monotheism. The symbolism of the story of the bush gives concrete expression to the religious idea that was revealed to Moses in the desert of Sinai. God appeared in a flame burning in a dry thorn bush; the bush burned but it was not consumed — something transcending nature was at work. Here is a symbol of a deity who rules and governs over everything, even nature, and by whose will a dry bush survived the fire.

In the story of the burning bush there appears at once and for the first time those features which provided the historical framework for Israelite monotheism throughout the ages: the name "YHWH," the People of Israel, the election of Israel, apostolic prophecy, and the battle with heathendom. This story, it may be stated, marks the beginning of an epoch.[87] The skeptic asks: Why was Israel unique among all the peoples in its religious world view? The believer answers: Israel was chosen. The empirical historian can only say: Here is revealed the creative genius of the nation. For the birth of every original idea is a mystery which defies attempts to account for it. The task of the historian is not only to account for what he can but also to see clearly what is beyond his capacity to explain. We may be able to describe the historical circumstances of its appearances; that is the most we can hope for.[88]

In the light of the new evidence, many scholars are no longer ready to believe that monotheism was invented by the pioneering spirits of the literary prophets. As Peake writes: "It becomes more and more difficult to believe that the monotheism of the 8th century B.C.E. prophets could have evolved naturally from polytheism, as was formerly supposed, and we are driven more and more to postulate on the one hand some divine thrusting-in of revelation, whereby the Hebrews were elevated from one plane of apprehension to the higher; and, on the other hand, some great personality to interpret the thrusting-in. In other words, we are being driven back to take seriously what the Hebrews said in our book – that God entered into a covenant with their forefathers at Sinai which determined not only their relation to Him, but also the form of their society. Their emphasis, unique in the ancient world, upon justice and righteousness, derived from a character of a God who revealed himself there, and not from growing insight into what was humanly desirable."[89]

All savants are willing to accept that Jeremiah was a pure monotheist, because he clearly described the idols as "nothings." He said: "They are vanity, a work of delusion; in the time of their visitation they shall perish."[90] In the second chapter of Isaiah the idols are likewise described as nothing at all; they are man-made.[91] The later chapters of this prophetic book continued to depict the idols as "nothing."[92] They refused to accept lip service as a substitute for active faith and upright life. Thus, Isaiah proclaimed: "Bring no more vain offerings. Sacrifice is an abomination to me. . . . I cannot endure iniquity along with solemn assembly . . . wash yourself, make yourself clean . . . cease to do evil . . . learn to do good. Seek justice. Relieve the oppressed. Take up the cause of the fatherless. Plead for the widow."[93] Jeremiah like all other later prophets likewise denounced mere lip service and empty ritual. On one occasion Jeremiah proclaimed: "Thus says the Lord of Hosts, the God of Israel; add your burnt offerings to your sacrifices· and eat the flesh. For I did not speak to your fathers or command them in the day I brought them out of the land of Egypt concerning burnt offerings and sacrifices. For this thing I commanded them saying, 'Obey my voice, and I will be your God, and you shall be my people and walk in all the ways that I command you, that it may be well with you.' "[94] The close connection between inward thought and outward action is stressed in Isaiah, when he wrote: "And the Lord said: 'For as much as this people draw near and with their mouth and with their lips do me honor, but have removed their heart far from me and the fear of me, is a commandment of men learnt by rote.' "[95]

The basic principle, that the law has to be obeyed in spirit together with the letter, was already implied in the Decalogue. For a most important mark of monotheism is that God is benign and ethical, and therefore a distinction between inward thought and outward action is imperative. The ethical binding to the Godhead is most important.

These elements of the Hebraic religion are already present in the Mosaic legislation.[96] The Decalogue proclaims: "I am the Lord your God who brought thee out of the land of Egypt. Thou shalt have no other gods before me." Some scholars claim that the first commandment, by stating "have no other gods," gives expression to recognition of their existence. Kaufmann shows, however, that later Hebrew writing, as for instance the complaint of David, whose monotheistic outlook is unimpeachable, uses similar phraseology. Thus, David said, "For they have driven me out this day from abiding in the inheritance of the Lord, saying, 'Go, serve other gods.' "[97] The same notion of compulsory service in exile to foreign gods is found in Jeremiah as well. Thus, Jeremiah stated, "Therefore will I cast you out of this land unto a land that you know not . . . and there shall you serve other gods." [98] In these sources there is no doubt that the people speaking denied belief in other gods; yet they speak of them as if they existed, using terminology similar to that of Moses in the Decalogue.

We must remember when dealing with Hebrew sources that the Bible is not a philosophical book. It teaches religion through historic experience. The phrase in the first commandment merely gives expression to the fact that the other people believe in the existence of these gods. Israel is neither to deify nor to worship those gods. Israelite monotheism was not derived from philosophical speculation concerning the one and the many but from the knowledge of God's power, as expressed in His powerful acts in history. It was by the power of this one God that a people was redeemed, given a law, and molded into a nation. When in later history the gods of the nation are mocked as no-gods or "nothings" or "non-entities," there is no abstract or metaphysical emphasis on the existence or non-existence of these gods, but the emphasis, in keeping with the ancient, unlike the modern, mind, is on their lack of power to intervene in the history of man. A god without power was only worthy of derision.

Thus, monotheism, as it came to Israel, was not as the critical school maintained a product of development but rather, as Kaufmann puts it, "its monotheistic world view has no antecedent in paganism . . . It was the fundamental idea of a national culture and influenced every aspect of that culture from its very beginning."[99]

Albright likewise agreed that Moses was a monotheist to all intents and purposes, the term "monotheist" meaning "one who teaches the existence of only one God, the creator of everything, the source of justice, who is equally powerful in Egypt, in the desert, and in Palestine; who has no sexuality and no mythology, who is human in form but cannot be seen by human eye and cannot be represented in any form." [100]

Likewise Orlinsky writes: "In sponsoring monotheism, Moses was actually not introducing a new concept to the Hebrews. He had a familiar developing Hebraic idea of monotheism to work with, and there was nothing fundamental in his approach to the Deity which was not already to be found in the patriarchal period. Even the Covenant of Sinai represented not so much a change in kind as a change in degree from the old way of binding oneself to the Deity." [101]   Likewise Segal writes: "Abraham and not Moses was the founder of Israel's monotheism. Moses gave Israel the Torah with its commandments, but as to her God, Israel inherited Him from the Patriarchs." This is an oft-repeated assertion in Israel's Biblical and post-Biblical literature, and it is without doubt based upon historical fact. Nowhere do we find the designation of God as the God of Moses. This is a final proof that Israel never associated her first knowledge of her God with a revelation to Moses. God is always described as the God of Abraham and of Isaac and of Jacob, and after them as the God of Israel. [102]   Speiser in his *Anchor Bible* commentary on Genesis likewise argues for a monotheistic impulse behind Abraham's initial decision to leave Ur itself.[103]

The prophets, the earlier as well as the later, took their stand on two fundamental ideas; first that there was a covenant between God and His people, Israel; and second, that this covenant bound the Israelites to a completely ethical relation to one another. It will be recalled that the Patriarchs individually had entered into a covenant with God so that they would worship Him alone and that He would protect them. This personal covenant was broadened in the era of Moses as a consequence of the Exodus from Egypt, so that the entire population of Israel became God's chosen people to recognize and serve Him as the only God in the world. This covenant, it should be noted carefully, was voluntary on both sides. God elected Israel in His love and grace, and Israel freely undertook to carry out the will of God. This covenant imposed specific demands on Israel, for the binding to the God was an ethical one, as it is written: "I am holy therefore you shall be holy." [104]   This is the keynote of the Israelite monotheism which Moses already taught to his people. Hebrew monotheism, it must be stressed, was not the outgrowth of philosophical reasoning but the result of an encounter with the one ethical God, who demands moral conduct in all spheres of endeavor.

Because Israel constituted a special religious community, the concepts of law and covenant were of particular importance. Owing to the discovery of Babylonian, Assyrian, and Hittite legal codes, the legislation of Moses appears in clearer perspective.

The Biblical religion used the idea of a covenant to express its concept of law. A covenant is a solemn promise made binding by an oath, which may consist in a verbal formula or may be accompanied by a symbolic action. Such an action or formula is recognized by both parties as the formal act which compels the actor to fulfill his promise.

There were many different kinds of covenant relationships in the

Ancient Near East.[105] Recent archaeological research has shed much light on the covenant relationship between God and Israel.[106] Such legal undertakings between a great king and a vassal were very frequent in the international treaties of the 2nd millennium B.C.E. The legal undertakings between a king and a vassal commenced with a preamble which identified the author of the covenant and furnished his credentials. This was followed by an outline of the historical relations between the contracting parties. Then came the obligation to be imposed upon, and accepted by, the vassal, including a prohibition against the latter's engaging in foreign alliances. A further provision stipulated that the document should be in the deposit of the vassal and read publicly at intervals. A concluding portion listed the deities as witnesses and enumerated the blessings or curses which depended on whether the covenant was kept or violated. Accordingly, the Sinai covenant really fits into a very early period of history; presumably it was, and could have been, enacted by Moses at Sinai, for this was the manner of making a covenant in that age and time.

The most frequent type of covenant relation in the Bible is the "patron" covenant. The classical and probably original covenant of the "patron" type is the Abrahamic covenant in Genesis xv and xvii. This covenant tradition is of great historical importance, for it became the model for later covenant traditions in the Bible.

Law in the Bible is nothing else but the enumeration of the obligations of the vassal to his lord. The analogy is of a petty king and a world power; God is the world power and Israel is the petty king. The lord enumerates the acts of benevolence he performed for his vassal, and in exchange for these favors he expects the vassal to obey his laws. The commandments, which we shall show as varying in content, outline clearly what is expected of the vassal.

The most frequent word for covenant in the Bible is *brit*. It occurs 286 times in Scripture. There are numerous references to covenants and covenant relationships in the Bible where this term is not used. The etymology of the term *brit* is uncertain. The most generally accepted one is the derivation from Akkadian *biritu* ("fetter") or a cognate root.[107]

The first commandment proclaims that God bestowed a great favor upon His vassal, Israel, and redeemed him from the House of Bondage. The Lord who saved Israel from slavery, who was thus his benefactor and redeemer, has a claim on his gratitude and obedience. Already in the Decalogue we see that the law, or Torah, best translated as "instruction" is concerned with the behavior of the vassal, not only toward God but also with his conduct toward his fellow vassal.[108] Israel is forbidden to worship or make images of any other gods, and is also warned not to take the name of God in vain. This is a reference not to use God's name for magical purposes. The practice of magic was very widespread in the ancient world. The Bible inveighs strongly against these practices stating: "There shall not be found among you . . . one that uses divination, a soothsayer, or an enchanter, or a sorcerer."[109] Isaiah likewise decried magical practices, especially those connected with the dead: "And when they shall say unto you: 'Seek unto the ghosts and the familiar spirits, that chirp and that mutter, should not a people seek unto their God on behalf of the living unto the dead?' "[110]

The Bible contains laws regulating the behavior of the subject toward his God and toward his fellow man. In Talmudic terminology this is designated as laws between man and God and laws between man and man.

The laws which describe the building of the tabernacle and who may enter it show God's transcendency. As the Psalmist wrote:

Who shall ascend into the mountain of the Lord,
And who shall stand in His holy place?
He that has clean hands, and a pure heart;
Who hath not taken My name in vain,
And hath not sworn deceitfully.
He shall receive a blessing from the Lord,
And righteousness from the God of his salvation.[111]

This psalm, as well as the prayer of Solomon, Isaiah vi, and Ezekiel xiii:8, dwell on the transcendent character of God. Yet, He is also immanent and concerned with one vassal's behavior toward the other. The vassal must remember that his conduct toward man affects God as well. The laws of the Bible deal with one man's relation to the other and with the attitude toward the poor and the needy, the widow, orphan, and stranger.

The Decalogue contains laws regulating man's behavior toward God and man. These laws are written in the "apodictic" form, which scholars claim is unique to the Bible. These laws are brief and to the point, thou shalt or thou shalt not; whereas the "causuistic" law or case law is phrased, "If a man . . . then thus shall he pay . . . " This form of law is found in all Ancient Near Eastern legislation.[112]

The last five commandments are brief and emphatic. Our relation to our neighbors requires no elucidation; since we feel the wrongs which others do to us, we have a clear guide how we ought to act toward others.

These duties have their root in the principle, found in Leviticus xix:18, "Thou shall love thy neighbor as thyself," applied to life, house, property, and honor.

It has become customary to designate Exodus xx:22—xxiii:23 as the Book of the Covenant; it contains both casuistic and apodictic laws. The divine law recognizes and makes use of every honest attempt to dispense justice among men. What was right and just in the customary law was incorporated into the Biblical law.

The Book of the Covenant, which is by common consent the oldest collection of Israelite law, comprises "judgments" and "statutes." The judgments take the form of case laws: "If a man does so-and-so, he shall pay so much." The statutes take the categorical or apodictic form: "Thou shalt do so-and-so." Intermediate between those types are the participial laws (so called because they are expressed by means of the Hebrew participle), of the type: "He that doeth so-and-so shall surely be put to death." This type frequently replaces the "If a man . . . " type when the death penalty is prescribed.

Scholars have pointed out similarities and differences between Biblical law and the other ancient codes. Archaeological researches have brought to light many ancient Oriental codes. The best known are the codes of Hammurapi, Lipit-Ishtar, the law of the city Eshnunna, and a few others included by Pritchard in his volume *Ancient Near Eastern Texts, ANET.* [113] All these compilations contain chiefly regulations of the "causuistic" type starting with "if . . . " There is, therefore, a certain resemblance between the ancient Oriental codes in general and some of the Biblical injunctions, especially in the Book of the Covenant.

The material resemblances have been greatly exaggerated; even the most quoted example, the law concerning the "goring ox," is not at all convincing; there are seven points of difference between the Biblical and the Mesopotamian regulations. [114] A close study of the law concerning the goring ox by van Selms clearly shows that the Hebrew law cannot be a derivation from the Babylonian code; we will quote but one of the seven significant differences enumerated in this article by van Selms. Whereas the blood money ostensibly appears to be a feature, characteristic of both Exodus xxi:28—32 and Hammurapi, paragraphs 250—252, a closer study indicates that this conclusion is erroneous. In Babylonia money is paid in order to compensate for the life of the man killed by the ox; in Israel the blood money serves as a ransom for the owner, who otherwise should be put to death. [115]

It is well to remember that there are basic differences in the aims of the two systems of law. To maintain the rights of ownership is the goal of the Code of Hammurapi. Even criminal law as a whole has been affected by this general idea. The main objective is not to prevent crime or to punish criminals but to provide a compensation for the loss the other party has suffered.

The Israelite law is altogether different. An ox which has killed a man, woman, or child, be they free or slave, must be stoned, for Biblical law strove to protect the innocent by exposing the guilty party. In this case the guilt is put on the head of the ox. The reason the ox is stoned is not only to prevent a recurrence of the fatal incident, otherwise it could just have been slaughtered in the usual manner and its meat eaten. When human death is involved, the ox is unfit for consumption. The totality of the community is free from blood guilt when it can be placed at the door of the real culprit – in this case, the ox. That this is the spirit in which criminal procedure was undertaken appears quite clearly in the stories like that of Achan in the Book of Joshua. [116] The way to protect the community is by exterminating the actual sinner. It is now clear why the ox had to be killed – not because the Israelite lawgiver had an idea about animals being responsible for their deeds, as some wish to state, but to protect the whole of the community. By killing the ox it was publicly proclaimed that nobody from the community could be involved in a blood feud. Therefore, it becomes clear why the method of death had to be stoning. The whole community, by being present at this act, declared that no one but the animal is guilty of the blood of one of its members. So the law about the ox that gored proves again that the Book of the Covenant cannot be derived from the Code of Hammurapi and that Hebrew law has some ideas that are unique to it alone."[117]

A close reading of the Code of Hammurapi and the Bible will indicate that differences between the two by far outweigh the similarities. It is correct to mention that common laws are often due to common human experiences. Therefore, as stated earlier in this chapter, what was right and just in customary law was included in the Biblical law. Thus, analogous features occur in the casuistic laws. However, the article by van Selms makes us realize that, even in this sphere, one must study the case very closely before pronouncing judgment either way.

To quote a few more differences between the two codes. In Israel, the people are in possession of sovereign rights; the king is under the law. In Babylon, a limited monarchy would have been deemed a contradiction in terms. In the Covenant code, the death penalty for property crimes is abolished; and whether the theft be from king or commoner, freeman or slave, the fine is the same. In direct contrast, the Code of Hammurapi still demanded the death penalty for theft. [118]

A further difference worth noting is in relation to the famous *lex talionis*. This law has been greatly misunderstood and misquoted in the Western world. The principle of "an eye for an eye," is not a law of revenge in the Bible but a law of justice and protection. The enunciation of the principle "eye for eye, life for life" is today recognized as one of the most far-reaching steps in human progress. It means the substitution of legal punishment, and as far as possible the exact equivalent of the injury, in place of wild revenge. It declares that retaliation was a law of justice not of hatred; one eye, not two, for an eye; one tooth, not ten, for a tooth; one life, not a whole family, for a life. Albright writes: "The original ethical intent of Mosaic law also has been badly mangled by misinterpretations of the so-called *lex talionis* — 'Life for life, eye for eye.' " This is often considered as a vindictive cruelty which survived somehow from the barbaric past. Actually, it is the first formal enunciation of the principle of equal justice for all, and it put an end to the pre-Mosaic practice of exacting heavier penalties from the lower classes than from those of higher social rank. The "eye for eye" meant, in fact — let the punishment fit the crime, "and had nothing to do with the idea of revenge." [119] This law declared that all citizens are equal, and that injuries of every human being are valued according to the same standards. In this Biblical law the poorest peasant has the same rights as his most aristocratic friend. It deems the tooth of the poorest inhabitant as valuable as that of the nobleman.

It should be mentioned that monetary commutation had already begun. This is illustrated by the prohibition of accepting monetary compensation for malicious murder: "Ye shall take no ransom for the life of a murderer, that is guilty of death." [120] The literal application of the "eye for eye" was excluded in Rabbinic law; and there is no instance in Jewish history of its literal application ever having been carried out.

Very different is the manner in which the *lex talionis* was applied in the Code of Hammurapi. The whole code is based on it. Instead of it being merely a general principle, as in Hebrew jurisprudence, it is here taken literally and translated into cruel practice. Thus, it is written: "if a seignior has knocked out a tooth of a seignior of his own rank, they shall knock out his tooth." [121] The same rule is applied in fourteen other cases. [122] It is true that here likewise the beginning of monetary compensation appears; but not for the aristocrat or free born — only for slaves. The status of the slave in this Code, as compared with the Biblical law, will be discussed later in this chapter. In the Code of Hammurapi there is only equality for the ruling class, and not for the people who find themselves in the lower strata of society. There was a difference in executing the law, depending on the status of the people involved.

More important than certain accidental resemblances between separate paragraphs is a comparison between Biblical and Oriental law in general. In Biblical law the Divine origin is stressed nearly everywhere, giving to the injunctions their authority. Indeed, the whole of the Torah is considered as the most striking instance of the Lord's favor to His Chosen People. In the Oriental codes religion plays only a subordinate part; it is the king, not the divinity, who gives his authority to the code.

In popular literature it is often mentioned that the bas-relief at the top of the stele of Hammurapi depicts the sun-god giving his laws to the king; in reality this scene shows us the god investing the king with the symbols of rulership. [123] In general, the Oriental codes deal with legal matters only, leaving morals and religious exhortations to other branches of literature. In the Biblical Torah legal, moral, and religious prescriptions issue from one inseparable unit.

To the modern mind this unity of ethical values, religious ritual, and judicial prescriptions makes a baffling impression; in this respect the Oriental codes are more "modern" than the Biblical ones. For the Biblical mind, however, the separation of religion from morals, and of morals from law, which we see today, would be proof of a most unhealthy condition of society. One of the effects of the blending of religion, morals, and law is the admonitory character Biblical law often assumes. In contrast to all ancient Oriental codes, Biblical prescriptions often contain some motivation which appeals to the religious and ethical sense of the reader – the so-called motive clauses which, though superfluous from a legalistic standpoint, are essential parts of the Biblical law.

A striking feature in Biblical legislation is the numerous paragraphs which protect the rights of the indigent and the needy. An excellent example of the Bible's concern for the oppressed in society is the law concerning the fugitive slave. The Bible commands: "Thou shalt not deliver unto his master a bondman that is escaped from his master unto thee." [124] This command stands in sharp contrast to the Babylonian law, which makes the return of the fugitive slave compulsory. [125]

Biblical legislation shows great concern for the widow or fatherless child. They were bereft of any human protector. They could not institute legal action to defend their rights. Women could not appeal to the king for mercy and institute legal action to defend their rights. Therefore the Bible shows concern for them, stating: "Ye shall not afflict any widow, or fatherless child. If thou afflict them in any way – for if they cry at all unto Me, I will surely hear their cry. My wrath shall wax hot, and I will kill you with the sword; and your wives shall be widows and your children fatherless." [126]

The Bible always commands the Israelites to be good to the stranger for they know the heart of the stranger, since they were strangers in the land of Egypt. In the ancient world the stranger was especially liable to become a victim of injustice, and therefore the Bible commands: "And a stranger shall thou not oppress; for ye know the heart of the stranger, seeing you were strangers in the land of Egypt."[127]

The laws concerning the Sabbath, the Sabbatical year, and the Jubilee, and those regulating religious festivals, point to the same social attitude, in sharp contrast, for example, to the Code of Hammurapi, in which the tendency to secure the interest of the ruling classes is paramount.[128]

The Bible also provides cities of refuge to serve as a "sanctuary" to the manslayer. In this way the immemorial custom of blood revenge, that to this day rests like a curse upon many Bedouin tribes, is curbed; and the heathen conception of "sanctuary" for the wilful murderer is abolished.[129]

The Bible likewise shows great concern for the animal kingdom. In the Decalogue it already commands that one should give rest to everyone, even the beast of burden. It likewise shows sympathy to the mother bird commanding us that "If a bird's nest chanced to be before thee in the way, in any tree or on the ground, with young ones or eggs and the dam sitting upon the young, or upon the eggs, thou shalt not take the dam with the young; thou shalt in any wise let the dam go, but the young thou mayest take unto thyself; that it may be well with thee, and that thou mayest prolong thy days."[130] The ground of sympathy is the sacredness of the parental relationship. The mother bird is sacred as a mother; and length of days is promised to those who regard the sanctity of the motherhood in this sphere, as it is promised to those who observe the fifth commandment. When the mother is sent away, she does not see the taking of her young ones, and does not feel any pain. We see that the Bible provides that such grief should not be caused to cattle and birds; how much more careful must we be that we should not cause grief to our fellowman.[131]

Thus, we have seen in Biblical legislation, which according to Segal, Cassuto, Harrison, and the writer can be attributed to Moses with certain reservations, that the ritual and ethical, the criminal and civil, are all intermingled and intermixed. It is also significant to note that whereas the other Ancient Near Eastern codes were concerned with political and economic matters, and especially with the protection of property, the Biblical legislation was unique because of the supreme value it set on human life in a religious context. It is now clear from archaeology that detailed legal codes such as those found in the Pentateuch are not anachronistic, as was supposed formerly; nor is it any longer necessary to assign the origin of many Mosaic enactments to the 8th or 7th centuries B.C.E., as was the custom with the school of Wellhausen and others. For Pentateuchal and other Near Eastern legislation must now be envisaged against a background of a common intellectual and cultural heritage, from which an understandable similarity of antecendents emerges. Despite this, striking differences exist between these ancient codes and Mosaic law. The Hebrews were unique in antiquity for their attempts to interpret their entire national life in terms of a solemn convenantal relationship with a single Deity. While it reflected many features of contemporary legal agreements, the bond of union between God and Israel, which was forged at Sinai by Moses, was underpinned by concepts of ethical monotheism whose nature was completely foreign to the peoples of the Ancient Near East.[132]

While archaeology cannot offer direct evidence for the life of Moses, it has brought back an abundance of indirect information to enhance the trustworthiness and substantial historicity of the Biblical traditions associated with him. Apart from the various particulars, archaeology's contribution can be summed up by saying that it has provided an actual, historical context and setting for interpreting Moses' life or that of the Patriarchs, instead of using the *a priori* philosophic one on which Wellhausen had largely depended. As Bright writes: "Over all these events towers the figure of Moses. There can be no doubt that he was, as the Bible portrays him, the great founder of Israel's faith. Attempts to reduce him are subjective in the extreme. The events of the Exodus and Sinai reflect a great personality behind them. A faith as unique as Israel's demands a founder. To deny that role to Moses would force us to posit another person of the same name!"[133]

NOTES

[1]   Gn. xxxvii: 2ff.
[2]   Josephus, F. *Against Apion,* 1–14, pp. 863ff, translation by W. Whiston.
[3]   *ANET,* pp. 230ff.

[4] Wright, G.E. *Biblical Archaeology*, 1957, pp.56-57.

[5] *ANET*, pp. 23 ff.

[6] Gn. xxxvii:28; 36.

[7] Kitchen, K.A. *Ancient Orient and Old Testament*, 1966, pp. 52ff.

[8] Gn. xxxvii:36.

[9] Gn. xli:45.

[10] Gn. xli:45.

[11] Ex. ii:10.

[12] *Views of the Biblical World*, 1961, Vol. 1, p.101.

[13] Gn. xl:2.

[14] Gn. xl:20.

[15] *Views of the Biblical World*, 1961, Vol. 1, p. 105.

[16] Gn. xli:40.

[17] Gn. xli:42ff.

[18] *Views of the Biblical World*, 1961, Vol. 1, p.106.

[19] Gn. xlvi:34.

[20] Gn. l:2.

[21] Gn.xlvii:31.

[22] See *ANET*, p. 22, for the Story of Sinuhe. See also Gn. xlix:33; Am. vi:4.

[23] *ANET*, p. 18.

[24] *ANET*, p. 3.

[25] *ANET*, p. 259.

[26] *ANET*, p. 23.

[27] Finegan, J. *Light from the Ancient Past*, 1969, p. 96.

[28] Ex. xii:40. Compare Gn. xv:13, which speaks of four hundred years. The Septuagint speaks of four hundred and forty years. See Burrows, M. *What Mean These Stones?*, 1957, p. 72, where he endeavors to reconcile these numbers.

[29] Ex. 1:1-6.

[30] Ex. 1:8-12.

[31] *Ibid.*

[32] Montet, P. *Le Drame d'Avaris*, 1940.

[33] Ex. 1:12-22.

[34] *ANEP*, p. 229, fig. 729; *Views of the Biblical World*, Vol. 1, p. 128.

[35] Ex. v:6-19.

[36] *ANET*, p. 295.

[37] The biblical commentator, Rashi, offers an interesting homiletical explanation for the two names under discussion. He claims that Shiphrah is Jochebed, the mother of Moses. She was thus called because she spent much time beautifying the child. Puah is Miriam, the sister of Moses, thus named because she spoke and murmured to calm the crying newborn babe.

[38] Bright, J. *A History of Israel*, 1964, p. 111.

[39] I Ki. vi:1.

[40] The figure is given as 440 in the Septuagint: *Ibid.,* note 28.

[41] I Ki. xi:42.

[42] Breasted, J.H. *A History of Egypt,* 1959, pp. 761ff.

[43] Ex. ii:5-10.

[44] Kenyon, K.M. *Digging up Jericho,* 1957; *Archaeology in the Holy Land,* 1970.

[45] Winton, T.D. *Archaeology and the Old Testament Study,* article by Bruce, F.F., Tel el-Amarna, 1967, pp. 3ff.

[46] Ex. xxi:1ff.

[47] Gn. xxxiv.

[48] Breasted, J.H. *A History of Egypt,*1959, pp. 392ff.

[49] Hertz, J.H. *Pentateuch and Haftorahs,* 1962, p. 95.

[50] Nu. xiii:22.

[51] Winton, T.D. *Archaeology and Old Testament Study,* pp. 8ff; *ANET,* 1967, pp. 255ff.

[52] Joshua xvii:16, 18; Judges i:19.

[53] Albright, W.F. *Archaeology of Palestine,* 1935, pp. 110-112.

[54] Van Zyl, A.H. *The Moabites,* Brill, Leiden, 1960; Glueck, N. *Rivers in the Desert,* 1959; *The Other Side of the Jordan,* 1945.

[55] *ANET,* p. 378.

[56] *Views of the Biblical World.* 1961, Vol. 1, p. 113.

[57] Ex. xiii:17; Wright, G.E., and Filson, F.V. *Westminister Atlas to the Bible,* 1953, p. 38.

[58] *ANET,* p. 119.

[59] Ex. ii:1—10.

[60] Yahuda, A.S. *The Accuracy of the Bible,* 1935, pp. 70-71.

[61] Ex. ii:10.

[62] *ANET,* p. 471.

[63] Ex. xii:12; vi:6; vii:4.

[64] Nielsen, E. *Oral Tradition,* 1954.

[65] Kitchen, K.A. *Ancient Orient and Old Testament,* 1970, pp.136ff.

[66] Nielsen, E. *Oral Tradition,* 1954, Engnell, I. *Gamla Testamentet I.* 1945.

[67] II Ch. xvii:9.

[68] Nielsen, E. *Oral Tradition,* 1954, pp.24ff.

[69] Segal, M.H. *The Pentateuch,* 1967; Cassuto, U. *The Documentary Hypothesis, The Composition of the Pentateuch,* 1961.

[70] Kaufmann, Y. *Religion of Israel, 1961, p. 1.*

[71] James, O.E. *The Old Testament in the Light of Anthropology,* 1934, pp. 83ff.

[72] Harrison, R.K. *Introduction to the Old Testament,* 1970, p. 382

[73] Rowley, H.H. *The Growth of the Old Testament,* 1969.

74 Kitchen, K.A. *Ancient Orient and Old Testament*, 1970, pp. 116ff; Likewise articles by this author in the *T.S.F. Bulletin*, No. 59, 60.

75 *Ibid.*, p. 20.

76 Gordon, C.H. *Ugaritic Literature*, 1949, pp. 6ff; *Higher Critics and Forbidden Fruit*, Christianity Today, 1959, iv, No. 4, pp. 131ff. Harrison, C.K. *Introduction to Old Testament* 1970, p. 516.

77 Meek, T.J. *Hebrew Origins*, 1936, pp. 195ff.

78 *Ibid.*, pp. 195ff.

79 *ANET*, p. 369; Gordon, C.H. *An Introduction to the Old Testament*, 1953, p. 78.

80 Breasted, J.H. *A History of Egypt*, 1959, pp. 355ff.

81 *Views of the Biblical World*, Vol. 1, p. 153.

82 *Ibid.*

83 Freud, S. *Moses and Monotheism*, 1959, pp.35ff.

84 Wright, G.E. *The Old Testament against its Environment*, 1950, p. 15.

85 Kaufmann, Y. *Great Ages and Ideas of the Jewish People*, 1956, pp. 16ff.

86 Burrows, M. *What Mean These Stones?* 1957, on the Elephantine Papyri. Wright, G.E. *Biblical Archaeology* 1957, pp. 112, 116f.

87 Kaufmann, Y. *Great Ages and Ideas of the Jewish People*, 1956, pp. 16ff.

88 Kaufmann, Y. *The Religion of Israel*, 1961, p. 225f.

89 *Peake's Commentary on the Bible*, 1965, p. 208.

90 Je. x:8,15; xvi:19; ii:5.

91 Is. ii:8.

92 Is. xl:18; xliv:9ff.

93 Is. l:13ff.

94 Je. vii:21ff.

95 Is. xxix:13.

96 *Ibid.*, note 70.

97 I Sa. xxvii:19.

98 Je. xvi:13;
Kaufmann, Y. *The Religion of Israel*, 1961, pp. 129ff.

99 *Ibid.*, p. 3

100 Albright, W.F. *From the Stone Age to Christianity*, 1957, pp. 271ff. *Archaeology and the Religion of Israel*, 1942, p. 116.

101 Orlinsky, H.M. *Ancient Israel*, 1956, p. 41.

102 Segal, M.H. *The Pentateuch*, 1967, p. 125.

103 Speiser, E.A. *Genesis, Anchor Bible*, 1964.

104 Lv. xix:2.

105 Mendenhall, G.E. *The Interpreter's Dictionary of the Bible*, 1972, Vol. 1, p. 714. *Law and Covenant in Israel and the Ancient Near East*. 1955, pp. 24ff. Kitchen, K.A. *Ancient Orient and Old*

[106] *Testament,* 1970, pp. 92ff.

Ibid.

[107] Mendenhall, G.E. *The Interpreter's Dictionary of the Bible,* 1972, Vol. 1, p. 714.

[108] *The New Bible Dictionary,* article on Law by van Selms, A., 1962, p. 718.

Herford, R.T. *The Pharisees,* 1962, pp. 54ff.

[109] Dt. xviii:10; Ex. xxii:17.

[110] Is. viii:19; xlvii:9, 12; Je. xxvii:9.

[111] Ps. xxiv:3ff.

[112] Kitchen, p. 147; *ANET,* p. 183, note 24.

[113] *ANET,* pp. 159ff; Hertz, *Pentateuch and Haftorahs,* 1960, pp. 405ff.

[114] van Selms, A. *The Goring Ox in Babylonian and Biblical Law,* Archiv Orientalni, 1950, pp. 321ff.

[115] *Ibid.*

[116] Jos. vii:1ff.

[117] *Ibid.,* notes 115, 166.

[118] *ANET,* p. 167, paragraphs 22ff.

[119] Albright, W.F. "The Law that Bound Israel," *Life,* Vol. 38, No.7, p. 60.

[120] Nu. xxxv:3.

[121] *ANET,* p. 175, paragraph 200.

[122] *ANET,* p. 175, paragraphs 200 ff.

[123] Wiseman, D.J. *Illustrations from Biblical Archaeology,* 1966, p. 27, figure 24.

[124] Dt. xxiii:16. The Code of Hammurapi states: "If a seignior has helped either a male slave of the state or a female slave of the state or a male slave of a private citizen or a female slave of a private citizen to escape through the city-gate, he shall be put to death" (Paragraph 15). The last law of the Code also deals with a slave whose ear must be pierced for rebelling against his master. It is interesting to compare this to the Biblical legislation which pierces the ear of a slave who refuses to go free. (Ex. xxi: 2-6).

[125] *ANET,* p. 166, paragraphs 15ff.

[126] Ex. xxii:21; Dt. xxiv:17ff.

[127] Ex. xxiii:9; Lv. xix:10. It is interesting to note that the laws stressing the obligations toward the "stranger" always use the word *gēr* and sometimes *tōsāb,* but rarely the word *nokrī.* So they deal with people dwelling permanently in somebody else's soil.

[128] Lv. xxv:1ff; Dt. xiv:29; xvi:11, 14.

[129] Nu. xxxv:9–34; Dt. iv.:41ff; xix:2ff.

[130] Ex. xx:12; Dt. xxii:6, 7; v:16.

[131] Ex. xx:10; Dt. xxii:6, 7; Lv. xxii:28; Dt. xxv:4; Pr. xii:10.

[132]   Freedman, D.N. and Greenfield, J.C. *New Directions in Biblical Archaeology*, article by Albright, entitled "The Impact of Archaeology on Biblical Research," 1966, pp. 1ff, especially pp. 13 and 14.

[133]   Bright, J. *The History of Israel,* 1964, p. 116.

CHAPTER FOUR

Joshua—Canaanite Culture
and Conquest

Redemption from slavery in Egypt and the gift of a good land were the two most important events in the history of the People of Israel. These are celebrated in song and story, poetry and prose throughout the Bible. Before describing Joshua's role in the conquest of the land and the difficulties connected with it, let us see what insights Biblical archaeology gives into the Canaanite civilization and religion. Israel's struggle against Canaanite culture is vividly depicted throughout the pages of Scripture. Only within recent years has the progress of archaeological study reached the point where we can speak with some confidence about the beliefs and practices of ancient polytheism around Israel, and understand the reasons for this clash of cultures. Archaeology has discovered three sets of texts, namely the Execration, the Amarna, and especially the Ugaritic; and these finds shed fascinating new light on life in Canaan from the earliest times until the arrival of the Hebrews.

The Execration texts date from the 20th century B.C.E., and indicate that Egypt already then had vested interests in the land of Canaan. These curious documents are vases and statuettes, inscribed with the names of the enemies of Egypt. If Pharaoh was threatened by rebellion, he had only to break the object on which were written the names of his foes and accompanying formulae, to the accompaniment of a magical ceremony, and the power of his adversaries would be crushed immediately. The exorcised elements mentioned in the texts, among others, are Asiatics and familiar names of rulers of cities such as Shechem, Hazor, and Jerusalem feature prominently. To cite a few lines from the texts: "The ruler of Jerusalem, Yaqar-Ammu and all retainers who are with him; ... All men, all people, all folk, all males, all eunuchs, all women, and all officials, who rebel, who may plot, who may fight, who may talk of fighting, who may talk of rebelling ... shall die."[1] These texts clearly indicate that in very early times the Egyptians were connected with Canaan. It also shows the widespread use of magic. These documents indicate that they believed that

75

magical cursing and physical smashing of objects, obviously resembling the enemy, would bring them to grief.

The Amarna letters, referred to above, contain a wealth of information about the political conditions prevailing in Canaan in the 14th century during the reigns of Ikhenaton and his father in Egypt. We learn from these documents that though nominally Canaan was part of the Egyptian Empire, it needed a strong man on the throne of the Pharaohs to uphold Egyptian rule effectively. After Amenophis III, Egyptian foreign power declined. When Ikhenaton, the dreamer, neglected his Empire and political matters and devoted himself to his religious revolution, Egyptian rule declined. The kings of Canaan automatically became independent rulers trying to maintain themselves against the invasions of Bedouin tribes. The Amarna letters found at Ikhetaton, the city that Ikhenaton had built as his holy city and where his palace had been located, indeed reflect the intrigue, the jealousies, and the feuds between the local rulers of Palestinian towns and offer a wealth of information about the politics, trade, commerce, and warfare of those times.

The tablets are mostly letters exchanged between Pharaohs and the rulers of Asia. The latter include the kings of Babylonia, Assyria, the Hittites, and, especially of interest to the Bible student, the kinglets of the Canaanite city-states. The city-states of Syria, Phoenicia, and Palestine had been made tributary to Egypt since the earlier kings of the 18th Dynasty. But by the time of the Amarna correspondence, the Egyptian grip was slackening; some of the vassals were being attracted into the Hittite sphere of influence; some were being attacked by marauding bands and found it difficult to secure Egyptian aid against them; some were making local arrangements for their own advantage. When writing to the Egyptian Pharaoh, however, they all eloquently protest their absolute loyalty; some complain of the slanderous reports sent in by their neighbors and suggest that those neighbors themselves are the real rebels against their Egyptian overlord.

Six of the vassal letters are addressed to the king by Abdi-hapa, ruler of Jerusalem, who protests his utter loyalty. He then continues to explain to Pharaoh that he is distressed by the malicious reports which his detractors are sending to the king, and also by the menace of people whom he calls Habiru (Apiru). He goes on to ask: "Why do you favor the Apiru and oppose the governors? . . .O king, my lord, there are no garrison troops here! So let the king take care of his land! . . .The Apiru plunder all the lands of the king."[2] He continues to imply that the rulers of the nearby cities and states or their relatives are in league with the Apiru; in particular Lab'ayu, ruler of Shechem, has surrendered everything to them.

They are trying to capture Jerusalem, but other rulers have fared even worse. So the letters continue to reflect the bickering and quarreling between the petty kings of Canaan. As indicated previously, there is no relationship between the Apiru, Habiru, and Hebrews.[3]

Needless to say, Canaan is described by these letters as being with no central government. Each city considered itself an independent entity with no obligation toward the other city. In a few cases we notice small coalitions of cities against common foes, but on the whole there was no coordination of forces whatever. This explains how Israel was able to infiltrate into the country and to attack the Canaanite cities one after another. In a few instances some of the Canaanite cities joined forces against their common enemy, as the Book of Joshua claims.[4]

The Amarna letters also offer us interesting information about the language of Canaan before the conquest. When the scribes were not sure about the Babylonian word to be used to render the Canaanite word dictated to them by their king, they added the Canaanite word itself between "brackets" after the Babylonian rendering, and these are the so-called Canaanite glosses in the Amarna letters. A study of these words has shown that Hebrew was, as mentioned once by Isaiah "the language of Canaan."[5] After the conquest, the Israelites took over the language of the country. In their mouth it changed in some respects, but not enough to form a separate branch of Semitic language; Biblical Hebrew is regarded as one of the Canaanite dialects.

The Ugaritic texts offer the most fascinating information about the people and gods of Canaan. Ugaritic is closely related to the language revealed by the Canaanite glosses and is therefore of the utmost importance in the study of Hebrew. It is true that it possesses some sounds, many words, and a few grammatical forms which are foreign to the more Southern Canaanite dialects as represented by Hebrew, Moabite, and others, but it is doubtless a Canaanite language. It is certainly not the father of Biblical Hebrew, but could be called its uncle.

As indicated previously, accident played an important part in the discovery of the Amarna tablets. It is well known that the Dead Sea Scrolls were supposed to have been brought to light by the unintentional straying of an innocent goat. The Bedouin boy called Muhammed followed the goat and came upon the caves which eventually yielded some of the most fantastic discoveries of our age. Likewise the discovery of ancient Ugarit was made accidentally by a peasant digging on the Northern Syrian coast. Schaeffer excavated there, and at nearby Ras Shamra (ancient Ugarit), for twenty-two seasons between 1929 and 1960. Among the important finds were many fine objects. These included ivories, weapons, statues, and stelae, as well as two temples — one dedicated, according to the excavators, to Baal and one to Dagon, dating from the 14th century B.C.E. There were found many inscriptions in Cuneiform (Sumerian, syllabus scripts, Babylonian and Hurrian), Egyptian, and also texts written in a hitherto unknown Ugaritic Cuneiform alphabet.[6]

From this sudden and spectacular discovery, there has arisen an entirely new branch of Semitic studies called Ugaritic after the ancient name of the town where the texts were found. These Ugaritic studies are now regarded as a discipline on their own, which has a grammar, a lexicon, and a long shelf of specialized studies on philology, history, and literature.

Before these discoveries practically nothing was known of the theological organization of the various gods and goddesses worshiped in Canaan. From these texts we learn that the gods of Canaan were arranged in a highly organized system, each having his function and authority. This pattern of relationship among the gods is expressed in mythological terms. The general Canaanite word for "god" was *El*, and thus the gods were called *Elim*, which is the plural of this word.

The head of all the gods was "El." El is known by a number of names in the Ras Shamra texts. He is designated as "The Creator of Creatures," "Father of Man," or "The Bull." The last is a characteristic metaphor of El, for he is likened to a bull in a herd of cows and calves.[7] El's epithets in the Ugaritic texts are "the benign one," or "the kind one." He is rather a shadowy figure who apparently takes little part in the affairs of men. He lives far away "at the source of the two rivers, in the midst of the fountains of the two deeps." Nevertheless, the gods and goddesses come to him with their entreaties and demands, or send their messengers. The actual rule of the world, however, appears to be divided between Baal in the heavens and on earth's surface, Mot in the netherworld, and Yam in the sea. These three gods are at times in conflict, and El seems to vacillate in favor of now one and now another of the rivals. El retained his ancient titles and prestige without any real power, except in an advisory capacity. It is clear that Baal is the rising young god at Ugarit. The battles between Baal and the gods Mot (Death) and Yam (Sea) will be described later. The wife of El was Asherah. El apparently treated his wife Asherah with great respect and consulted her on all matters. For instance, when Baal was dead, El discussed with her whom to appoint as king in place of Baal.[8] When Baal wanted a house she knew how to flatter El to get his consent and approval for carrying out this project.[9] El also had relations with other women, which are described in a very obscene passage of text 52. He seduced these women and then allowed them to be driven into the desert after the birth of two children, "Dawn" and "Sunset." The description of the act of

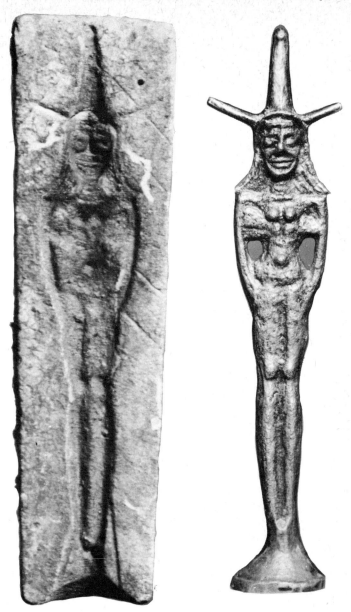

Figure 12. Stone mold for casting figurine of what is believed to be the Canaanite goddess Asherah, and a modern bronze cast made in this mold. From a Middle Bronze temple at Nahariyyah.

Figure 13. Stele of "Baal of the lightning" from Ras Shamra (Ugarit) depicting the god with a mace in his right hand and a lance in the form of stylized lightning in his left hand. Below the left hand appears a small figure on a podium — probably a deity or a person under the protection of the god

seduction is one of the frankest and most sensual in the Ancient Near East.[10]

In the Bible we have a number of allusions to Asherah, though her name is hidden in the authorized version by the translation "grove." Jezebel introduced into Israel four hundred prophets of Asherah,[11] and Manasseh had an image of her put in the temple.[12] The symbol of her presence at a place of worship was apparently a sacred tree or pole standing near the altar. One was either set up or planted in Samaria by Ahab,[13] another in Jerusalem by Manasseh[14] Such objects must have been very familiar to the people, for we constantly hear the injunction that they should be cut down, burned, or pulled up because they led Israel astray.[15] Under these trees the goddess was worshiped by immoral practices, temple prostitution.

The figure of Baal dominated the Ugaritic pantheon. This young and strong god eventually replaced El, who lived far away playing only a minor role in the affairs of the gods and of man. The word *Baal* means "to own," "to rule," and "to possess."[16] Baal was a god who was closely connected with fertility, fields, and cattle. By giving rain he enabled growth to take place, and thus made man and beast fertile and fecund. Baal is designated by various names in these myths. When the texts were first dug out at Ras Shamra, the excavators were of the opinion that the names Baal and Aliyn Baal designated different gods.[17] However, closer study of the sources now indicates that they were one and the same god. Baal is also designated as "The Prince, Lord of the Earth;" "The Rider of the Clouds," "Son of Hadad," "The son of Dagan," and "Lord of Sapan." The area where Baal lived was called "Mount Sapan" These names of Baal are used interchangeably in the texts.[18]

The wife, consort, and sister of Baal is Anat. She is the goddess of love and fertility. She has a very warlike nature and has many similar features to the goddess Ishtar. One text describes her as ruthlessly butchering men, and then bathing happily in their blood. The text states :

> She locked the gates of Anat's house
> And let the picked fighters in ...
> Now Anat dost battle in the plain,
> Fighting between the two towns;
> Smiting the Westland's peoples,
> Smashing the folk of the Sunrise.
> Under her, hea(ds) like sheaves;
>
> Her liver swells with laughter,
> Her heart fills up with joy,

Figure 14. Cuneiform tablet of the 15th—14th cent. B.C.E. from Ugarit, dealing with a message from Baal (here called *Aliyn Baal*) to his sister Anat.

> Anat's liver exults;
> For she plunges knee-deep in knights' blood,
> Hip-deep in the gore of heroes. [19]

The goddess Anat is always at Baal's side, ready to aid and assist him. Love scenes between the two gods are frequently described. One text, of which only a fragment is preserved, has a graphic account of a sexual union between Baal and Anat, and is followed by a description of the resulting fertility in the herds: "Calves the cows drop: an ox for the Maiden Anat."[20] The example of the gods, who through sexual union brought about fertility in the flocks, and the family was followed by similar acts of sexual union among humans in the temple of the gods. This belief led to the practice of sacred prostitution here and throughout the Ancient Near East. The prophets of Israel, particularly Amos and Hosea, bitterly inveighed against it.[21]

The religion of Ugarit was polytheistic, mythological, and ritualistic, and was centered to a large degree in promoting the fertility of family, field, and flocks. The god Baal and goddess Anat play dominant roles in the mythology of Ugarit. Baal's connection with rain, vegetation, and fertility is stressed in these texts. In this context it is interesting to study a limestone stele dating from the 2nd millennium B.C.E.[22] This stone pillar picturesquely depicts Baal's functions in Ugaritic mythology. It portrays Baal standing on what might be both heaven or earth. He brandishes a club in one hand and holds a stylized thunderbolt ending in a spearhead in the other. The club is a symbol for thunder, and is connected with his function as the god of rain. The stele, in short, aims to show that Baal is closely connected with rain, vegetation, and growth.[23] The text which describes the death and revival of Baal is most interesting to study in this connection. When Anat, the mistress and consort of Baal, wished to resuscitate her beloved companion, she proceeded first to war with Mot, the god of sterility and aridity. Only after she succeeded in overcoming this adversary did the god Baal return to life once more. What is significant is the manner in which Anat killed Mot. The detailed description of this act of the goddess, conveys the impression that with his dissection and planting of his remains in the earth the forces of destruction will be eliminated and growth and abundance will take place. The relevant text reads as follows:

> She seized Mot
> With a sword she crushed him
> With a pitchfork she winnowed him
> With fire she burned him
> With millstones she ground him
> In the field she planted him
> In order that the birds might eat his remnants
> In order that the fowl might consume his portion
> Remnant called to remnant.[24]

Then Baal is revived, and with his resuscitation fecundity returns to all spheres of life. As the text puts it :

> The heavens rain oil,
> The wadies run with honey,
> So I know that the mighty one, Baal lives
> Lo, the Prince, Lord of the Earth exists.[25]

Baal is described as being delighted with the victory over Mot and says to Anat: "We have planted our enemies in the ground."[26]

Love scenes between Baal and Anat are frequently described in these texts. The tender love of Anat for Baal is described thus :

As the heart of a cow for her calf
And the heart of a ewe for her lamb
So is the heart of Anat for Baal. [27]

But in another text a description is given of Baal mating with a cow and an offspring is born. [28] In fact this incident appears to indicate that bestiality was practised in ancient Ugarit. It is possible that this text was a kind of mythos to a sacred rite of fertilizing the herd by having sexual intercourse with the cows. Practices of this nature were strictly forbidden by Biblical law. The Book of Exodus states : "Whoever has unnatural connection with a beast shall be put to death." [29] It is these lascivious practices, such as bestiality, temple prostitution, and child sacrifice, that are associated with Baal, which evoked the bitter invective of the prophets against the sensual Canaanite cult. [30] Thus Hosea cried:

Your men sacrifice on mountain-tops
and burn offerings on the hills,
under oak and poplar
and the terebinth's pleasant shade.
Therefore your daughters play the wanton
and your sons' brides commit adultery.
I will not punish your daughters for playing the wanton
nor your sons' brides for their adultery,
because your men resort to wanton women
and sacrifice with temple-prostitutes. [31]

The myths of Ugarit, like other mythologies of the Near East, pictured the gods in human forms, having similar aims and aspirations, desires and passions. The amazing thing about these gods and about Baal himself is that they appear to have no standard of morality governing their actions. Goodness and godliness did not go hand in hand. Though the texts deal with deities, there is no stress whatever on ethics or morals. The gods themselves indulge in all pleasures, eating, drinking, and lovemaking, and perpetrate some of the most abominable deeds. They lived immoral lives, hated, warred, and killed often only for fun, as we saw in the case of the goddess Anat. They certainly were not models for man to emulate, either ethically or religiously. The only tablets which contain ethical ideas are the Keret and Aqht texts, which speak about these semi-divine beings, or kings e.g., Keret and Dnil judging the widow and pleading the cause of the orphan. [32]

The primary purpose of these myths was to explain the world and how it functioned to the men of their generation. This is in fact what ancient mythology has in common with modern theology. It endeavored to explain the meaning of life and the mystery of the universe to mortal man. It aimed to help him face up to the challenges and the perplexities of life. These polytheistic texts explained the secrets of the universe by claiming that there were opposing forces continuously at war with one another in the world. As Wright put it: "The primary purpose of the stories about the gods was to explain the world and how it works. Basically, the mythology has this in common with some modern theology: namely, that the world was created through conflict and continues its operation in the continual struggle of opposing forces – health, light, and order being perpetually arrayed against the forces of death, darkness, and chaos. Thus, we hear of the stories of battle between Death, Life or Vegetation, between Night and Day, between Chaos and the forces of the Cosmos."[33] The myths of the ancient world, as well of those of ancient Ugarit, try to furnish an explanation for this phenomenon. They claim, for instance, that when Baal was dead, aridity and sterility reigned in the land, because Mot, the god of these forces, ruled in the land. When the god of rain and vegetation was revived, then fertility and fecundity returned to the earth. This myth of the dying and rising god was common throughout the Near East. In Babylonia he was called Tammuz and his mistress was Ishtar. In Egypt it was Osiris and Isis, and in Greece Adonis and Aphrodite. While the stories about these gods and goddesses were greatly elaborated in these countries, the basic plot remains the same. There is no doubt that the Hebrews knew this myth, and we find warnings directed against it as well. That explains why the Hebrew Bible always stresses that "YHWH" is the "living God."

The prohibition by the lawmaker and prophet against the making of idols also suggested the prevalence of idolatry in Canaan. Indeed, remains of images have been found in large numbers at the excavated sites. Numerous nude female figures made from clay have been found. These images are crude, but always emphasize the distinct feminine aspects of the human figure. Male figures were also found. These were made of metal, always fully dressed and mostly portrayed in a seated position. Most scholars believe that these images served some vital religious or magical purpose in the Canaanite cult. The discovery of these idols on Canaanite soil makes clear the reason for the Biblical prohibition of making graven images. By force of this command the God of Israel was to be comprehended without any effigy, as a deity far beyond all human visualization, "Who has no body, nor can He be conceived in bodily terms."[34] This, as indicated in Chapter Three, made the religion of Israel fundamentally different from all the embryonic forms of monotheism that appeared in various parts of the Fertile Crescent. The finding of these Canaanite images in such large numbers on Palestinian soil gives us a new perspective and is further confirmation of the aniconic passion of the ancient Hebrews. Religion in general, as practiced in Canaan, must have been a rather sordid and degrading affair, and so it seems to have appeared to the teachers and spiritual mentors of ancient Israel. However, the masses at large were fascinated by this sensuous nature cult and continously went "awhoring after foreign gods." [35]

The Ugaritic literature not only is concerned with the life of the gods but also describes the actions of some human heroes, the most important being, as mentioned earlier, the epics about King Keret and Aqht.

In the Ugaritic texts, the craving for progeny appears twice. The story of a king called Dnil narrates an unusual incident of childlessness. The other is the narrative about the tragedy of King Keret, who is apparently of semi-divine descent. In this instance the king appears to be bereaved of all family, wife, and children.

The legend of Aqht deals with the story of King Dnil, who longed for a male heir. His name means "God judged." Perhaps he is thus called because according to the text, judging the cause of the widow and the fatherless was his special concern, as it is written:

> He judged the case of the widow,
> And adjudicated the cause of the fatherless. [36]

This Dnil is probably the hero of the Hebrew tradition, the righteous man mentioned together with Job and Noah in the Book of Ezekiel. [37] The texts also describe what service the father could expect from a son:

> One who sets up his standing stela,
> Who takes his hand in drunkenness,
> Who carries him when sated with wine,
> Who eats his meal in Baal's house,
> His portion in El's house;
> Who plasters his roof on the day of rain,
> Who washes his clothes on the day of mud. [38]

This passage outlines the varied and numerous duties that a father could expect from his son in life and after death. The care of a person after death was a most important matter with all ancients. All excavated graves indicate that the dead were buried with all necessary supples that they might need in the netherworld. Dnil's deep concern for male offspring derived from the fact that only the son could perform the last rites toward the father at Ugarit. This reminds one of the tradition in Judaism, where only the son is able to recite the Kaddish, the prayer for the dead, for both father and mother.[39] Eventually Dnil's prayer as well as that of Keret are answered and they both are blessed with progeny. The stories about these humans or semi-divine figures are enlightening, as they alone give us a glimpse of some ethical content in Canaanite life.

The forms of poetry found at Ugarit are of great interest to the student of the Bible, for they resemble the poetic forms found in Scriptures. It is interesting to compare Psalm xcii, where it is written:

"For lo, thy enemies O Lord,
For lo thy enemies perish,"[40]

with the Ugaritic sources, where it is stated:

Lo, thine enemies O Baal
Lo thine enemies wilt thou smite.[41]

It is clear that the Hebrew poets were familiar with and made use of the literary forms of the Canaanites. But it is well to remember that the Psalmist merely used a well-known expression to teach new ideas. The verse in Psalms has an ethical significance. The text about Baal has no moral value. The Biblical writer used accepted literary forms to express novel truths about God and man and their role in the universe. For when studying the Bible and comparing it to Ugaritic literature, we must be aware of the great gulf that separated the religious contents of Canaanite poetry from the message of the Bible: polytheism versus monotheism; magic versus devotion; moral indifference versus sublime ethical teachings. Israel's struggle against Canaanite culture extended over many centuries. It started with the invasion of Canaan by Joshua at the end of the 13th century B.C.E., and to this we must now turn our attention.

The Book of Joshua, named after the national leader who succeeded Moses, relates the conquest of Canaan and its division among the tribes of Israel in accordance with the divine promise to the Patriarchs. It had been a constant preoccupation in their long and weary wanderings in the wilderness, and the basis of their hope for the future. The forty years were not a period of aimless wandering, but a preparation — spiritual, physical, and mental — for a fulfilment which was largely but not completely achieved by Joshua.

Five times Joshua comes before us as the protégé of Moses, and in each case as one intimately connected with the great prophet, leader, and lawgiver. When the Amalekites attack Israel, Moses commands him to choose men and fight the enemy.[42] Later at Sinai he accompanies Moses up to the mountain, and as they come down after forty days it is Joshua who first detects the uproar in the camp, mistaking the noise of idolatrous feasting for the clamor of war.[43] It is the young man Joshua whom Moses leaves in charge of the Tent of Meeting.[44] His devotion to Moses manifests itself in a jealous rebuke over the unauthorized exercise of prophetic gifts by Eldad and Medad: "My Lord Moses, stop them!" Moses replies to him in a most kindly fashion: "Are you jealous on my account? I wish that all the Lord's people were prophets and that the Lord would confer his spirit on them all!"[45] There can be no doubt that tradition regarded the two men as united by a close bond of affection and depicted the older man as preparing the younger to take up the responsibility of leadership. We are therefore not surprised to find Moses at the end of his life passing on to Joshua the arduous task of bringing the Children of Israel into the Land of Promise, and saying to him through the mouth of the Lord; "Be strong, be resolute; for you shall bring the Israelites into the land which I swore to give them, and I will be with you."[46]

What new light does archaeology shed on Joshua and his campaign to conquer Canaan? Recent excavations of sites in Palestine, especially at Jericho, Ai, Bethel, Shechem, Lachish, Debir (Kiriath-sepher), and Hazor have much to tell of the general period in which Joshua carried out his work.

The Canaanites were the inhabitants of Canaan, the older native name of Palestine. As a geographical designation the Hebrew form of "Canaan" seems to be derived from the Hurrian word meaning "belonging

Figure 15. Ivory of the Late Bronze period engraved with celebration of victory with feasting and mirth and a procession of prisoners.

to the land of the red purple." As early as the 14th century B.C.E., this term came to be used of the country in which the "Canaanites," or Phoenician traders, exchanged for their wares their most important commercial commodity, red purple dye, which was obtained from the murex shells found on the shores of the Mediterranean.[47] Accordingly, in the Amarna letters, "the Land of Canaan" is applied to the Phoenician coast, and the Egyptians called all Western Syria by this name. By the time of the Conquest, however, the term Canaan was in vogue as the general designation of the territory later called Palestine. The language of Canaan[48] refers principally to Hebrew, but embraces the general West Semitic languages spoken in this territory, of which Phoenician and Moabite were dialects. The name Palestine as a geographical term is of later origin and is derived from the Philistines who settled, as we shall see, in large numbers along the southern coast in the 12th century B.C.E. The area which they settled became known as Philistia,[49] and from that in turn came the Greek name Palestine.[50]

The Book of Joshua, which is part of the history of Israel which extends through the Books of Judges, Samuel, and Kings, gives the following description of the actual invasion of the land.[51] The book's view of the conquest was that a long and drawn-out struggle took place, but that ultimate success was possible only because of an initial, spectacular, and successful campaign led by Joshua. This attack on Canaan was carried out in three phases. The Israelites first secured a foothold west of the Jordan river, accomplished through the capture of Jericho and Ai.[52] This initial campaign was followed by an attack on the southern parts of Palestine but avoided the strong Jebusite fortress of Jerusalem. Finally, a northern campaign was launched, which, though gaining territory, actually destroyed none of the fortified cities except Hazor.[53]

This Biblical picture of a rapid occupation of Canaan under Joshua is substantially correct when studied in the light of archaeology. The greatest difficulty in the story of the Conquest is presented by the city of Jericho. The prominent part that Jericho played in the account of the Israelite entry into Palestine under Joshua has induced many archaeologists in the last hundred years to excavate this site. Already in 1867 an excavation was undertaken by Warren. However, the first systematic examination of Jericho, the modern Tell es-Sultan, which is near the spring of Ain es-Sultan about one mile northwest of modern Jericho, was undertaken by Sellin and Watzinger in 1901–1909.[54] These two scholars revealed to the world that they had discovered two concentric rings of fortification, the inner ring surrounding the ridge of the hill. It appeared as a masterpiece of military defense made of sun-dried bricks in the form of two parallel walls about ten or twelve feet apart. The inner wall, which is particularly massive, is about twelve feet thick throughout. The outer ring of fortification runs along the foot of the hill and consists of a six-foot-thick wall, about twenty to thirty feet high, with strong foundations. These were supposed by Sellin and Watzinger to be the famous walls of Jericho.

The two lines of fortifications, their exact historical placing, the dates of the erection and destruction have given rise to vehement disputes among scholars, who advance pros and cons in a welter of opinions, hypotheses, and arguments. The battle that raged over Jericho began with the announcement issued by Sellin and Watzinger which claimed that the outer wall fell about 1200 B.C.E., and therefore must be the city wall which Joshua destroyed. To shed new light on the whole affair, a British expedition under Garstang set out for Tell es-Sultan in 1930. After six years of digging, further portions of the fortification were exposed. Garstang noted every detail with utmost precision and described graphically the violence with which the inner circles of parallel fortifications had been destroyed.

Unfortunately the most recent work at the site, from 1952 to 1961, by Kenyon throws very little light on the period of Joshua, and differs appreciably from the findings of Garstang, who believed that he had found ample evidence of destruction under Joshua. Garstang in his expeditions devoted much attention to the mud-brick town walls of which the line following the crest of the mound of the north,west, and south sides had been traced by previous expeditions, and through which he cut a number of trenches. He assigned them to four stages, two to the Early Bronze age, one to the Middle Bronze age, and one to the Late Bronze Age. The destruction of the latter by fire and earthquake he attributed to the time of Joshua, which he dated to 1400 B.C.E. He wrote: "Jericho lies particularly in an earthquake zone and on that occasion violent shocks were recorded on four days out of seven. Theoretically, then, the possibility of the walls of Jericho having been damaged or destroyed by earthquake is to be admitted . . . traces of intense fire are plain to see, including reddened masses of brick, cracked stones, charred timbers, and ashes . . . as to the main facts then, there remains no doubt: the walls fell outwards so completely that the attackers would be able to clamber up and over their ruins into the city . . .meanwhile the impression remains uppermost that the walls fell at about that place because it had been partly undermined."[55] In other words he claimed that the walls of Jericho were not breached but sank down in their place exactly as the Bible claims, and this was caused by earthquakes.

Kenyon has shown that the walls which Garstang, and before him

Sellin, had claimed belong to the period of Joshua actually belong to the Early Bronze Age. A double wall of the Late Bronze Age simply does not exist anymore. This may have been there in the days of the Conquest and was worn away by erosion. All archaeologists are agreed that this area is subject to a great amount of denudation. However, Kenyon stresses that no relics of such a wall were found.

A very interesting piece of evidence, agreeing with the account in the Bible, is that Jericho was indeed the gateway to Canaan for thousands of years. Both for the end of the 4th millennium and of the 3rd, excavation has produced evidence that Jericho was a point of entry for all nomadic tribes. Joshua told his spies: "Go view the land, and Jericho." [56] This record of Joshua's plan fits in perfectly with what is known of invasions or entry into Canaan of those ancient times. Any leader of a group of invaders would make Jericho his starting point. Jericho was a vantage point for all infiltrators because of its position opposite the main ford through the lower Jordan, defending the main passes up out of the Jordan valley and controlling a vital water supply.

Since this area was subject to earthquakes and tremors, it is permissible to assume that there was a town on the eastern part of the mound during the days of Joshua in the 13th century B.C.E., which was later wholly eroded away. It could be that the once powerful Hyksos fortress, which they erected when they were expelled in 1550 B.C.E. from Egypt, had by the days of Joshua become little more than an outpost, but still an imposing one in appearance. Such a possibility is not just a harmonistic or heuristic view, but one suggested by the evidence of considerable erosion of the older settlements of Jericho. The tombs conclusively prove the importance of Middle Bronze Age, although on the city mound most of the Middle Bronze town and even much of the Early Bronze one before it were eroded away between 1600 and 1400 B.C.E. When so much damage was done by the elements in barely two hundred years, it is easy to see how much havoc natural erosion must have wrought on the deserted mound in the four hundred years that separated Joshua from Jericho's refounding by Hiel the Bethelite. [57] For the narrative of Joshua about Jericho, as it is depicted in the Bible, reflects faithfully the general conditons and topography of the area. It seems likely that the washed out remains of the last Late Bronze Age city are lost under the modern road and cultivated land along the eastern side of the town mound, as the main slope of the mound is from the west down to the east. It remains highly doubtful whether excavation here, even if allowed, would yield any further evidence on this rather thorny problem of Jericho.

To sum up, excavations at Jericho indicate that no wall was found that could be attributed to the Canaanite city captured by Joshua. The terminal date, according to Kenyon, for Jericho's destruction is 1325 B.C.E. Current scholarship prefers a date for the Exodus in the 13th century, 1225 B.C.E. as indicated in Chapter Three. To resolve this discrepancy, some scholars suggest that the mud-brick wall was washed away by rain during the long period that it stood in ruins. Others maintain that the Canaanite city did not possess its own wall but reused the wall of the earlier city; and still others consider the Biblical tradition to be an etiological story to explain the destruction of the earlier city. At all events, archaeological evidence from Jericho is inconclusive, and it is not too much to suppose that this situation may be one result of the havoc caused by the Conquest itself. We must look elsewhere for more decisive evidence of Joshua's conquest in about 1225 B.C.E.

Excavations at the sites of Ai, Bethel, Lachish, Debir, and Hazor have furnished important evidence for their destruction in the 13th century B.C.E. and of these only Ai poses its own peculiar problem. It seems that the site that has been identified with Ai was destroyed about 2350 B.C.E., and it lay in ruins at the time of the Israelite invasion.[58] Its very name means "ruin." Various suggestions have been offered to account for the fact that it is mentioned as being taken by Joshua. One is that it was merely an outpost of Bethel under the control of a military captain. He is styled "king," but this need occasion no difficulty as the Hebrew root simply means "ruler." If Ai was only a military outpost there may not have been any substantial buildings there, and so nothing tangible would remain. However, the Biblical narrative clearly indicates that Ai was an inhabited city. Thus, from an archeological point of view this city is still one more problem that needs elucidation.

In the north, the town of Hazor is singled out in Joshua for special mention.[59] Here a coalition of Canaanite kings was defeated. It was only in recent times that the excavation of Hazor was undertaken by Israeli archaeologists. Reconstructing its history, these savants, headed by Yadin, found that Hazor had been a modest settlement since its establishment on the mound, and it started to develop only with the construction of the lower city round about 1750 B.C.E. The lower city flourished throughout the Late Bronze Age, reaching its zenith in the 14th century B.C.E., when it was the largest city of all Canaan. The final destruction by conflagration, both of the upper and lower cities, occurred probably in the middle of the 13th century B.C.E. This destruction is quite definitely to be ascribed to the Israelite Tribes as related in detail in the Book of Joshua.[60]

Excavations at Bethel under Albright in 1934 revealed that the city enjoyed considerable prosperity during the Middle and Late Bronze Ages.

It was destroyed by a tremendous conflagration during the 13th century B.C.E., as indicated by the huge qualities of charred debris, burnt brick, and ashes that were unearthed at lower Late Bronze Age levels.[61]

The reconstruction of a fragmentary bowl recovered from the site of Lachish proved that it was also destroyed in the 13th century. The pieces of pottery were inscribed with a notation, possibly made by an Egyptian tax collector, in which the fourth year of a certain Pharaoh was mentioned. Despite the absence of a specific name, the script is clearly contemporary with Merneptah; and since the bowl was broken when the city was taken, it would appear that Lachish fell about 1220 B.C.E. [62]

There is no mention of conquest in the center of the land. This fact has puzzled scholars and they have suggested that Shechem belonged to friends or relatives of the Hebrews, or perhaps they surrendered willingly like the Gibeonites. That this area was under Israelite control is clear, for Joshua's farewell addresses to the people take place at Shechem. According to the information contained in the Amarna letters, the king of Shechem was a man called Lab'ayu. He communicated regularly with the king of Egypt, but he often adopted a very aggressive tone in his letters. He even quoted to the king an old Canaanite proverb about the ant. He wrote: "If ants are smitten they do not accept it passively, but they bite the hand of the man who smites them. How could I hesitate this day when two of my towns are taken." [63]

Proverbs about the ant appear in the Bible in other chapters as well. [64] We have no means of identifying who this King Lab'ayu was, and if he was in any way related or friendly to the Hebrews. Likewise the marauding Apiru mentioned in these texts were discontented mercenaries, but there is no mention of an invasion of Palestine in these sources; and these people and their activites cannot be connected in any way with the invasion of Canaan under Joshua. [65]

Archaeology lends support to the story of the Gibeonites, who surrendered to the Israelites without fighting. The Bible states: "When the inhabitants of Gibeon heard how Joshua had dealt with Jericho and Ai, they adopted a ruse of their own. They went and disguised themselves, with old sacking for their asses, old wine-skins split and mended, old and patched sandals for their feet, old clothing to wear, and by way of provisions nothing but dry and moldy bread. They came to Joshua in the camp at Gilgal and said to him and the Israelites, 'We have come from a distant country to ask you now to grant us a treaty.'" [66] They pretended to have come from a far away land because they had heard of the greatness of the God of Israel, and wished to become friends of this nation. Joshua accepted them peacefully and granted them a treaty promising to spare their lives. The chiefs pledged their faith to them on oath. But within a few days the Israelites learnt that they were in fact neighbors and lived nearby. However, they were no longer able to attack them as they had made peace with them. But Joshua, after he discovered their deception, cursed them saying that they would be "hewers of wood and drawers of water."[67]

The site of modern el-Jib has been thoroughly excavated by Prichard.[68] Among the principal discoveries made at this site was a great pool, water tunnels, collection of inscriptions, royal stamps, the winery, handles with the word Gibeon inscribed on them, and a number of storage rooms. Indeed, the Bible, in both the books of Samuel and Jeremiah mentions Gibeon as a place which had a pool.[69] Thus, it would seem that the Gibeonites were indeed "drawers of water" — not "hewers of wood", but rather of stone cellars in the cleft of the rocks. Excavations show that one of the principal sources of the prosperity of Gibeon was the wine industry. It gives us a picture of Gibeon as a center for wine making. The Bible describes the clash between Jeremiah and the false prophet Hananiah from Gibeon.[70] We can now sense the reality of this tradition which pictures Jeremiah as an admirer of the Rechabites, a sect in Biblical times who, among other prohibitons, abstained from drinking wine. Jeremiah contrasted the loyalty of the Rechabites to the commandments of their forefather with Judah's disobedience to God's prescripts.[71] It is now easier to understand the conflict between the two prophets. Is it possible that the strife between the true prophet and the false one involved not only theological matters but economic ones as well?

Another factor which emerges clearly from archaeology is that this city of Gibeon was never ravaged by any war or destruction. This agrees with Scripture, which claims that the inhabitants surrendered peacefully without putting up a struggle.

To sum up on Joshua's campaigns — it is clear that they were carried out during the third quarter of the 13th century B.C.E. That Israel was roaming in the Sinai desert at this juncture in history is evident from the Egyptian stele of Merneptah. From this reference we may assume that Israel began the conquest of the land not later than about 1225 B.C.E.

Joshua's campaign exhibits sound military strategy as well. In conquering Canaan, Joshua did not waste his strength on the strongest military fortresses such as Jerusalem and Gezer, which came only later, when David and Solomon incorporated them into Israelite territory. David conquered Jerusalem from the Jebusites.[72] Solomon received Gezer as part of the dowry his Egyptian wife brought with her.[73] The strategy Joshua employed was the same as that used later by the Assyrians and

Babylonians. This was to conquer first the string of fortresses in the Shephelah which guarded the approaches to the Judean hill country. After that was achieved, the capture of the hill country was a comparatively simple operation.

One final point of archaeological interest is that even after Israel had secured a good footing in the land, there were many pockets of resistance that still remained: "There remaineth yet very much land to be possessed." [74] The extent of this unconquered land is also mentioned in chapter one of the Book of Judges. Some of the towns named in this list have been excavated. Two in particular, Megiddo and Beth-shan, tell the story that they were in Egyptian and Canaanite hands until after 1200 B.C.E. Only after the lapse of some years did the typical Israelite culture, as shown by pottery, appear in these towns. Archaeology indeed shows that the culture that succeeded the Canaanite one in all these cities was much poorer, as is evidenced by masonry, building plans, and pottery. From a material standpoint the Israelites had an inferior culture to that of the Canaanites, but a superior one spiritually. [75] The archaeological evidence brought to light has resulted in new respect for the general picture of the Conquest as narrated in the Book of Joshua. Thus, it is apparent that there was a rapid succession of attacks made by Joshua only after he received intelligence reports from the spies and evaluated them. [76] He had many successes in the central, southern, and northern parts of the country. But the Bible quite rightly makes it clear that the conquest of the land by Israel was incomplete at the time of the death of Joshua, and much was still left to be done. [77]

With the story of the Conquest we have already entered the days of the Judges. The land was divided among the various tribal groups both to the east and the west of the Jordan. It was to be about 1000 or so B.C.E., before there was any semblance of stability and centralized control in the Land of Israel.

When we turn to the period of the Judges we find that the keynote is anarchy. A verse which occurs four times in the Book of Judges conveys the spiritual climate of the times. It states: "In those days there was no king in Israel; each man did what was right in his own eyes." [78] According to the Book of Judges, the people, when settling down to life in Canaan, succumbed in a large measure to the seductive nature worship which we described earlier in this chapter; in consequence they lost their sense of unity and broke up into separate tribes each fighting only for its own existence. Individual tribes had their own form of governmental organizations and cities appointed their own leaders. Several tribes might as a result of outside pressure combine for joint action; but not until the end of the

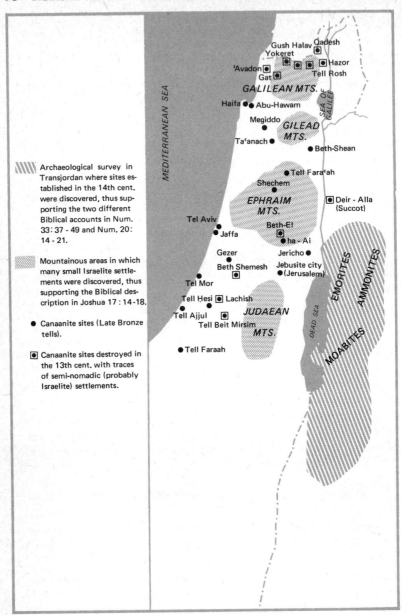

Figure 16.   Canaan in the 12th century B.C.E.

period of the Judges do we find the whole nation joined together for united action. Confusion and disorganization are the keynote to the period of the Judges.[79]

Throughout the book we find the fourfold themes of Sin, Suffering, Supplication, and Salvation. When the people forgot their devotion to the Covenant and went "awhoring after foreign gods," the Lord sent oppressors to oppress them. When the people's measure of suffering reached a high-water mark, they would again turn unto the Lord, and He would raise up to them a leader who would save them from the hand of their enemies. In other words: "The more paganism they adopted, the weaker the Covenant bond between them became, and the more each tribe tended to live by and for itself, isolated from the other tribes. This disunity made subjection and oppression by outsiders relatively easy."[80]

Complete disaster for the People of Israel in those dark days was avoided by the spontaneous leaders who were called "Judges." The term *shophet* in Hebrew has a wider connotation than the English word "judge," or the corresponding noun in Greek or Latin. The Hebrew word denotes both *judicare* and *vindicare,* the latter in the double sense of defending, delivering, avenging, and punishing. The *shophet* was judge and ruler. These figures have been called "charismatic" leaders, because they were believed to possess some special gift of God's grace. They were set apart from the others by special responsibilities. Such an appointment would involve them in Samuel's outline of the obligations of the nation to a king and his autocratic nature, as characterized by contemporary Canaanite kingship.[81] The Israelite kings, commencing with the tragic King Saul, were never allowed to become too despotic. Whenever a king endeavored to exploit his subjects and overstep his authority the prophets arose to rebuke him and curb his power. To cite some examples: David is rebuked by Nathan after his sin with Bath-Sheba,[82] Elijah castigates Ahab for "killing and taking possession" illegally of the vineyard of his subject Naboth,[83] and Jeremiah's invectives are directed against Johoiakim when he uses slave labor to build himself a palace emulating the king of Egypt.[84] King and commoner were subject to obedience to God's word, and whoever flouted the law came in line for the prophet's rebuke. In the next chapter we will deal with the ways of the Israelite kings and what light archaeology sheds on their activities.

NOTES

1   *ANET*, p. 329.
2   *ANET*, p. 487.
3   See Chapter Three.
4   Jos. chapters x and xi.
5   Is. xix:18.
6   For a description of the Ugaritic texts, the student is advised to consult Gordon's *Ugaritic Literature;* also *Ugaritic Textbook for the Grammar, Texts in Transliteration,* cuneiform selections, glossary and indices, 1965; *The World of the Old Testament; ANET*, p. 129ff.
7   Bronner, L. *The Stories of Elijah and Elisha,* 1968, pp. 21ff.
8   *Ugaritic Texts,* text 49:1.
9   *Ibid.,* text 51, IV, 30ff.
10   *Ibid.* text 52, 28;
     Albright, W.F. *Archaeology and the Religion of Israel,* 1946, p. 73.
11   I Ki. xviii:19.
12   II Ki. xxi:7.
13   I Ki. xvi:33.
14   II Ki. xxi:3.
15   Dt. vii:33; xii:3; xvi:21; Mi. v:14.
16   Smith, W.R. *The Religion of the Semites,*1959, pp. 92–104
17   Schaeffer C.F.A. *The Cuneiform Texts of Ras Shamra – Ugarit,* Plate 1939, p. 69.
18   Gordon, C.H. *Ugaritic Texts,* 1949, pp. 1ff.
19   *ANET*, p. 136.
20   *ANET*, p. 142.
21   Ho. vi:13, 14; Am. ii:3.
22   Schaeffer C.F.A. *The Cuneiform Texts of Ras Shamra–Ugarit,* Plate XXXII, figure 2.
23   Bronner L. *The Stories of Elijah and Elisha,* 1968, pp. 55ff.
24   *Ugaritic Texts,* text 49, II, 30–37.
25   *Ibid.,* text 49, 11, 2–9.
26   *Ibid.,* text 76, 11, 24.
27   *Ibid.,* text 49, 11, 28ff.
28   *Ibid.,* text 76, 1, 11.
29   Ex. xxii:19; Lv. xviii:23; xx:15, 16; Dt. xxvii:2.
30   Lv. xviii:21, 27; Dt. xii:31; xviii:9ff; II Ki. xvi:3; xvii:8, 17; xxi:2.6; II Ki. iii:27; Je. xix:5; Ps. cvi:37ff.
31   Ho. iv:13–14; Am. ii:3; Dt. xxii:18–19.
32   *Ugaritic Texts,* text 2 Aqht, V, 4–8.
33   Wright, G.E. *Biblical Archaeology,* 1957, p. 110.
34   *Views of the Biblical World,* Vol. 1, p. 153. The belief in an

incorporeal God became a basic tenet of Judaism. It is included in Maimonides' Thirteen Principles of Faith and incorporated into the daily prayer which states: "Eternal, inconceivable is He.

No form, or shape has the incorporeal One."

[35] Dt. xxxi:16; Koehler-Baumgartner *Lexicon in Veteris Testamenti Libros* on the root *zanah,* 1958.

[36] *Ibid.,* note 33.

[37] Ezk. xiv:14; It is worth noting that the name Daniel is spelled with a *yod* in the Book of Daniel and without a *yod* in Ezekiel. The Dnil in Ezekiel is somebody from the remote past. In the Book of Daniel he is a person described as living during the Babylonian exile.

[38] *Ugaritic Texts,* text 2 Aqht, 1, 27–34.

[39] Luban M. *The Kaddish, Studies in Torah Judaism,* 1970.

[40] Ps. xcii:10.

[41] *Ugaritic Texts,* text 68, 7ff.

[42] Ex. xvii:8ff.

[43] Ex. xxiv:13; xxxii:17.

[44] Ex. xxxiii:11.

[45] Ex. xi:28ff.

[46] Dt. xxxi:23.

[47] Maisler, B. "Canaan and the Canaanites," in *Bulletin of the American Schools of Oriental Research,* 1946, pp. 7–12.

[48] Is. xix:18.

[49] Joel ii:4.

[50] Finegan, J. *Light from the Ancient Past,* 1969, p.135.

[51] For the authorship of the book see Harrison, R.K., *An Introduction to the Old Testament,* pp. 666ff; Peake's *Commentary to the Bible,* 1962, pp. 289ff. *The Interpreter's One-Volume Commentary on the Bible,* 1971, pp. 122ff.

[52] Jos. viff.

[53] Jos. x, xi.

[54] Sellin, E. and Watzinger, C. *Jericho,* 1913.

[55] Garstang, J. *Joshua – Judges,* 1931; pp. 144, 5, 6; Rowley, H.H. *From Joseph to Joshua,* 1948.

[56] Jos. ii:1.

[57] I Ki. xvi:34; Kenyon, K.M. *Digging up Jericho,* 1957, pp. 170ff.

[58] Albright, W.F. *Archaeology of Palestine,* 1957, p. 76.

[59] Jos. xi.

[60] *Ibid.,* Yadin, Y., BA, 1956, xix, No. 1, pp. 2ff, xx, No. 2, pp. 34 ff, 1957.

[61] Albright, BASOR, 1934, No. 56, pp. 2ff.

[62] Finegan, J. *Light from the Ancient Past,* 1969, pp. 161ff.

[63] *ANET,* p. 486.

[64] Pr. vi:6; xxx:25.

65 See our discussion above on the Amarna letters.

66 Jos. ix:3−7.

67 *Ibid.*, ix:27; This translation is the author's and is not taken from the *New English Bible.*

68 Winton, T.D. *Archaeology and the Old Testament,* 1967, pp. 231ff.

69 II Sa. ii:12−17; Je. Li:12.

70 Je. xxviii:1.

71 Je. xxxv:1ff; *De Fructu Oris Sui, Essays in Honour of Adrianus van Selms,* edited by I. Eybers; see article by Bronner, L., "The Rechabites, A Sect in Biblical Times," 1971, pp. 6ff.

72 II Sa. v:6ff.

73 I Ki. ix:16.

74 Jos. xiii:1ff.

75 Albright, W.F. *The Archaeology of Palestine and The Bible,* 1935, pp. 101ff.

76 The story of Joshua in the Bible makes it abundantly clear that the Israelite attack was launched after the collection and evaluation of intelligence data. Joshua sent spies to search out the land and lay the groundwork for the forthcoming invasion. A familiar manner of preparation for war is found in the time of Hammurapi and Homer. See Gordon, *Before the Bible,* 1962, pp. 294ff.

77 Jos. xiii:1; xv:63; xvi:10.

78 Jdg. xvii:6; xviii:1; xix:1; xxi:25.

79 For authorship see the same authors mentioned in note[51]

80 Wright, G.E. *Westminster Atlas to the Bible,* 1953, p. 19.

81 Mendelsohn, I. *Samuel's Denunciation of Kingship in the Light of Akkadian document from Ugarit.* BASOR. 1956, No. 143, pp. 17ff.

82 II Sa. xii:1ff.

83 I Ki. xxi:19. The whole chapter is relevant to the issue of the prophet's rebuke but the words "Hast thou killed and also taken possession" are both famous and most moving.

84 Je. xxii:13ff.

CHAPTER FIVE

David—The Way of the Kings

David, the man who lived in and ruled Israel in about 1000 B.C.E., was an outstanding general, statesman, and diplomat, the architect of the Jewish nation. He was also known for his piety and poetical musical talents. Archaeology has shed light on the activities of David and confirms that he was a great leader, organizer, and conquerer. There is no story in the Bible that is more beautiful and romantic than that of David, the shepherd boy of Bethlehem, who won a king's favor, then lost it and became a hunted outlaw, only eventually to be made king himself and to turn a small people into a proud, almost leading nation of those days. For a very short time, the kingdom created by David was a world power, in the context of Western Asia at that time.[1] Artifacts retrieved from excavated sites and written material associated with David and all the other kings have provided interesting sidelights on the political, economic, military, and religious life of those times.

The Biblical sources for information on the lives of Samuel, Saul, David, Solomon, and the later kings that ruled Israel and Judah come from the Books of Samuel, Kings, and Chronicles. These present students with many problems, particularly the Book of Samuel, which displays a tendency to give what appears a double account of the same story. It is beyond this book to attempt to reconcile these apparent discrepancies, and the reader is directed to the numerous books available on the subject. Nevertheless we will quote but one example, relevant to our discussion, of duplications in the Book of Samuel. Two accounts are given of David's introduction to Saul.[2] The first tells how David was invited to play before Saul and dispel the king's depression by his music.[3] His playing proved a cure for the king's black moods, and Saul in fact developed a great affection for the lad.[4] The longer and better known story is of David's fight with Goliath. Because of his victory over the Philistine, Saul took him into his military service and appointed him over the men of war. Many critics claim that these two accounts cannot be reconciled, unless one follows the lead of the Greek translators of the Bible, who saw the contradictions and boldly omitted from the Goliath story everything inconsistent with the shorter account. Others have tried to reconcile the two versions by stating that Saul pretended not to recognize David, or that his particular mental condition occasioned such non-recognition. In connection with the second of these theories it is true, of course, that mental imbalance can affect recollection and recognition, and this could be especially true in the case of Saul, who was evidently suffering from paranoid schizophrenia, and not from the manic depressive condition assumed by most scholars and commentators. Nevertheless, neither of these suppositions is really necessary in order to reconcile the apparent discrepancy. Whereas on the first occasions Saul was made aware of David as an individual, on the second the inquiry of the king concerned the lineage and social status of David, presumably as a prerequisite to the admission of the conqueror to the royal company and court. Had King Saul only been interested in the name of the hero and that of his father, the apparently lengthy conversation between Saul and David would have been quite unnecessary.[5] It is true that the Biblical writings are replete with problems of one kind or another that perplex Western minds, but it must be stated that many of the alleged discrepancies in Scripture can be reconciled if the text is closely studied and analyzed.[6]

But the purpose of this book is to continue our study of archaeological material and evaluate how, or if at all, it illuminates the setting for the lives of the Biblical personalities. We saw at the end of Chapter Four that the transition from the period of the "Judges" to that of the "Prophets" is made by Samuel. When he became old the people demanded that he should appoint a king over them. Samuel eventually acceded to their demands and anointed Saul as the first king of Israel. While at first Saul inspired confidence and destroyed the Ammonites, who threatened Jabesh-gilead, and later at least bruised the power of the Philistines, it eventually became apparent that Israel's first king was not equipped with the temperament or the ability to unify the tribes and ensure peace.

Two conflicts that broke out between Samuel and Saul led to the fall of the latter. Saul's first rift with Samuel came when he did not wait for the prophet at Gilgal, and when he saw people abandoning him he offered up sacrifices and prepared to go into battle. Samuel regarded this action as an intrusion into his office. This flagrant act of disobedience caused the first breach between Samuel and Saul.[7]

Later, after Saul's victory over the Philistines, which was occasioned by Jonathan's signal valor at Michmash, Samuel directed Saul to wage a war of extermination against the Amalekites. Saul undertook the war, but failed to exterminate the enemy. He spared the king and the best of the flocks.[8] This called forth the prophet's well-known dictum that to obey is better than sacrifice, and to hearken than the fat of rams.[9] With this second act of disobedience, he had further proved that he could not be trusted to serve as God's instrument. He was dominated by his own will and therefore he was emphatically rejected as king. Samuel was commanded to go to Bethlehem and anoint David.[10] The sympathy of the reader is usually with the tragic Saul rather than with the stern Samuel. It is interesting to note that in both instances, when Saul is rebuked by Samuel for failing to fulfill his instructions, Saul lays the blame on the people. When Samuel asked him, "What have you done?", Saul answered, "I saw that the people were drifting away from me, and you yourself had not come as you had promised, and the Philistines were assembling at Michmash; . . . so I felt compelled to make the whole-offering myself." When returning from the war with Amalek he happily greeted Samuel, saying, "I have obeyed the Lord's commands." But when the prophet said "What are the sheep I hear bleating in my ears?", Saul merely answered once again, "The people have taken them from the Amalekites . . . to sacrifice to the Lord your God." His behavior in both instances displayed a measure of weakness, for a leader must influence his flock and not the reverse.[11]

The prophet's rejection of Saul caused him to suffer fits of depression, and eventually he became possessed of a mad jealousy against David, who was originally brought before him to dispel his black moods. The most tragic step in the king's downfall was his recourse to the witch of Endor. The seriousness of this act, the king's final plunge into ruin, derives from the fact that was resorting to an illegitimate means of discovering the future, which was characteristic of the polytheistic nations surrounding Israel but utterly at variance with the faith of the God of Israel. The fact that Saul himself had outlawed these occult practices, and that he dared to have recourse to them himself, clearly indicates the measure of his tragedy.[12] The king's doom is announced by Samuel in this last tragic meeting between prophet and king. In sum, Saul was a tragic figure; Samuel broke him by declaring him rejected by God. Nevertheless, Saul's good traits are depicted in the early scenes of his life. For instance, when he was anointed king he was scorned by some scoundrels who said: "How can this fellow deliver us?" After his first victory against Nahash the Ammonite, who besieged Jabesh-gilead, the people wished to punish these wicked men who insulted the king. But Saul said: "No man shall be put to death on the day when the Lord has won such a victory in Israel."[13] However, once he attuned himself to the life of a king, and the glory that went with it, the thought of being deprived of it threw him into fits of raving madness. The rift between Saul and David came about when the women meeting the returning warriors sang: "Saul made havoc among thousands. But David among ten thousands."[14] From that moment David became an object of suspicion and hate, and Saul's pursual of David led him to neglect his kingdom and duties as king. Hatred of David became a monomania which eventually destroyed him. It is true that Saul lacked self-control and foresight. He was hasty at times, as when he was ready to put his son to death or to kill the priests because they had assisted David; nevertheless his greatness perhaps lies in the fact that his conscience always pricked him for all the evil actions he perpetrated. His life vividly illustrates that power corrupts.[15]

Excavations were carried out at Saul's home town, Gibeah, by Albright, and they revealed a fortress which represented the second occupation of the site, the first town having been destroyed in the period of the Judges.[16] At Gibeah were found the remains of a palace, a remarkable and romantic discovery! True, it was in ruins and forts had been built on top of it. True, it was far from being a magnificent building. Indeed it was more of a fortress than a palace and, while strongly fortified, could scarcely have been considered a comfortable and suitable residence by the standards of the monarchs of the Ancient Near East. Nevertheless it was the royal residence of Saul, and its nature was quite in keeping with what we know of him from the stories in Samuel. Saul was no wealthy, learned cosmopolitan statesman. He was first and foremost a warrior and the rustic simplicity of this fortress fits in well with his life. It was two stories high, the family living on the second floor. A double wall surrounded the palace fortress. The furnishings of the building were very simple, and among the debris were found cooking pots, a variety of pottery vessels, arrow heads and sling stones which were the usual weapons of war of those days. And most significant, an iron plowshare was found in the debris as well. In short, this two-story building was serviceable rather than luxurious. Saul was only a rustic chieftain as far as architecture and amenities of life were concerned.

From a political point of view Saul had the unenviable task of not only uniting the tribes but of facing a ferocious foe without adequate weapons. The secret of smelting iron was strictly guarded by the Philistines. "No blacksmith was to be found in the whole of Israel, for the Philistines were determined to prevent the Hebrews from making swords and spears. The Israelites had to go down to the Philistines for their plowshares, mattocks, axes, and sickles to be sharpened . . . So when war broke out none of the followers of Saul and Jonathan had either swords or spears; only Saul and Jonathan carried arms." [17] The earliest iron plowshare was discovered at Saul's fortress in Gibeah, and this has caused some scholars to claim that he did eventually break the Philistines' hegemony and wrested the monopoly of iron manufacture from them. The result of this was to have tremendous beneficial effects for the days of David and Solomon, when this metal began to be widely used.

The story of the war between Jabesh-gilead and the King of Ammon, where the latter demanded that the people submit to the humiliation of having one eye struck out, finds a parallel in Ugaritic sources. The legend of Aqht describes a conflict between this young lad and the goddess Anat. Aqht possessed the bow which the goddess coveted. She asked Aqht to give her the bow. Aqht not only flatly refused to accede to her request but added insult to injury by informing her that the bow was a weapon for men only. The cruel goddess became annoyed with the young lad and had him killed. His father, the righteous Dnil, mourned bitterly for him and cursed the town of Abiluma because it was the site where his son was murdered. The righteous Dnil cried: "May Baal make thee one-eyed." [18] Thus, in both the Bible and in Ugarit we see the existence of a barbaric custom in the ancient world where the idea of punishing or humiliating a city by blinding its inhabitants in one eye was known. The town's responsibility for a crime perpetrated within its territory is, in turn, an institution attested in the Bible and cuneiform records and persists in the Middle East until today. [19]

David's lament over Saul and Jonathan is couched in the poetic forms that are well known today from Ugarit. David sang:

Ye mountains of Gilboa,
Let there be no dew nor rain upon you
Neither fields of choice fruits. [20]

It is interesting again to note in Ugaritic literature that when Dnil curses the site of Aqht's murder, he uses similar words:

Woe unto thee, arbor of dead clusters!
Alongside which Aqht the hero was smitten!
May thy roots not flourish in the earth. [21]

This unmistakable parallel is of special importance because it provides the key to the origin of Hebrew historiography. Other nations of the Ancient Near East had annals, but no real history in which personal character and motivation were delineated. Such delineation had been limited to the epics that dealt with the gods and legendary men. We have observed that historic events such as Deborah's victory were celebrated in poetry as well as in prose. David's dirge, as the Ugaritic parallel proves, is in the epic tradition. Thus, the Hebrews achieved true historical composition by transferring human values from the epic to current events. In reading the account of the battle of Gilboa, we see that while the political and military developments are mentioned, the real interest is in the fate of Saul and Jonathan, and in how their fate affected the hero David. With the rise of the monarchy, Hebrew historiography comes into its own, for the sense of national greatness evoked a pride in the story of the nation. The composition of real history is one of the greatest achievements of that period. It antedates Greek historiography by over 500 years. Prior to the Ugaritic discoveries, the origin of Hebrew historiography was a mystery. But now that we know it was created through the application of epic values to current events, it still remains a miracle that it was not the large nations, such as Babylonia, Assyria, or Egypt, but tiny Israel which made that momentous contribution to civilization. National, like individual, genius cannot be explained by analysis in a test tube. Every nation in the Bible world had epic traditions and experienced current events. It took the genius of Israel to create historiography by combining them! [22]

Archaeology has added one more touching point to the end of Saul's life. After he died so tragically on Mount Gilboa, the Philistines desecrated his body and that of his sons which they found lying on the ground as they had died. They cut off Saul's head and placed it in the temple of Dagon in Bethshan. [23] Scholars believe that one of the two temples excavated at Bethshan during 1921–1931 by Rowe and Fitzgerald was this actual temple. Here were typical temples of the day where the cult of the gods of Canaan was carried out. Numerous articles of religious significance were found in these temples. Which one of the two temples was the one referred to in the story about Saul is, of course, impossible to say. It is now quite clear, however, that there was a temple in Bethshan at that time. [24]

David's most important contribution to Biblical history is that he created the Israelite nation. The romantic manner in which his life unfolds in the Bible has been briefly referred to above. David possessed a magnetic and winning personality and showed a remarkable gift for attracting friends and appeasing his enemies. Even a son and a daughter of King Saul were enchanted by him. Saul had turned David into an outlaw who had to flee his country and to take up residence eventually in the land of Gath. David gathered around him four hundred fellow tribesmen, all desperadoes who had not gotten along with organized society. When David became their chief he really began his career as a leader, and this leadership was to culminate in the establishment of a long dynasty. Though during his exile David had a couple of opportunities to kill Saul, he never availed himself of them. He refrained from laying his hand on God's anointed. This action is in keeping with David's character; rarely did he fail to do what would command the respect of the public. David, as distinct from many orientals of the Biblical world, and even of later times, was not bent on extirpating the line of his predecessor. On the contrary, he vowed he would not destroy Saul's seed, a vow of which he was later mindful. Upon Saul's death he uttered a most eloquent dirge commemorating the valiant acts of the king and his son. David's way was then clear to becoming king. He was first elected king of Judah in Hebron and seven years later king over all Israel.

David's life henceforth was filled with a number of magnificent achievements. On every side he was able to push back the enemies of Israel. He defeated and broke the power of the Philistines. Then he subjugated the Moabites, Edomites, Arameans, and Ammonites.[25] At his death, David left a kingdom at peace with her foes. In addition to these military successes there were outstanding advances made in the spheres of government, commerce and trade, religion, and international affairs.

In the realm of religion, David brought the Ark to Jerusalem and wished to build the Temple. This privilege was not vouchsafed to him, as the Chronicler puts it: "You have shed much blood in my sight and waged great wars; for this reason you shall not build the house in honor of my name. But you shall have a son who shall be a man of peace; I will give him peace from all his enemies on every side; his name shall be Solomon, "Man of Peace," and I will grant peace and quiet to Israel in his days. He shall build a house in honor of my name; he shall be my son and I will be a father to him, and I will establish the throne of his sovereignty over Israel forever."[26]

One of David's greatest achievements was the conquest of Jerusalem, and the turning of this city into his capital. Archaeology offers some new light on the subject. The Book of Samuel describes the capture of Jerusalem very briefly and in obscure language. The Jebusites were so confident in the strength of their city that they jeered at David's boasting. They taunted him that even if they manned the walls only by blind and lame men it could not be captured. It appears that David was desperate to capture this city and he said: "Whosoever smiteth the Jebusites and getteth up to the gutter and taketh away the lame and the blind, that are hated of David's soul — Wherefore they say: 'There are the blind and the lame; he cannot come into thine house.' "[27] The first verse seems incomplete, and in Chronicles it apparently explains that David said: "Whosoever smiteth the Jebusites first shall be chief and captain. And Joab the son of the Zeruiah went up first, and was made chief." [28] How David conquered this fortress has always puzzled scholars. Two suggestions have been offered. The one claims that the word *ẓinnor*, which is translated as "gutter", is the water tunnel through which the Israelites conquered the city. The verses appear to imply that there was a route to the spring from within the wall which was penetrated by Joab, who thus took the defenders by surprise from the rear and enabled the attacking force to break in. Access to a spring in a valley outside the city site is a commonplace phenomenon in Palestinian towns. The most famous are to be found at Megiddo, Gibeon, and Gezer.

The first archaeologist to excavate at the site of Jerusalem was Warren in 1867. The basic discoveries concerning the tunnels connected with the Gihon spring in the Kedron valley came from his work in that area. The interrelation of the numerous tunnels and shafts was elaborated by Vincent in his study of the clearances of the 1911 excavation. There was discovered a tunnel about 230 feet in length, which runs from the spring of Gihon to the top of the hill, on which the ancient fortress of Zion must have been situated. The purpose of the tunnel was to enable the garrison to draw water from the spring from within the fortress, especially in the event of a siege. This tunnel, or part of it, may have been that *ẓinnor* or gutter that the Israelites discovered. Through it they made their way into the fortress in order to surprise the Jebusites. In other words, the position of the head of the shaft was inside the town, while the spring was outside the wall. Access to the Gihon spring was made by tunnel and shaft and was the way of reaching it from within the city in times of danger, but archaeologists maintain that there was a simpler approach to it in times of peace. There probably was a water gate which must have been the main gate of entrance to the spring. [29]

An alternative explanation for the conquest of Jerusalem has been offered by Albright. He showed that the word *ẓinnor* translated as "gutter" or "watershaft," is a Canaanite word meaning "hook," and implied that access to Jerusalem was gained by means of grappling hooks. According to this explanation the capture of Jerusalem was effected by quite a different method. [30] Whatever the method, the stronghold of the Jebusites was subjugated and turned into David's capital. This was a masterly diplomatic move on the part of David. In this manner he founded a capital that was neutral in relation to all of the quarrelling tribes, since it was entirely his by right of conquest. In addition to this, Jerusalem's natural strategic strength, its central geographical position, and its situation connecting the north and the south made it an excellent choice as a capital. It also had religious significance, for it was in all probability, according to tradition, the place which had honored associations with Abraham. Excavations carried on by Kenyon at the site in the 1960's discovered a wall which must have been that of the Jebusite town that was captured by David. It was thereafter repaired by him as the wall of his own city. Kenyon claimed that the line of the northern and northeastern part of the wall of the original Jerusalem had been established with reasonable certainty.

Kenyon writes: "The Jerusalem captured by David is revealed, with all reservations demanded by the limitations of the evidence, as an elongated triangle, with east and west sides following the shape of the ridge, the northern base of the triangle crossing it transversely on the arbitrary line. The area enclosed is c. 10.87 acres. This area consisted of two very different parts – a narrow summit plateau, at its widest not much more than 100 m. across, and on the east a slope running deeply down to the central valley. This lopsided development was undoubtedly dictated by the need to control access to the spring. The wall is in fact sited with some skill. In time of war, the inhabitants could obtain their water under cover by means of a tunnel and a shaft. There is every reason to suppose that this is the method by which the Jebusites had access to the spring in the time of war, and it was the means whereby the capture of the town by David was achieved. The position of the head of the shaft would be inside the town, while the spring would be outside the walls. But however carefully the external entrance to the spring was disguised, they could not expect that spies or traitors would not disclose its position to an enemy. The town wall had therefore to be close enough to the spring for the defenders to inhibit or discourage interference with it by attackers. On the other hand, it could not be so low on the slope, and certainly not low enough to enclose the spring, as to come under fire from enemy stationed on the eastern side of the Kedron valley."[31]

Thus, the city captured by David was a promontory projecting south from the main summit ridge, the ridge defended by steep valleys to the east and west, with a north wall crossing the ridge at a point just far enough north to secure access to the vital spring in the eastern valley. David then paid specific attention to what is called the *millo*. The meaning of the word is "filling," but the translations from the Hebrew made its meaning so uncertain that they transcribed the word as it stood. The present archaeological evidence suggests that *millo* was the terrace structure, or a filling, and on it was situated nearly half of the whole town of Jerusalem. The literary evidence suggests that David repaired the city

Figure 17. Excavations in the south hill at Jerusalem (Ophel) which revealed the Jebusite city wall (1) and the Israelite city wall above it (2).

that he captured. There is no evidence that he developed it or expanded it. With this, archaeological evidence agrees. Politically, this is also entirely acceptable. David was far too deeply involved in conquest, stretching from Damascus to the north to the gulf of Aqaba in the south, to engage in major architectural schemes in his capital. The expansion of Jerusalem, and turning it into a city of splendor, was left to his son Solomon.

Archaeology sheds interesting light on the tradition which connects David with music and psalmody. On archaeological grounds there is no reason to doubt what has been handed down — that he was a lover of music and poetry, and that he was designated as the sweet singer in Israel.[32] It must be remembered that even Talmudic tradition attributed to David only some of the psalms, and stated that the book included the works of fifteen other men.[33] It was accordingly recognized that the psalter was a composite effort. Most probably David gave firm definition to the concept of poetry in Israel, as Moses had done for the law; and it may be that his poetic compositions, along with any which may have been attributed to him in parts or in whole, formed the basis of the Hebrew psalter. On the other hand, modern criticism tended completely to reduce David's role in this particular sphere, and relegated the psalter to post-exilic times. Until the recent discoveries came to hand, this position was not easy to refute because of lack of evidence on the subject. Now, however, archaeology has shed so much new light on the matter that there is nothing incongruous in regarding David as the patron saint of Jewish hymnology, and "the organizer of the Temple music," as the Bible has it. Egyptian and Mesopotamian sources provide ample evidence that Palestine and Syria were well known in antiquity for their musicians. The Beni-Hasan relief from Egypt depicts a black bearded nomad walking behind his donkey to the accompaniment of music which he makes upon a lyre.[34] The knowledge of music and musical instruments among the early Hebrews and their pre-diluvian ancestors in extremely early times is borne out in the account of Jubal in Genesis.[35]

The discoveries at Ugarit have brought forth interesting information on Hebrew psalmody and poetry. They have illustrated that Hebrew singing was not influenced at all by Babylonian or Egyptian sources, but reveals a close relationship with that of Ugarit. It is now apparent that the earliest poetry of the Bible is replete not with Babylonian or Egyptian forms, but with rhythmical patterns that are thoroughly characteristic of the Canaanite poems of Ugarit. As already mentioned, far-reaching parallels in grammar and syntax, as well as literary style, have served to emphasize the closeness of relationship between Ugaritic and Hebrew poetry and to minimize the connection with other areas of the Ancient

Near East. Thus, for instance, the epic religious literature discovered at Ras Shamra in ancient Ugarit in northern Syria speaks of a group of *sarim* or singers who formed a special class of temple personnel there as early as 1400 B.C.E.[36] Even the Greeks are supposed to have borrowed certain musical instruments along with their names from the musically talented Phoenicians. The *kinnor*, which was used for sacred and secular occasions, corresponded to the *cithara* of the Greeks and the Romans. This newly discovered external evidence reinforces the view that the institution of Temple musicians goes back to an early date.

The Bible itself offers strong evidence in support of David's musical interest and talent. Coupled with his pious devotion to the Lord, David's interest in music presents an ideal background for the Chronicler's assertion that he organized the guilds of Temple musicians. David is repeatedly represented as a skillful performer on the lyre and a composer of beautiful poetry. He is described as jubilantly dancing before the Ark when he brought it to Jerusalem and set up the Tabernacle to house it.

However, there is not only strong evidence of the existence of Temple music in early Israel but there is incontrovertible archaeological evidence for the existence of the musical guilds themselves. The Canaanites outshone their contemporaries in music, and the Israelites were influenced by them. Musical guilds among the Hebrews may be traced back, in some instances, to the old Canaanite families whose designations, such as Heman and Ezrahite mentioned in Chronicles, became a part of the later Hebrew family names. In addition, such terms as "Asaph," "Heman," and "Ethan" or "Jeduthun" are evidently used by the Chronicler to designate musical guilds, and in the case of "Heman" and "Ethan" are closely paralleled by scores of abbreviated names found at Ugarit and elsewhere. They are characteristically Canaanite and early, not appearing in later Hebrew lists of contemporary names.[37] Thus, Hebrew Temple music was recognized in Israel as going back to pre-Israelite sources and, although archaeological evidence does not prove that David organized the first religious music in Israel, it does show that the Chronicler's attribution of such activity to Israel's shepherd king contains nothing inconsistent with the spirit of the times or at variance with the contemporary historical scene.

Abundant light has been shed on the Hebrew psalter by the religious literature from Ugarit which shows that many of the psalms, such as lxviii and xcii are suffused with Canaanite stylistic and literary parallels and even with direct quotations. Just as the Israelites took their music from their precursors, so they borrowed the metric form, vocabulary, and style of their sacred lyrics from their Canaanite neighbors.[38]

The Canaanite material in many of the psalms does not necessarily prove an early date, since strong Canaanite influences can be shown to have taken place in two distinct periods — in the 11th century and the 6th—4th centuries B.C.E. But the Canaanite context of such psalms as lxviii and its striking parallels with such an obviously ancient poem as the Song of Deborah in Judges,[39] which cannot be dated under any consideration later than the 11th century B.C.E., shows that this psalm and certainly many others may go back to David's time or earlier. In fact archaeological evidence points to the high probability that the entire Book of Psalms spans the whole of Old Testament history from Moses to Malachi, as its internal evidence would lead us to conclude, and supports the traditional role of David as a musician, poet, and organizer of sacred music in Israel. To sum up on David the musician, we can say that the historical narratives about David depict him as a person possessing gifts of leadership and friendship, poetical and musical imagination, and the evidence from archaeology lends considerable support to this glorious image.

Biblical tradition regarding the age of Solomon has received similar confirmation in recent years as the result of archaeological activity. The age of Solomon was certainly one of the most flourishing periods in the material civilization in the history of Palestine. The creation of Jerusalem as a city of splendor belongs to the time of Solomon. It would take us too far afield to describe the eclipse of all the powerful nations in the Fertile Crescent which made possible the rise of the Kingdom of Israel; yet archaeological discoveries plainly illustrate that precisely during this period, from about 1100—900 B.C.E., the power of all these great nations of the Ancient Near East relating to Palestine was either eclipsed or laid low for a while, so that Solomon could rule with the splendor and wisdom divinely promised to him.[40] A vivid illustration of the power of Solomon and the dwindling influence of Egypt can be seen from the fact corroborated by archaeology that Solomon married an Egyptian princess. This marriage was given special emphasis in the Bible.[41] Malamat, in a very interesting article, shows that it was unusual for the kings of Egypt to give their daughters in marriage to foreign rulers, even though they themselves were in the habit of taking the daughters of such rulers as wives. It was known from the Amarna letters that, when the king of Babylon sought the hand of the daughter of Amenhotep III, the Egyptian monarch rejected his suit on the grounds that "from of old, a daughter of the king of Egypt has not been given to anyone," i.e., to a foreigner. It is therefore most likely that the Biblical reference to Solomon's marriage to the daughter of Pharaoh is meant to stress the power and the high esteem in which the kingdom of Israel was held by the Egyptians and throughout the whole

Ancient Near East in that period of history. Solomon, who had inherited a large empire from his father, apparently conducted no major military campaigns. His task was to maintain Israel's extensive boundaries and to exploit his position of strength during the power vacuum that was created by the temporary eclipse of Egypt and Assyria. The two main pillars of Solomon's foreign policy were friendly alliances, sometimes sealed by marriage, and the maintenance of a formidable army. [42]

The life of Solomon stands in complete contrast to that of his father, David. The latter had to struggle to reach the crown and conquer his own empire. Solomon encountered but few difficulties in the form of rivalry from his brothers before ascending the throne. It was then left to him to devote himself to peace and prosperity. The narratives in the Bible about him love to depict his wealth and magnificence. People from near and far came to behold his splendor and wisdom. Whereas David is depicted as an intensely human figure, the stories about Solomon describe him as a distant grandiose person, draped in the splendid robes of power, proceeding in a stately fashion across a magnificent stage. First Solomon devoted himself to eliminating his enemies and then to his ambitious building and business enterprises. Though his reign opens amid glory, it ends amid murmuring and discontent. His ambitious building projects, which we shall describe, caused discontent and after his death the whole magnificent structure which David had built up came tumbling down.

The Bible describes in one verse the ambitious building projects that Solomon undertook upon ascending the throne. "This is the record of the forced labor which King Solomon conscripted to build the house of the Lord, his own palace, the Millo, the wall of Jerusalem, and Hazor, Megiddo, and Gezer," [43] A few other verses describe Solomon as an enterprising merchant who controlled all the leading routes of the Fertile Crescent and sent ships equipped with smelted ore to the far ends of the earth, which came back with splendid cargo for his own realm: "King Solomon built a fleet of ships at Ezion-Geber near Elath on the shore of the Red Sea, in Edom. Hiram sent men of his own to serve with the fleet, experienced seamen to work with Solomon's men; and they went to Ophir and brought back 420 talents of gold; ... brought also cargoes of almug wood and precious stones. The King used the wood to make stools for the house of the Lord and for the royal palace, as well as harps and lutes for the singers." [44]

The description of Solomon's Temple and palace is given in great detail in the first book of Kings. [45] As one reads the descriptions, one's impression is of exotic magnificence, the full significance of which in the culture of Israel can only be appreciated if one remembers how simple

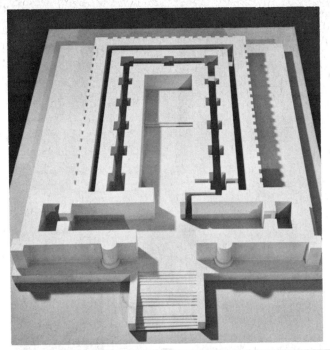

Figure 18a-b. Two models of tentative reconstruction of Solomon's Temple, prepared by the Israel Museum.

Figure 19. Model of the Israelite temple at Arad showing: (1) entrance hall *(ulam)*; (2) altar; (3) columns; (4) main hall *(heikhal)*; (5) Holy of Holies *(devir)*.

were the origins of Solomon's father, David. Israel in the days of Solomon had indeed moved into the category of a world power. The plan of the Temple was relatively simple, a porch, a basilical main chamber consisting of a central hall flanked by multi-story side rooms, and at the end of it the Holy of Holies in which the Ark was housed. It was the ancillaries to the Temple that were exotic. The entrance to the vestibule was flanked by two great bronze pillars. In front of the whole building stood the bronze "sea." This fixture was of special ritual importance, since the washing of the hands and the feet was a necessary preliminary to the priests' officiating in the sanctuary. In the center of the court was the bronze altar which is only mentioned in the description of the inauguration ceremony carried out by Solomon.[46] Solomon received from Hiram, king of Tyre, the material for building this elaborate edifice as well as the skilled craftsman and the ornamental motifs. Though no relics of Solomon's Temple have as yet been found, discoveries of similar edifices in Palestine and its neighborhood indicate that such a building was possible. Excavations carried out in Palestine at Bethshan, Megiddo, Lachish, Hazor, and most recently Arad, and also at sites in Lebanon and Syria, have brought to light the remains of various Canaanite temples.[47] The one that most resembles Solomon's Temple in plan was excavated at Tell Tainat in Syria and is from the 9th century B.C.E. Like Solomon's Temple it was also divided into three sections, and at its entrance had two pillars. A Cannanite temple from the end of the Late Bronze Age, which might be considered as a prototype of the Solomonic Temple, has been recently excavated at Hazor. This, too, consisted of three parts, namely the vestibule, the nave, and the inner sanctuary. In the latter various ritual implements were found. The excavations at Arad revealed the most thrilling discovery by bringing to light an ancient sanctuary which once again resembled that of Solomon's Temple. A reconstruction of it can be seen in the Israel Museum. The temple at Arad is really the first Israelite sanctuary discovered in the Land of Israel.[48] Thus, although the archaeological evidence for Solomon's Temple in Jerusalem is still regrettably slight, the evidence for the culture of Phoenicia and the neighboring countries does provide a visual interpretation for the literary evidence of Solomon's buildings at Jerusalem. The general picture of this city is clear. To the town conquered by his father, Solomon added buildings, the Temple, his palace, and the palace of his principal wife, the daughter of Pharaoh, in a style using all the most exotic elements of the more advanced civilizations of Phoenicia and Syria. Probably the Temple dominated the sight of Jerusalem.[49]

A special status is given to three other towns, namely, Hazor, Megiddo, and Gezer, by the fact that they are linked in the verse with

Jerusalem. Both Megiddo and Hazor are very old cities which appeared to have suffered destruction between the 13th and 12th centuries B.C.E., followed by a gap in occupation. That Solomon rebuilt all these cities is evident from the fact that the design of the gateway of all three cities is exactly the same. From this we are entitled to infer that all three were built by royal command on a single master plan, and possibly by the same architect. [50]

The backbone of Solomon's military defense was a ring of cities strategically located near the borders of Israel and manned by squadrons of charioteers. [51] His militia included 4,000 stalls for horses. At Megiddo archaeologists discovered 450 stalls with elaborate systems of feeding and watering the horses. However, some scholars now question the customary crediting of these stables to the age of Solomon. Yadin has discovered a construction which resembles the Solomonic walls at Hazor and Gezer, but differs from the stables, which he now attributes to Ahab. [52] Thus, while Yadin has cast some doubt as to whether the ruins at Megiddo did in fact belong to Solomon and not rather to Ahab, the appearance of Solomon's stables may be understood from the ruin at Megiddo. Speaking of stables, it must be mentioned that Solomon carried on a lucrative trade in horses. The passage in the Authorized Version of the Bible has an odd ring about it when it says: "And Solomon had horses brought out of Egypt and linen yarn." The word for "linen yarn" could mean "from Kue" (Cilicia). In the light of new discoveries we can translate this passage differently. Horses were imported from Egypt and Kue (Cao) for Solomon; in other words Solomon's business acumen took advantage of Israel's location when he became the exclusive agent through whom the Neo-Hittite petty kingdoms of Moab – Syria had to negotiate in order to buy horses from Kue. [53]

We still must describe Solomon's maritime enterprises, as well as his mining activities. Nelson Glueck, during his excavation activities in the Negev, uncovered the first copper refinery ever found in the Near East. It was built for Solomon by Phoenician workmen who were experienced in the construction of copper furnaces and the refining of ore, and it was located at Ezion-Geber (modern Tell el-Kheleifeh), between the hill country of Sinai and the land of Edom. The archaeological finds from this site show that it was once an important industrial center, with a highly efficient metallurgical furnace for the smelting of copper. Thus, archaeology bears further evidence of the industrial activities of Solomon, who did so much to develop the crafts, industry, and foreign trade of Israel.

Scholars maintain that the ore from the mines of the Arabah, after

Figure 20. Aerial view of the Solomonic gate (1) and the casement wall (2) at Hazor.

being smelted and refined at Ezion-Geber, constituted the principal commodity exported from there by Solomon's ships. The phrase in the Bible "ships of Tarshish" is probably to be translated "refinery ships," that is ships equipped to carry smelted ore. Once again it was the king of Tyre who built these ships at Ezion-Geber and manned them with Tyrian sailors for Solomon who, together with the Israelites, traveled to countries rich in gold, spices, and precious stones. They took the ore to faraway countries, and in return the ships brought back splendid cargo: gold, silver, hardwood, jewels, ivory, and a variety of birds. [54]

One valuable piece of written evidence from this age is the now famous Gezer calendar, written in the old Phoenician script on a piece of limestone. According to some scholars it was an exercise tablet belonging to a learned scribe. According to others it was an actual calendar, i.e. a list of agricultural activities engaged in during the different months of the year. A recent translation by Albright reads as follows:

> His two months are (olive harvest)
> His two months are late planting;
> His month is hoeing up a flax,
> His month is harvest and feasting;
> His two months are wine-tending;
> His month is summer fruit. [55]

It can be seen that Solomon's reign is characterized by its tendency to toleration toward alien ideas and cultures. The Israelites began to have intellectual and cultural contact with the Canaanites under his rule. The Canaanite elements were responsible for the main divergences from the worship of the Lord. Economic and political cooperation between Israel and Phoenicia led to a free exchange of cultural and religious practices as well. The worship of Baal and other prominent Phoenician deities, including some of their orgiastic elements, spread in Israel. Intermarriage with the Phoenicians and other non-Israelite peoples became less rare now. The king himself "loved many foreign women, besides the daughter of Pharaoh, women of the Moabites, Ammonites, Edomites, Sidonians, and Hittites." [56] It is true that Solomon's acquisition of many of the alleged total of 700 princesses and 300 concubines was motivated, as royal marriages frequently are, by the dictates of diplomacy. But these marriages with foreigners brought in their train additional concessions to alien gods.

The Biblical writer did not overlook the fact that Solomon built shrines to the various gods whom his wives worshiped. The author of the Book of Kings blamed Solomon for this apostasy from the Lord, which in his opinion accounted largely for the disruption of the kingdom and the other disasters which followed Solomon's death. Recent discoveries have greatly enhanced the historical value of the Biblical account of the activities of Solomon, and enriched its story with its considerable new material. It is told that the Queen of Sheba after she met Solomon is reported to have exclaimed: "The report which I heard in my own country about you and your wisdom was true, but I did not believe until I came and saw for myself. Indeed I was not told half of it; your wisdom and your prosperity go far beyond the report which I had of them."[57] These words of the Queen of Sheba might well be used to express the mood of modern scholars when they re-read Biblical stories about the reigns of David and Solomon in the light of the most recent revelations.

However, Solomon's reign which began with such promise, was to end tragically. For though we have illustrated how remarkably the biblical account of his reign has been corroborated by modern archaeological discoveries, the Bible gives a sad picture of its collapse on his death. Yet to a certain extent it was Solomon the wise himself who sowed the seeds of rebellion which overtook the country upon his death. But the worst aspect about Solomon's program was its social effect; it destroyed the happiness of the people. The heavy taxation, the levy with its enforced removal of men from home and work, the handing over of Israelite cities to a foreign master – these are the kinds of acts that in all ages have brought misery wherever they have been put into practice. While Solomon's wisdom and greatness could hold the people in harness, from the moment he died his foolish son brought the kingdom to division. Thus, from the material point of view he brought Israel to a high-water mark, while from a social standpoint he caused much heartache and grief. To use a metaphor employed by the prophets, he did not feed the sheep entrusted to him. The fact is he was not thinking enough of his people. He was dazzled by his own accomplishments and splendor and especially by his buildings. His mind, like that of many another great builder, was on stones and mortar more than on men and women. The passion for building is apt at times to blind men to the true importance of their tasks. They forget that the important structures cannot replace national and human happiness. Solomon nevertheless left a permanent legacy to his people. He became the father of its wisdom, and he gave it its temple. The division of the kingdom came during the days of his son Rehoboam. The people demanded that he lighten the burdens of taxation, and instead of hearkening to the advice of the old men he listened to his cronies and threatened to increase their burdens. When all Israel saw that the king would not listen to them they answered:

What share have we in David?
We have no lot in the son of Jesse.
Away to your houses, O Israel;
Now see to your own house, O David. [58]

The division of the kingdom opened a new phase in the history of Israel's relations. Whereas the Judeans continued to worship in the Temple we observe the rise of new sanctuaries at Dan and Bethel in the Northern Kingdom. [59] Jeroboam, the founder of the separate monarchy in the north, elevated these two places to the status of royal shrines. In the latter places golden bull calves provided the visible pedestal for YHWH's invisible throne, the functions fulfilled by the cherubs in the Jerusalem Temple. However, some scholars feel that these bulls were not meant to be only the footstool of God but were actually intended to represent God himself. For the king told his people: "Behold thy God, O Israel." [60] Further support for the latter view is Hosea's denial that the "calf of Samaria was a god." His statement: "A smith made it, and it is not God," shows that the people considered the image as being God. [61] The Northern Kingdom established by Jeroboam was characterized by continuous strife and the rise and fall of leaders. In the 200 years of its independent existence, there sat on its throne no less than 19 kings. These men belonged to nine different families. There was great insecurity in government. If we wish to use the term "dynasty" for a ruling house, then we can say that only the 4th and the 5th Dynasties achieved any stability at all.

During this time, Israel had periods of conflict and periods of friendship with her neighbor and brother kingdom Judah. The great Assyrian nation lay in the background like a giant which was to awaken soon and eventually swallow up little Israel. These were the days of the great preaching prophets like Elijah, Elisha, Hosea, Amos, Isaiah, Micah, Jeremiah, and Ezekiel. In the next chapter we turn to the activities of Elijah in light of archaeology.

NOTES

[1]   Kenyon, K.M. *Royal Cities of the Old Testament,* 1972, p. 36.
[2]   Harrison, R.K.   *An Introduction to the Old Testament,* 1970, pp.700ff.
[3]   I Sa. xvi:14ff; xviii:1ff.
[4]   It was believed then, as psychiatrists claim today, that music can produce good and bad effects in patients. In II Ki.iii:15, Elisha asked that the musicians play before him and this induced the prophetic spirit to descend upon him.

5   I Sa. xvi:14ff; I Sa. xvii:55ff; xviii:1ff.

6   *Ibid.*, note ².

7   I Sa. xiii:13ff.

8   I Sa. xv:1ff.

9   I Sa. xv:22.

10 I Sa. xvi:1ff.

11 I Sa. xiii:9; xv:14.

12 I Sa. xxviii:2–25; Lev. xix:31; xx:6, 27 ; Dt. xviii:10, 11. These occult practices were forbidden by the laws of the Pentateuch.

13 I Sa. xi:13; x:16, 22. Saul's modesty and kindness are evident in these verses.

14 I Sa. xviii:7.

15 I Sa. xiv:39ff; xxii:18ff; xxiv:16ff.

16 Jdg. xix:20;
    Kenyon, K.M. *Archaeology in the Holy Land,* 1970, p. 238;
    Albright, W.F. *The Archaeology of Palestine,* 1956, p. 122.

17 I Sa. xiii:19ff.

18 I Aqht : 167; Krt 99, 187.

19 Dt. xxi:1ff.

20 II Sa. i:21. This translation is taken from the Soncino Bible.

21 I Aqht : 160ff.

22 Gordon, C.H. *An Introduction to the Old Testament,* 1953, pp. 152ff.

23 I Sa. xxxi:9ff; I Ch. x:9ff.

24 Kenyon, K.M. *Archaeology in the Holy Land,* 1970, p. 309.

25 II Sa. v, viii, x, xi.

26 I Ch. xxii:8ff.

27 II Sa. v:8, 9; The Sages of the Talmud claimed that the lame and the blind were the idols the Jebusites worshiped.

28 I Ch. xi:6.

29 Kenyon, K.M. *Royal Cities of the Old Testament,* 1971, pp. 25ff.

30 Albright, W.F. *The Old Testament and Archaeology, Old Testament Commentary,* 1954, p. 149.

31 Kenyon, K.M. *Royal Cities of the Old Testament,* 1971, pp. 31ff.

32 Am. vi:5; Ezr. iii:10; Ne. xii:12, 24; I Ch. vi:31; xvi:7. These verses attribute poetic and musical ability to David.

33 *Baba Batra* 14b.

34 *ANEP,* p. 3.

35 Gn. iv:20–22

36 Albright, W.F. *The Religion of Israel,* 1946, pp. 225ff.

37 Harrison, R.K. *An Introduction to the Old Testament,* 1970, pp. 982ff. I Sa. xvi: 14–23; II Sa. i:17–27.

38 *Ibid.* Also Albright, W.F. *The Religion of Israel and Archaeology,* 1946, pp.225ff.

39 Albright, W.F. "The Song of Deborah in the Light of Archaeology,"

BASOR April 1936, No. 62. It might be said, though, that Canaanite influence in the 6th—4th centuries B.C.E. looks very doubtful. It was invented because many scholars date Is. xxiv-xxvii to post-exilic times. Ugaritic parallels to Is. xxvii:1, xxvi:19 suggest rather a much older date for this so-called Isaiah apocalypse.

40 I Ki. iii:1ff.

41 Malamat, A. "The Kingdom of David and Solomon in its Contact with Egypt and Aram Naharaim," *The Biblical Archaeologist Reader*, 1964, 2, 89.

42 I Ki. iii—xi; *Ibid.*

43 I Ki. ix:15.

44 I Ki. ix:25-28; x:11—12.

45 I Ki. vi-vii.

46 The "Sea" is described in Ex. xxx:17ff; the altar in I Ki. viii:22, 54, 64.

47 *Views of the Biblical World*, 1960, Vol. II, p. 213;
Kenyon, K.M. *The Royal Cities of the Old Testament*, 1971, pp. 53ff;
Archaeological Discoveries in the Holy Land, published by The American Institute for Archaeology, 1967, see Hazor, pp. 64ff, Arad. pp. 97ff.

48 *Israel Exploration Journal*, Vol. 17, Number 4, pp. 247ff;
Aharoni, Y. *The Israelite Sanctuary at Arad, New Directions in Biblical Archaeology*, 1971, pp. 28ff.

49 Excavations are being carried out near the Temple site but no relics of Solomon's Temple have yet been found. See Mazar, B. *The Excavations in the Old City of Jerusalem*, The Israel Exploration Society, Jerusalem, 1969.

50 Kenyon, K.M. *The Royal Cities of the Old Testament*, 1971, pp. 53ff.

51 I Ki. x:26.

52 Yadin, Y. "New Light on Solomon's Megiddo," *The Biblical Archaeologist Reader*, 1964, 2, pp. 240 ff.

53 I Ki. x:28; The name is spelt as Koa or Cue.

54 I Ki. ix:26—28;
Glueck, N. *The Other Side of the Jordan*, 1940, pp. 93ff; *Rivers in the Desert*, 1959, 146ff. Albright's explanation of "Tarshish" as "refinery" has been criticised by many scholars.

55 *ANET*, p. 320.

56 I Ki. xi:16ff.

57 I Ki. x:6, 7. The queen of Sheba probably came to see Solomon for political and economic reasons.

58 I Ki. xii:16ff.

59 I Ki. xii:1; x.

60 I Ki. xii:28.

61 Ho. viii:6; cf. also Ho. xiii:2.

CHAPTER SIX

Elijah—The Struggle against the Baal Cult

The age of Ahab and Jezebel is remembered in the Bible for the activities of the fierce and fiery prophet Elijah, who denounced the royal pair for promoting the Baal cult and perpetrating injustices against their subjects. This period in Biblical history has been enriched greatly by archaeological and manuscript discoveries. But before we describe the clash between king, queen, and prophet in the light of the new sources, let us survey the events which led to the decline of the Hebrew kingdom.

The death of Solomon and the division of the Israelite kingdom caused a dwindling of Hebrew prestige in the Fertile Crescent. The power vacuum which had existed between 1100 and 900 B.C.E. and which enabled the glorious rise of the Israelite nation, owing to the eclipse of Egypt and Assyria, speedily vanished, with these latter nations reasserting their influence. Shishak, king of Egypt, invaded Judah, and seized the Temple treasure of Jerusalem in the fifth year of Rehoboam's reign.[1] He also attacked Israel and perhaps he caused Jeroboam to leave Shechem and move his capital to Penuel in Transjordan. Evidence of his devastating Israel is found on his broken stele discovered at Megiddo.[2] At the temple of Amon at Karnak, Shishak left a triumphal relief scene commemorating his victories in the towns of Palestine.[3]

At the same time the Aramean dynasty in Damascus reasserted itself and ravaged the Northern Kingdom. The ruler here now was the able Ben-Hadad I, who had invaded and caused havoc in the Galilee area. A stele of his, found near Aleppo, shows that by 850 B.C.E. his dominating influence reached as far as the northernmost part of Syria. The fact that his stele was dedicated to Baal Melkart of Tyre suggests that Ben-Hadad was then in treaty relationship with this Phoenician state.[4] The Arameans were to be the thorn in the flesh of Ahab all the days of his rule, except for the short period when they united against a common enemy, Assyria, at Qarqar. Thus, both kingdoms of Israel were in a reduced and threatened state.

It was the dynamic and ambitious Omri, father of Ahab, who brought about the resurgence of the power of the Northern Kingdom, ushering in a period of restored glory, strength, and influence in the Fertile Crescent. From Omri's reign onward northern Israel always appears in the Assyrian inscriptions as "the land of the house of Omri," attesting to its might and important role in political affairs of those days. For though this dynasty incurred the wrath of the prophets Elijah and Elisha, external sources indicate that politically and militarily speaking their kings were very wise and victorious and commanded respect throughout the Ancient Near East.

Until Omri the numerous kings who reigned and were deposed had different cities for the capitals, including Shechem, Penuel, and Tirzah. It was at the last city that Omri started his reign in about 878 B.C.E., after he had usurped the power of Zimri. Up to that point, the ruling house in Israel had been as transient as the capital, but Omri, who was to rule for some 30 years, changed the situation and decided to provide the Northern Kingdom with a permanent capital at Samaria. Omri's choice of Samaria as his new capital was a master stroke.[5] The beautiful site's strategic position enabled the Israelites thenceforth to repulse successive Aramean and Assyrian sieges. It commanded excellent trade routes. Thus, contact with Phoenicia was established; and also with Syria via the Plain of Jezreel.

The Bible tells us that "Omri bought the hill of Samaria from

Figure 21. Fragment of ivory plaque, probably from an article of furniture, from Ahab's palace at Samaria, 9th century B.C.E.

Figure 22. Memorial stele set up by King Mesha of Moab at Dibon, c. 850 B.C.E. The text extols Mesha, who liberated Moab from the Omride Dynasty of Israel.

Shemer for two talents of silver, and built a city on it which he named Samaria, after Shemer the owner of the hill."[6] Excavations have confirmed that he built the city on virgin soil, and this was probably the only completely Israelite city in Palestine. Wishing to turn Samaria into a rival of Jerusalem, he emulated the example of Solomon and also called in Phoenician craftsmen to build his palace. For Solomon, who employed foreigners on all his building schemes, we have only the literary evidence of the Bible; for Omri the evidence is purely archaeological. The material and the style of the artifacts unearthed at Samaria were completely Phoenician. The building projects commenced by Omri were no doubt completed by his son Ahab.[7] The Bible sums up Ahab's acts and events of Ahab's reign: "the ivory house and all the cities he built, are recorded in the annals of the kings of Israel."[8] Scripture, which is concerned with the ethical and religious aspects of the activities of its heroes, does not elaborate on their temporal attainments. Excavations at Samaria have indeed brought to light fragmentary relics of the most exquisite ivory ornaments that no doubt covered the furniture and walls of Ahab's palace. It was not likely that Ahab's house was built of ivory, but the lavish decorations of ivory on walls and furnishings gave it the impression of being built of ivory. His palace was not only spectacular, but exotic-looking, with this sumptuous display of magnificent ivory carvings. The picture that archaeology conveys of Ahab's palace and city is one of an autocrat living in a luxurious royal residence, which had many rooms and to which Ahab added defenses that converted it into an acropolis.

Ahab is mentioned in connection with one of the biggest clashes of the ancient world, namely the Battle of Qarqar in 853 B.C.E. The Assyrian annals show that in that year Ahab joined a grand alliance of Arameans, Cilicians, Egyptians, Arabians, Ammonites, and others to stem the advance of Assyria. Ahab contributed to this joint military effort an impressive force of 10,000 men and 2,000 chariots. Thus, we can accept what Yadin claims — that Ahab had stables at Megiddo. This grand alliance of nations succeeded in inflicting at least a temporary defeat upon Shalmaneser, king of Assyria.[9]

There is no mention of this battle in the Biblical sources. The Moabite stone referred to in Chapter One also bears witness to the might of Ahab. He subdued the Moabites, and only after his death were they able to rebel against Israel and throw off her rule. Though the Moabite stone claims that King Mesha threw off the Israelite yoke in the middle of the reign of Ahab, according to II Kings,[10] this happened after the death of Ahab. Let Mesha speak: "I am Mesha son of Chemosh King of Moab, the Dibonite — my father had reigned over Moab thirty years, and I reigned after my father . . . As for Omri, king of Israel, he humbled Moab many years, for Chemosh was angry at his land. And his son followed him and he also said, 'I will humble Moab.' In my time he spoke thus, but I have triumphed over him and over his house, while Israel hath perished forever! Omri had occupied the land of Medeba, and [Israel] had dwelt there in his time and half the time of his son [Ahab], forty years; but Chemosh dwelt there in my time."[11] Thus, we see that Mesha's claim differs from the Biblical version. Nevertheless, the two accounts are not necessarily contradictory. The rebellion may have occurred during the reign of Ahab, but had been first mentioned in the annals of the Israelite kings after the death of Ahab when Moab refused to pay tribute and show respect to the new king. Ahab made no effective attempt to suppress the revolt because he first had to fight against the Arameans and then, in a coalition with the Arameans at Qarqar, against Shalmaneser III. Thus, we see that, from a secular point of view, Ahab was a powerful king and one to be reckoned with in the ancient world.

However, the Biblical records surveyed the attainments of each king not from a temporal point of view but from an ethical one. To them Ahab was remembered for two episodes which made him especially unpopular. He married a Phoenician princess who introduced the cult of Baal into Israel, and which eventually led to a life and death struggle between herself and the prophet Elijah. The story of the manner in which the queen faked a trial to dispose of Naboth in order to obtain his vineyard has marred Ahab's and her image in the eyes of posterity. [12] We turn now to the clash between Jezebel and Elijah which has been illuminated by the discovery of the Ugaritic texts.

It was the threat of foreign nations and their cultures which eventually influenced the Israelites to appoint a king and rid the country of these political and religious dangers. The division of the kingdom witnessed the introduction of the worship of golden bull calves at Dan and Bethel. The practice of this syncretistic cult in the Northern Kingdom which resembled idolatry evoked the bitter invectives of the later prophets. [13] One might state that there were three types of worship in the ancient Israelite states of Judah and Israel. There was the state religion both in Judah and the Northern Kingdom on the one hand, which was ostensibly the worship of YHWH; but the people introduced into it many Baalistic elements. On the other hand there was the Canaanite cult, especially of Baal, promoted by Jezebel and her followers. The third, as upheld by the prophets, was the type directed against both pure Canaanitism and the syncretistic state religion. Thus, there was the state religion, the Canaanite religion, and the prophetic religion. The prophets endeavored to introduce a pure prophetic religion of the worship of the God of Israel. Jezebel made the first attempt to introduce Canaanite worship into Israel on a large scale; and eventually her daughter Athaliah did the same in Judah. Elijah's activities were a reaction to the activities of Jezebel.

The Solomonic era already witnessed the introduction of many foreign cults into Israel, owing to his marriages to many alien women. Marrying foreign wives was politically, but not spiritually, expedient. The Biblical historian indeed censured Solomon's disobedience to Israel's monotheistic ideals. However, these ladies of the court never attempted to force the adoration of their respective deities on the People of Israel, and were content with the tolerance to worship according to their own beliefs.

Jezebel, the wife of Ahab, was of a very different temperament from the wives of Solomon. Everything we know about her shows her to have been a woman born to rule. She had a strong and domineering character, a fountain of energy and determination, stopping at nothing to effect her ends. Jezebel apparently was not satisfied with permission to worship her god Baal Melkart in the temple that Ahab had built for her [14] and her staff, which numbered 450 prophets of Baal and 400 prophets of the goddess Asherah. The ambitious and self-willed queen clamored for her god to have at least equal rights with YHWH, the God of Israel. This desire of Jezebel brought her into conflict with the prophet Elijah, whose actions show that he believed YHWH and Baal to be mutually exclusive. It was to Elijah an intuitive truth that YHWH can brook no rival; his spirit blazed out with contempt against all weak-kneed persons that "halted between two opinions." This evoked a violent religious clash in the Northern Kingdom. The Ugaritic texts describe in detail the powers that worshipers of Baal attributed to him, as we mentioned in Chapter Four. Elijah knew the myths associated with Baal, but like the other prophets of the Bible he never gave a systematic description of them. Nevertheless the verse which states: "Elijah mocked them: 'Call louder, for he is a god; it may be he is deep in thought, or engaged, or on a journey; or he may have gone to sleep and must be woken up' " [15] is telling. Elijah's satire in this verse is the raciest comment ever made in the Bible about pagan mythology. This illustrates his acquaintance with Ugaritic myths, as they describe Baal going hunting, sleeping, eating and making love. [16]

Before we proceed to illustrate, by citing a few examples from the Ugaritic texts, that Elijah's activities were probably intentional polemics against Baal worship, let us briefly describe what the Bible tells us about Elijah. Who was he, and where did he acquire his passionate zeal for the God of Israel? Elijah, whose name means "YHWH is my God," labored with every fiber of his being to serve God and expose the absurdity of Baal worship and discredit it in the eyes of his contemporaries. [17]

The unusual narratives about the fiery prophet of the Lord, Elijah, are found in the Books of Kings. [18] These stories offer very scanty information about the background of Elijah. There is one brief reference which states, "And Elijah the Tishbite, who was of the inhabitants of Gilead." [19] No mention is made of Elijah's parentage. The omission is in striking contrast to the wealth of detail with which the descent of some of the other prophets are given in the Bible. For instance, it is interesting to compare this with the copious genealogical material on Moses and Samuel. Even the later prophetical books afford more personal data on the prophets than do these narratives about Elijah. Tradition has preserved an interesting description of his appearance. He is depicted as wearing a garment of hair girt with a girdle of leather about his loins. [20] It was this solitary prophet, who had an austere appearance and ascetic spirit, who flung down before Ahab the gauntlet of YHWH's defiance, as "the Lord, the God of Israel, liveth, before whom I stand, there shall not be dew nor rain these years but according to my word."[21]

Elijah's religion presents some problems. It is also strange that he never mentioned the golden bull calves at Dan or Bethel nor the Temple worship at Jerusalem. Elijah ministered during the days of Ahab, who reigned from about 882 to 871 B.C.E.[22] Mention of him is made in two other instances — one which brings him into contact with Ahaziah, the son of Ahab; and the other that he lived on until the reign of Jehoram of Judah (852–845 B.C.E.). It is difficult to harmonize this chronology with that of II Kings, which makes it clear that Elijah's career ended and Elisha's began before the death of Jehoshaphat (872–852 B.C.E.). In II Kings iii Jehoshaphat and Jehoram go to war against Moab, and in II Kings i:17, Jehoram, the son of Jehoshaphat, is mentioned. It is possible that Jehoram reigned for a time during the life of his father, as the verse in II Kings viii suggests.[23] Only II Chronicles xxi:11 narrates that Jehoram, king of Judah, son-in-law of Ahab and Jezebel, having fallen under sensuous Baal worship, is rebuked by the prophet Elijah. Elijah sends a letter to the king warning him that God will bring a plague upon Judah, to which all the king's house will early fall victim. This is the only incident narrated in the Bible that brings Elijah into contact with the kingdom of Judah, and the only one which represents him as carrying on his work by means of writing. It is difficult to reconcile the document with the life of Elijah.[24] Thus, Elijah lived and labored during the reigns of Ahab and Ahaziah. From the position the translation of Elijah occupies in II Kings [25] and the answer to Jehoshaphat's question in II Kings, [26] we may conclude that it occurred probably about the time of the accession to the throne of Jehoram of Israel.

The thorny problem of how and whence monotheism came to the Hebrews was discussed in Chapter Three. As with Moses, so with Elijah, many critical scholars such as Wellhausen and Ewald claim that he was not a monotheist but a henotheist.[27] They maintain that, like the mass of people of his time, he regarded YHWH as the God only of Israel, a local God; and believed that every other nation had its own deity who ruled supreme in his territory.

It is true that the faith of many of his contemporaries was of this rudimentary order; the clash between God and Baal was to them a real struggle between rival deities. But Elijah's lofty conception of God virtually excludes all other objects of worship and makes all the gods idols. Elijah apparently proved by his actions that he believed the God of Israel not to be limited by the territory of Israel; he demonstrated that God can perform miracles in Phoenicia as well, thus showing his belief in a universal

Figure 23. Votive stele erected by Ben Hadad I, King of Damascus (Aram), to the god Melkart. It is dated c. 875–825 B.C.E. and was found in an open field north of Aleppo.

deity.[28] Gunkel likewise states that although Elijah never clearly enunciated the theory of monotheism, he was imbued with its spirit and was instrumental in spreading that doctrine in Israel.[29] The majority of scholars today will agree that Elijah was a monotheist and not a henotheist.

James writes: "A final point of resemblance between Elijah and Moses is that they both were practical monotheists. We have already seen that while Moses is frequently described by scholars as only a 'henotheist,' he acted as if the gods of Egypt, for instance, did not exist. So it was with Elijah. YHWH might be the God of Horeb, but he ruled also in agricultural Canaan and in commercial Sidon (cf. I Kings:xvii:8). When Elijah put before the people the alternative between YHWH and Melkart, it was in this form: 'If YHWH be God, follow Him, but if Baal, follow him.' He did not say, 'Israel's God,' but simply 'God' (I Kings:xviii:21)."[30] He spoke about Baal in such a scornful and mocking manner, as we indicated above, that we must conclude that one who speaks thus has little belief in the reality of such a deity. The view expressed by James would be echoed today by many other scholars. Albright states that, on the basis of archaeological findings, monotheism emerged with the Mosaic movement of the 13th century.[31] As Cornill wrote: "Elijah saw that man does not live by bread alone, nor nations through sheer power. He considered Israel solely as the bearer of a higher idea. If the people became unfaithful to this idea, no external power could help them; for the nation bore in itself the germ of death. Israel was not to become like the others; it should serve YHWH alone, so as to become a righteous and pure people. Elijah was in holy earnest about his Mosaic thought; he measured his age and its events by his standard; he placed things temporal under an eternal point of view and judged them accordingly. The crying evils existed plainly in the modes of worship and in the administration of the law. Undefiled worship and a righteous administration of the law are what God required above all things. Here, if anywhere, it was to be shown whether Israel was in reality the people of God."[32]

Elijah, like his great forebear Moses, appointed a successor prior to his translation to Heaven. When the Prophet felt defeated he journeyed to Horeb, where he got new strength from his God. Elijah is shown that God still has great work for him to do. He must shape the destinies of two great nations and provide for the continuance of the prophetic succession. Three commands were laid upon him at Horeb: to anoint Hazael to be king over Syria, Jehu over Israel, and Elisha to be his own successor. Thus, with faith restored, Elijah returned to his life's task. On his way to Damascus he found Elisha at Abel-Meholah at the plow and he threw his mantle over him, a symbolic action by which he claimed him as his son and invested him with prophetic office. Elisha at first appeared amazed at this sudden call, and bewildered by the necessity of making so tremendous a decision. But the young man's natural shrinking from so high a calling – a hesitation similar to that of Moses, Isaiah, Jeremiah – is quickly overcome by the consciousness that this is a call from God. He immediately ran after Elijah and declared his readiness to follow him, only begging permission to return and give the kiss of farewell to his father and mother.[33] Elijah rebuked Elisha for expressing such a wish, whereupon Elisha ran after him without displaying any regard for his parents anymore. Elisha left all to administer to Elijah, and from this time onward the prophet is never alone again. He has a companion, to whom he becomes a true spiritual father, receiving his filial affection as well as profound veneration. Of the three tasks placed upon him, Elijah was able to accomplish the very last one, anointing a successor. It was left to Elisha to complete the first two mandates,[34] namely, to anoint Jehu as king of Israel and Hazael as king of Aram.[35]

Elisha lived and labored during the reigns of four kings, namely, Jehoram, Jehu, Jehoahaz, and Joash.[36] However, it is impossible to arrange the events of Elisha's life in a chronological sequence. While the topography of the narrative is often precise, there is a singular want of definiteness as to personal names and dates. The only indication of time given by several of the anecdotes is the mention of "king of Israel." However, as no name is specified the reader is left to conjecture which of the four kings who were the prophet's contemporaries may be referred to. It is impossible to say in whose reign the cure of Naaman or the attempt of the Syrians to capture Elisha took place. In some cases occurrences are obviously grouped together, according to the connection of their contents.[37] In others no principle of arrangement is apparent and the loose connection of the narratives becomes very awkward. For instance, the siege of Samaria by the Syrians is described immediately after it has been stated that "the bands of Syria came no more into the land of Israel."[38] Gehazi appears in familiar intercourse with "the King of Israel" after the account of his punishment with leprosy;[39] and the visit of Joash to Elisha during the prophet's last illness is related just after the mention of the death of Joash.[40] Most of Elisha's deeds and experiences are set down before the account of Jehu's revolution, but the prophet lived 45 years after that event. His influence on the nation was certainly greater, and his deeds of beneficence probably more numerous, after than before the overthrow of his enemy. The narratives are for the most part a record of Elisha's activities as a seer, diviner, and occasionally a worker of miracles rather than as a prophet in the usual sense of the word.

Elisha, though he is Elijah's spiritual successor, nevertheless presented in many respects a striking contrast to his teacher. Only metaphorically did he wear Elijah's mantle. After its first display, it appeared no more. Elisha unlike Elijah was no son of the desert. Brought up at a peaceful farm in the Jordan Valley amid the sweet charities of home,[41] he always preferred human companionship. He was not a solitary figure as was Elijah. He was generally found in the city, sojourning in Jericho among the sons of the prophets or dwelling in his own house at Samaria or at Dothan.[42]

Elijah preferred the company of the bleak hills and lonely mountains and appeared in cities only when the necessity arose, to bring a message to his fellow countrymen. Elijah's power was derived from communion with God in lonely mountains and valleys. Elisha apparently also had a closer connection with the "sons of the prophets." He seemed to have gone beyond Elijah in his interest in the guilds. Elijah won their awe-struck devotion but remained aloof from their communities, inhabiting solitudes from which he emerged from time to time as from another world. Such, at any rate, is the impression conveyed by our sources. Elisha, on the other hand, became a household figure among these groups, looking out for their food supplies,[43] advising them as to building new houses, providing for their widows,[44] helping them in their difficulties,[45] making himself in a very intimate way their master.[46]

Thus, Elisha ensured the widening and the perpetuating of his own influence on behalf of his God. For the main object of Elisha's life, as that of Elijah's, was to promote loyalty to God. Elisha likewise took an active part in political affairs and inspired the revolution against Jehu. However, it is wrong for scholars to blame Jehu's cruelty in carrying out this mandate on the prophet. We know that the later prophet Hosea decried "the blood of Jezreel" as the crime to be atoned for only by the fall of Jehu's house.[47]

Thus, to sum up, one could say that differences between Elijah and his disciple Elisha abound. Elijah loved the ascetic life, the quiet mountains, and he kept away from the cities and remained untouched by Canaanite influences. Elisha liked city life, enjoyed the company of men, and took a more active part in politics.[48]

Numerous Biblical commentaries deal with the problem of the transmission, recording, and redaction of these narratives, but this will not be dealt with in this book.[49]

The prophet Elijah was the chief opponent of Jezebel, and he taught the people the belief that God and Baal were mutually exclusive.[50] The Lord, God of Israel, tolerated no rivals. Jezebel at first wished to acquire equal status for her god with that of the God of Israel. We notice that she allowed Ahab to honor YHWH by naming their children, Ahaziah, Jehoram, and Athaliah. However, Elijah's absolute and uncompromising rejection of her deity apparently turned Jezebel into a true religious persecutor. She began to hound and harass the prophets of the Lord, killing them ruthlessly. For Elijah claimed that: "I, even I only, am left a prophet of the Lord; but Baal's prophets are 450 men."[51] We are also told that Obadiah, who was over the house of Ahab, hid 100 prophets of the Lord and fed them.[52] When Jezebel heard of Elijah's slaughter of her prophets on Mount Carmel, she was not intimidated; on the contrary, she became more determined and warned the prophet that she would take his life.[53] Jezebel was not the first religious persecutor in history. The story of Ikhenaton, discussed in Chapter Three, presents us with an interesting example of a religious fanatic who preceded Jezebel by many centuries.[54]

The stories that mirror the miraculous activities of Elijah and then Elisha are probably the most supernatural sections of the Hebrew Bible. We will deal only with a few of these tales and illustrate that they contain polemics against Baal worship. The most famous wonders attributed to Elijah and Elisha are that both increased oil and meal and both revived a dead child. The miracles ascribed to these prophets baffled scholars. There was a tendency among savants either to rationalize the marvelous in them, or to state that they were legends added to the original kernel of historical fact in these series of tales. The reason for these embellishments was explained as a means of adding prestige to these prophets, and magnifying them in the eyes of their contemporaries.[55] In the light of the newly discovered Ugaritic texts a new and different interpretation can be given. These stories appear as important weapons, employed by the narrator of these cycles to expose the incompetence of Baal and the numerous creative functions that the myths ascribe to him.

In Ugaritic literature Baal is called the Prince, Lord of the Earth, and Ben Dagon.[56] These two designations of Baal wish to inform us that this deity had dominion over agriculture and the produce of the land. In short, Baal was the fertility god responsible for fecundity in field, flocks, and family. When he died nothing grew. But when he is revived "the heavens rain oil and the wadis run with honey."[57] The phrase is not to be taken literally that the heavens actually poured forth oil and honey, but that rainfall enabled the growth of the fruits of the land.

Turning to the Bible, we find that Elijah, after he had proclaimed that a drought would come to the land, hid himself, so that neither king nor commoner could find him. It was not fear for his safety that moved him to take this action. He wished to be certain that Ahab should not find him. For he might then capture him and force him to pronounce the word which would release the rain.[58] First Elijah is fed miraculously by ravens who bring him bread and meat to eat. Some commentators have rendered the word "ravens" as "Arabs," in order to reduce the miraculous element in the story. This form of exegesis is unnecessary. The miraculous is in keeping with the general mysterious air that surrounds the prophet Elijah, whose appearances are sudden and brief. Many of the miracles are polemics against Baal myths, as this chapter aims to show. When the river dried up, he went to Zarephath. There he performed a miracle with meal and oil. The widow who graciously assisted him in his need is blessed that "the jar of meal shall not be spent, neither shall the cruse of oil fail."[59] Oil and meal feature prominently in this miracle and with good reason, as we shall demonstrate. On his way to Horeb, Elijah is also fed miraculously. The disillusioned seer fled after the contest at Mount Carmel, for the queen swore to avenge the death of her prophets. He sits under a juniper tree in the desert and calls for death. Then an angel wakes him and feeds him, giving the prophet strength to carry on with his journey to Horeb.[60] Elisha also performs miracles with grain and oil. He increases the oil of a woman, a wife of one of the sons of the prophets, and thus prevents her sons being taken away from her in lieu of her debts.[61] A man brings Elisha bread of the first fruits, twenty loaves of barley and fresh ears of corn "in the sack."[62] Elisha states that it should be given to the sons of the prophets. However, his servant asks, "How should I set this before a hundred men?" But the prophet commands, "Give the people that they may eat, for thus said the Lord, they shall eat and they shall leave thereafter." So it was.[63]

All these incidents demonstrate Elijah's and Elisha's ability as prophets of the God of Israel to increase oil and multiply grain. When we compare these stories with the myths about Baal, polemical parallelism is apparent; Baal was called Ben Dagon, showing his relation to vegetation, and the Prince, Lord of Earth, who bestows the blessing of fertility. This belief took root among the people of Israel, especially under the reign of Ahab and Jezebel. Under Solomon closer contacts between Israel and Canaan had begun when he incorporated the Canaanite cities into his territory. But in the days of the fanatical Queen Jezebel, Canaanite influence reached its high-water mark. The author of these narratives endeavored to uproot these beliefs by demonstrating through concrete incidents that God, and not Baal, controls these forces.

According to the Book of Kings, oil and corn were exported to Phoenicia from Israel.[64] This was still the case in the times of Herod

Agrippa I.[65] This could even suggest a nationalistic element in the polemics about oil and grain. They are supposed to be gifts of Baal, according to the myths that circulated about him, but the land of the worshipers of Baal, Phoenicia, imported Baal's gifts, oil and meal from Israel, properly the land of Israel's God. The miracle of oil and meal had to take place in Phoenicia, in order to demonstrate that even in that land it was not Baal but the God of Israel who gave oil and meal. It is also worth mentioning that in I Kings xvii:14, it is stated explicitly that the God of Israel acts not only in Israel but in Zarephath as well. At the end of this narrative it is written: "Until the Lord will give rain on the earth." In other words, until the drought will cease, or until the rain will come, which will be given by the Lord of Israel and not by Baal. The writer of these stories endeavored to liberate the people from the illusion that the worship of Baal was necessary for the growth of crops.

Another interesting example of polemical parallelism between the stories of Elijah and Elisha and Baal is the power to give and take life. Since the dawn of history the belief that man continues some form of existence after life led to widespread care of the dead throughout the Ancient Near East.[66] Even Ben-Sira, a representative of those ideas which we later find embodied in the Sadducean party, supposed not to believe in a life beyond, said: "A gift is acceptable in the sight of every living man, and also from the dead withhold not kindness."[67]

The Siloam village tomb inscription further attests to the custom of storing a variety of objects in tombs. The words on the sepulcher which, it is conjectured, may be the grave of Shebna mentioned in Isaiah[68] reads as follows:

This is [the sepulcher of. . . .] yahu who is over the
house. There is no silver and no gold here but [his bones]
and the bones of his slave-wife with him. Cursed be the
man who will open this.

The fact that the inscription states that there are no treasures within shows that to put supplies into tombs was a common practice.[69] It is beyond the scope of this work to deal with the thorny question of how the Hebrew mirrored the life beyond. Archaeological excavations make it quite clear that all ancient people looked well after their dead and supplied the grave with food and drink.[70]

The Ugaritic texts claim that Baal can bestow the gift of progeny as well as revive the dead. In being acquainted with the myth of the dying and rising Baal, the people of Ugarit believed that the Baal who dies and then is resurrected has the power to resuscitate others. Baal, who was victorious over death, is regarded as having dominion over it.[71]

However, the Aqht legend describes the promise of eternal life to a human being and alludes to its realization. In Chapter Four we described the experiences of Dnil, an upright man, who desired a son. He propitiated the gods with sacrifices for a week in order to move them to grant his wish. The request of Dnil was fulfilled, and a son was born. The lad, called Aqht, was given a present by one of the gods, a wondrous bow. The goddess Anat desired to obtain this bow, and endeavored to persuade the lad Aqht to give it to her. In return for it, she promised him that she would bestow on him the blessing of eternal life. The passage reads as follows:

> And the maiden Anat replied:
> Ask for life O Aqht the youth
> Ask for life and I will give it to you.
> For deathlessness and I will bestow it on thee
> I'll make thee count years with Baal
> With the sons of El shalt thou count months
> Even as Baal when he gives life,
> Entertains the living,
> Entertains and gives him to drink
> And the lovely one sings and croons over him
> And responds to him
> So also I will give life to Aqht the youth.[72]

The above passage shows that the gods of Ugarit claimed to possess the power of bestowing eternal life. It also attests to the conviction that gods do not die. Nevertheless, we know that gods did experience death in these texts. But one cannot apply strict logic to ancient writings. Likewise, it is well to remember that Baal's death and subsequent revival made him appear more immortal than ever in the eyes of his worshipers. He had vanquished death for all times.

Anat was eventually enraged by Aqht because he refused to give her his bow. Then he added insult to injury by stating:

> Also another thing I shall tell thee
> The bow is a weapon for heroes
> Shall now a female hunt therewith?[73]

Aqht committed the grave sin of haughtiness toward a deity and chided her with the disabilities that go with her sex. Anat warned him that she would lay him low at her feet for his arrogant behavior toward her. Immediately, Anat went to El and extorted from him permission to fulfill her threat. She acquired the services of Ytpn and commanded him to assassinate Aqht. Her instructions were carried out, Aqht was murdered, and she got the coveted bow. Later she apparently regretted her action and restored Aqht to life.

> [For] his bow I destroyed him,
> on account of his darts,
> Him I will revive
> Only let his bow be given to me. [74]

Thus, the texts attribute both to Baal and Anat the power to revive the dead.

To interrupt our story: It cannot escape the reader that Anat's coveting of the bow and her cruel behavior is reminiscent of Ahab and his desire for the vineyard of Naboth. The king had approached his subject and asked him to sell his vineyard to him. Ahab promises to recompense him greatly. However, Naboth said: "The Lord forbid that I should let you have land which has always been in my family." [75] The king accepted the refusal as final but displayed his displeasure by going home, lying on his bed, and refusing to eat. This sort of behavior in the Bible symbolizes unhappiness; whereas partaking of food is a sign of satisfaction and contentment. His wife, inquiring why he was in such a depressed state of mind, was informed that Naboth was responsible for his unhappiness. His wife scornfully asked: "Are you or are you not king in Israel?" She tells him: "Come arise, eat and I will give you the vineyard of Naboth." Without any prick of conscience she faked a trial with scoundrels, and had Naboth put to death. [76]

This story and the one about Aqht and Anat desiring his bow reveal some parallel features. Anat also at first tried to persuade Aqht to part with his bow. Having failed by peaceful means, she also with the help of the gods enlisted the assistance of a man of brutal character, turned him into an eagle, placed him in a flight of eagles, and had him swoop down upon the young hunter Aqht and cause his death. She took the bow with impunity. The former is a historical event, while the latter is in the realm of legend. Might was right in Canaanite mythology as displayed in this incident. Jezebel, reared in this atmosphere, had no compunction about slaying Naboth. If the gods and goddesses behaved in this selfish manner, could it be expected that their worshipers would be any better? But in

Israel there were always the prophets who arose to challenge the power of autocrats and proclaim, as did Elijah to Ahab in this instance: "Have you killed your man, and taken his land as well." [77]

There is a Talmudic proverb which states: "Everything depends on one's *mazal* (luck)." This is indeed true of Ahab. The Bible mentions that he repented of his evil: "The word of the Lord came to Elijah the Tishbite: 'Have you seen how Ahab has humbled himself before me? Because he has thus humbled himself, I will not bring disaster upon his house in his own lifetime, but in his son's.'" But posterity never remembered Ahab's penitence – only his wickedness. With King David it was exactly the reverse. No matter what acts he perpetrated, they were forgiven and forgotten. It is true that he too repented of his sin immediately when rebuked by the prophet Nathan and said: "I have sinned unto the Lord." But history was very kind to David and cruel to Ahab – always condemning the latter's actions while condoning those of the former. Thus, even the story of Naboth receives some illumination in the light of Ugaritic mythology. But whereas Aqht is accordingly revived, Naboth's death is final.

To continue with our comparisons, the writer of the stories of Elijah and Elisha was well acquainted with the belief that prevailed in Ugarit that Baal who died and was resurrected could resuscitate. With his stories he demonstrates that the God of Israel controls life and death. The narrative about the two prophets depicts them reviving lads. The son of the woman of Zarephath fell sick, and his sickness grew so grave until there was no breath left in him. It is interesting to compare this verse to 3, Aqht 36, 37.

> His soul goes out like the wind,
> Like a gust his spirit,
> Like smoke out of his nose.

The bereaved woman turned to the prophet and bitterly protested against his coming to her house. For in her opinion that was the cause of her son's death. She and the prophet belonged to different classes of society. She was only a poor sinful woman and he was a man of God. In his absence her shortcomings had passed unnoticed in the sight of God. However, his arrival at her home had directed attention to her failings. In contrast to his holiness, she was a sinful being, and this caused the punishment of her son. In other words, here too we see the widespread belief that suffering comes as a result of sin. [78]

Elijah promptly stretched himself out on the child and prayed to

God: "O Lord my God, I pray thee, let this child's soul come into him again." [79] The Lord hearkened to the voice of his prophet and restored the child to life. His revival evoked the moving exclamation from his mother's mouth: "Now by this I know that thou art a man of God, and that the word of the Lord in thy mouth is true." [80]

The act of resurrection convinced the woman that Elijah was a man of God. In other words the man of God can perform godly acts to resurrect humans. He is God's instrument for giving or taking life.

Elisha had blessed a barren woman and she gave birth to a son. However, when the lad grew up he too fell ill one day and died. The grief-stricken mother reproached the prophet Elisha, stating: "Did I ask a son of my Lord? Did I not say 'Do not deceive me?' " [81] Elisha prayed fervently to God and then proceeded to stretch himself out on the child, so that his mouth, eyes, and hands lay on those of the boy. Finally, he succeeded in resurrecting the lad.

More astonishing, the lifeless body of Elisha revived a dead man. A band of people were burying a man when they were frightened from their task by the appearance of marauding bands from Aram. Hastily they threw the body in the grave of the prophet and fled. As soon as his bones touched Elisha's he was revived and he stood on his feet. [82]

The narrator wished to stress with these stories that:

The Lord killeth and maketh alive
He bringeth down to the grave and bringeth up. [83]

Even more significant, the story attributes power even to the dead body of the prophet. The latter's lifeless body can achieve more than the living Baal. They may be regarded as intentional polemics to undermine the belief in the myths circulating about Baal, that he or the other gods or goddesses of the Ugaritic pantheon could revive the dead. [84]

In the light of the Ugaritic sources the miracles discharged by Elijah and Elisha as increasing the oil and meal, withholding or releasing the forces of rain, restoring the dead to life, ascending to heaven, were deliberate actions carried out by Elijah and Elisha which were designed to undermine the belief prevalent in Canaanite circles that Baal was the dispenser of all these blessings. The narrator of these stories was well acquainted with Baal mythology and he deliberately indicated in his writings that the God of Israel through His prophets was the dispenser of rain, oil, corn, health and sickness, life and death. He showed that God alone makes man dumb or deaf, seeing or blind. Or as the Psalmist sang:

How manifold are Thy works, O Lord!
In wisdom hast Thou made them all.[85]

The eventual fall of the house of Ahab was brought about by Elisha, whose instrument was Jehu. However, it is wrong for scholars to blame Jehu's cruelty in carrying out this mandate on the prophet. The manner and mode of fulfilling the act was the product of Jehu's own tyrannical nature.[86] The later prophet Hosea decried "the blood of Jezreel" as a crime to be atoned for only by the fall of Jehu's house.[87] The rule of the latter, founded on usurpation and established in bloodshed, was never very strong. First he became a vassal of Hazael of Damascus,[88] and then of Assyria. Jehu is mentioned in the famous Black Obelisk of Shalmaneser III. It depicts the Assyrian king's triumphs over several kingdoms, including Syria and Israel. In the second row from the top is a figure dressed in the costume of the Western Semites, who pays homage by bowing to the ground, while his servants bring gifts. He seems to depict Jehu, who in the text is called "son of Omri."

The inscription on the Black Obelisk is in Assyrian cuneiform and reads:

The tribute of Jehu, son of Omri; I received from him
silver, gold, a golden bowl, a golden vase printed with
bottom, golden tumblers, golden buckets, tin, a staff
for a king and wooden . . . [89]

This is a most fascinating find. It is the earliest picture of an Israelite king which has survived. It shows Jehu, the Israelite king, wearing the Western Semitic dress, which included a low turban and long overgarment.[90]

Thus, archaeology has, through the excavations at Samaria, the discovery of the Ugaritic texts, and Assyrian annals, shed new and fascinating light on the images of Ahab, Jezebel, Elijah, and Elisha. The clash between them emerges in brighter and clearer colors. Ahab, from a political and material standpoint, was a strong and mighty king who greatly enhanced the power, prosperity, and prestige of his realm. The ivories and the stables of Megiddo bear eloquent testimony to his building activities. However, the ancient writers of Jewish history, whose work was preserved in the Book of Kings, were interested chiefly in spiritual facts and ethical attitudes. Political matters they relegated to the archives of the respective kings designated as the "Chronicles of the Kings of Judah," or the "Chronicles of the Kings of Israel." The impressive and unique aspect

Figure 24. The Black Obelisk depicting Jehu of the Omride Dynasty paying tribute to Shalmaneser III (828–824 B.C.E.).

of Bible history is that it was not the royal political and military archives which survived. It was religious history which became eternal. And because Scripture offers religious history and not political annals it became the "Bible." Only those temporal facts were introduced into the narratives which could teach a moral lesson. The activities of the prophets Elijah and Elisha were more important than the history of battles or the building of palaces. The spiritual took precedence over the material. Thucydides, the great Greek historian, said that "history is philosophy taught by example." That is to say that the facts which the philosopher records are merely those which can serve as examples to prove the philosophy which he believes is expressed through the experiences of the past. Biblical history is a selective one, which expresses the philosophy that ethical living and obedience to God's law is the crucial factor in determining the destiny of a people. If, then, history is philosophy taught by example, these histories in Scripture may be described as "prophecy taught by example." Let us hasten to stress that they are still history, for they preserve the records of ancient events. Archaeology is illustrating more and more that the facts given in the narratives are correct and dovetail well with what the spade busily continues to uncover. Archaeology is constantly filling in many gaps on the material side of the history of this world. Events like the battle of Qarqar, Jehu's tribute, Moab's defeat at the hands of Ahab, and many others are passed over in silence in the Bible. The ancient historian did not feel them important enough to include. Yet with the help of the spade and the scroll the diaries of the past continue to be unearthed and bring back the living world of the Biblical heroes.

To return to our story, it was during the reign of Jehu's descendant Jeroboam II (781–743 B.C.E), that the Northern Kingdom as well as Judah reached a height of material prosperity once again almost rivaling the glory of the kingdoms of David and Solomon. However, these events and what the spade reveals about them bring us into the age of Isaiah and Assyria.

NOTES

[1] I Ki. xiv:25; II Ch. xii: 2–12.
[2] *ANET*, p. 263.
[3] *ANEP*, p. 118, fig. 349;
    Kenyon, K.M. *Royal Cities of the Old Testament*, 1971, p. 67, 72.
[4] Bright, J. *History of Israel*, 1964, p. 221.
[5] I Ki. xvi:24.
[6] *Ibid*.
[7] Kenyon, K.M. *Royal Cities of the Old Testament*, pp. 71ff.
[8] I Ki. xxii:39.
[9] *ANET*, p. 279.
[10] II Ki. iii:5.
[11] *ANET*, p. 320.
[12] I Ki. xxi.
[13] It is indeed strange that the prophets of the Northern Kingdom, such as Elijah and Elisha, never referred to the golden calves set up by Jeroboam I.
[14] I Ki. xvi:31–33.
[15] I Ki. xviii:27.
[16] The following Ugaritic texts describe love scenes between Baal and Anat, text 76, 1, 11; 67:5. *ANET* offers a slightly different translation from that given by Gordon. The "waking up" of the deity is illustrated by an Ugaritic text published by Virolleaud, in which after each one of a series of choral stanzas and following a god's name occurs the choric "he has waked up." (hn 'r).
[17] Bronner, L. *The Stories of Elijah and Elisha*, 1968, pp. 23ff.
[18] I Ki. xvii:19; II Ki. i, ii.

[19]   II Ki. i:1.

[20]   II Ki. i:8.

[21]   I Ki. xvii:1.

[22]   The dates for the kings, as those for most other historical events, follow the chronology of the *Westminster Atlas to the Bible*, 1953, p. 15. Bengtson has shown that chronology is the "eye of history." Bengtson, H. *Einführung in die alte Geschichte*, Beck, 1965, p. 22.

[23]   II Ki. viii:16.

[24]   Curtis, E.L. and Madsen, A.A. *A Critical and Exegetical Commentary to the Book of Chronicles*, 1952, pp. 413—414.

[25]   II Ki. ii:11.

[26]   II Ki. iii:11.

[27]   Wellhausen, J. *History of Israel and Judah*, 1891, pp. 64ff.

Ewald, H. *History of Israel*, 1878, Vol. iv, pp. 68ff.

[28]   I Ki. xvii:13ff.

[29]   To quote Gunkel in the original: *"Aber die Stimmung des Monotheismus beherrscht ihn." "Dennoch ist Elias ein Markstein in der Entstehung des Monotheismus."* From Gunkel, H. *Elias, Jahve und Baal*, 1906, p. 54.

[30]   James, F. *Personalities of the Old Testament*, 1963, p. 181.

[31]   Albright, W.F. *Archaeology and the Bible*, 1932, p. 167; *From the Stone Age to Christianity*, 1957, p. 272.

[32]   Cornill, C.H. *The Prophets of Israel*, 1910, p. 34.

[33]   I Ki. xix:19ff.

[34]   II Ki. viii:7—15.

[35]   II Ki. ix:1—13.

[36]   *Ibid.*, note [22].

[37]   II Ki. ii:4.

[38]   II Ki. vi:23ff.

[39]   II Ki. vi:27; viii:4.

[40]   II Ki. xiii:13 ff.

[41]   I Ki. xix:20.

[42]   II Ki. vi:14.

[43]   II Ki. vi:38.

[44]   II Ki. vi:1; iv:1.

[45]   II Ki. vi.

[46]   II Ki. v, vi.

[47]   Ho. i:4.

[48]   Gordon, C.H. *An Introduction to the Old Testament*, 1953, pp.188ff.

[49]   Montgomery, J.A. *A Critical and Exegetical Commentary to the Book of Kings*, 1960, pp. 24—25;

Rowley, H.H. *The Old Testament and Modern Study*, 1956, pp. 102—105;

Fohrer, G. *Elia*, 1957, pp. 43ff;

Pfeiffer, R.H. *An Introduction to the Old Testament*, 1941, pp. 404ff;

Harrison, R.K. *An Introduction to the Old Testament*, 1970, pp. 719ff.

[50] Gunkel, H. *Elias, Jahve and Baal*, 1906, pp. 52–54. I Ki. xviii:22; xix:14.

[51] I Ki. xviii:22.

[52] I Ki. xviii:4.

[53] I Ki. xix:2.

[54] For more details see Breasted, J.H. *A History of Israel*, 1959, pp. 356–363.

[55] Kittel, R. *History of the Hebrews*, 1896, Vol. 11, p. 267.

Pfeiffer, R.H. *Introduction to the Old Testament*, 1941, p. 404.

[56] Bronner, L. *Stories of Elijah and Elisha*, 1968, p. 60.

[57] *Ugaritic Texts*, test 49, 111, 4–9.

[58] I Ki. xviii:10ff.

[59] I Ki. xvii:14.

[60] I Ki. xix:16.

[61] II Ki. iv:1ff.

[62] II Ki. iv:41; The word *bsql* appears in 1 Aqht, 62 ff. It is according to some, a plant, part of a plant, or fresh corn in its ears.

[63] II Ki. iv:42–44.

[64] I Ki. v:25.

[65] Acts xii:20.

[66] Charles, R.H. *Eschatology, The Doctrine of a Future Life*, 1963.

Bronner, L. *Stories of Elijah and Elisha*, 1968, pp. 106ff.

[67] Ecclesiasticus vii:33. (The book is also known as the *Wisdom of Ben-Sira.*)

[68] Is. xxii:16.

[69] Avigad, N. *The Epitaph of a Royal Steward from Siloam Village*, I.E.J., 1953, Vol. 3, Number 3. This author in his article cites numerous other inscriptions discovered in the Near East where similar warnings were written on the tombs.

[70] *Ibid.*, note [66].

[71] This myth of the dying-rising god was common throughout the Near East. In Babylonia he was called Tammuz, and his wife was Ishtar. In Egypt he was Osiris, and his consort Isis, and in Greece – Adonis and Aphrodite.

[72] *Ugaritic Texts*, text 2 Aqht, VI, 25–33.

[73] *Ibid.*, text 2 Aqht, VI, 39–41.

[74] *Ibid.*, Aqht, I, 14–17.

[75] I Ki. xxi:3.

[76] I Ki. xxi:7ff.

[77] I Ki. xxi:19.

[78] The Book of Job is devoted to investigating the problem why the wicked prosper while the righteous suffer.

[79] I Ki. xvii:22.

[80] I Ki. xvii:24.

[81] II Ki. iv:28.

[82] II Ki. xiii:20—22.

[83] I Sa. II:6.

[84] For parallel stories about revival of people, see *A Critical and Exegetical Commentary to the Book of Kings*, p. 294—295.

[85] Ps. civ:24ff.

[86] II Ki. ix:7ff. Here begins the story of Jehu and a description of his cruel destruction of the house of Ahab and all Baal worshipers follows.

[87] Ho. i:4.

[88] II Ki. x:32—33.

[89] *ANET*, p. 281. The word "son" here means belonging to the House of Omri, and not a son in our sense of the word.

[90] *ANEP*, pp. 120—122, Figures 351—355.

CHAPTER SEVEN

Isaiah—The Assyrian Advance

Assyria stands in the Bible for the nation whose invasions of Israel and Judah are described by the prophet as divinely permitted in order to carry out God's chastisement of His rebellious nation. However, Assyria according to Scripture fulfilled this divinely placed mandate with such vicious brutality that later she was to suffer violent destruction for her godlessness. The prophet Isaiah referred to Assyria as the rod, razor, flood, and preying bird with which God would punish his recalcitrant people.[1]

Already in the days of the Hebrew Patriarchs the Assyrians were an important recognizable group.[2] However, the Neo-Assyrian revival and expansion took place in the 9th century under the energetic Ashurnasirpal II (885–860 B.C.E.). He moved the capital from Ashur to Calah (Nimrud), and set out to organize the Assyrian army into the strongest military machine in the Ancient Near East. The descriptions in Isaiah and Nahum affirm the outstanding military instrument it was.[3] Bowmen, spearmen, and slingers made up the infantry. Its charioteers were dreaded by all warriors of antiquity. The prophet Nahum vividly depicted the Assyrian might:

> Hark to the crack of the whip,
> the rattle of the wheels and stamping of horses,
> bounding chariots, chargers rearing,
> swords gleaming, flash of spears.
> The dead are past counting, their bodies lie in heaps
> corpses innumerable, men stumbling over the corpses -
> all for a wanton's monstrous wantonness,
> fair-seeming, a mistress of sorcery,
> who beguiled nations and tribes
> by her wantonness and her sorceries.[4]

The Assyrians trained excellent cavalry and siege units. Their siege apparatus included battering rams, large wooden or cane shields to protect the attackers before the walls, scaling ladders, and great slings. They worked out special building techniques for erecting earthen ramparts on which the battering rams could be run up. They had units trained to cross rivers, climb mountains — to undertake anything that was necessary for the transport of their troops. In short, this was probably the best-equipped and the most efficient and ferocious fighting machine of antiquity. On the large four-paneled reliefs in the palace at Nineveh, where the later ruler Sennacherib made a detailed depiction of his capture of Lachish, we see a vivid picture of the Assyrian soldiers with all their ammunition and war maneuvers.[5]

The Assyrian kings were known for their ruthlessness. Ashurnasirpal II boasted about his brutality and the manner in which he treated his captives. He depicted the pain he inflicted with great pride: "I built a pillar over and against the city gates, and I flayed all the chief men who had revolted, and I covered the pillar with their skins; some I walled up within the pillar, some impaled upon the pillar on stakes, and others I bound to the stakes round about the pillar; many within border of my own land I flayed, and I spread their skins upon the walls; and I cut off the limbs of the officers, of the royal officers who have rebelled."[6] (This quotation is typical of the many more we find in the records of the Royal Archives of Assyria which sharply illustrate their brutality and savagery). The relentless Ashurnasirpal, who developed this army and expanded the extent of his territory, never reached the borders of Israel. It was his successor Shalmaneser III who exacted tribute from Jehu, which is artistically depicted on the Black Obelisk. This event happened in 841 B.C.E.[7] But after the death of Shalmaneser III the kingdoms of Israel and Judah had a brief respite as the Assyrian kings were busy with internal strife and raids nearer home. However, with the accession of Tiglath-pileser III to the throne of Assyria, he embarked upon a policy of conquest and deportation of the small nations with whom he came into contact. This new attitude of Assyria toward conquered peoples is likewise depicted on the Lachish relief, where we can see the inhabitants being deported in large numbers. Tiglath-pileser is also called Pul in the Bible.[8] The new policy of Assyria was eventually to have sad significance for the future fortunes of the kingdoms of Israel and Judah. The Assyrians exiled the inhabitants of the Northern Kingdom in 721 B.C.E. The Babylonians followed the Assyrian example and also removed their conquered subjects, leading to the exile of the Judeans to Babylon in 586 B.C.E.

Nevertheless the short lull in the expansion program of the Assyrian giant, owing to internal weakness, was richly exploited by these two nations. Jeroboam II of Israel and Uzziah of Judah took full advantage of the short breathing space afforded to them by the Assyrians' internal troubles and expanded their respective boundaries to rival the extent of the days of David and Solomon.

Excavations at Samaria reveal that Jeroboam II refortified Samaria with a double wall, which in the most vulnerable part of the city was nearly 33 feet wide. The fortifications were so strong that it took the Assyrian army three years to conquer the city (724–721 B.C.E.)[9] Jeroboam II successfully restored Israel's northern boundary to what it had been in David's time, by the defeat of the Arameans.[10] More information about his reign comes to us from the palace at Nimrud and the Samarian ostraca and a jasper seal. The latter was discovered by Schumacher at Megiddo in 1904, and on epigraphic grounds it is assigned to the days of Jeroboam II. This stamp seal is artistically engraved with a roaring lion and inscribed "belonging to Shema, servant of Jeroboam." The term "servant" on such seals designates "minister." Thus, at Lachish a seal was found stamped "belonging to Gedaliah who is over the house." This may have been the Gedaliah who was made governor over Judah by the Babylonians and was assassinated by Ishmael and his followers.[11] The penetration of Jewish enterprise into Arabia at this time is also attested by the discovery of a seal of Jotham, Uzziah's son and regent, in Glueck's excavations at Ezion-geber.[12]

Some of the ivories found in enormous quantities at the palace of Nimrud came from the days of Ahab, as well as Jeroboam II. We need but recall the castigation of Amos, who was horrified by the surfeit of luxury and the immorality and oppression of the poor that he saw around him. He rebuked the rich of Samaria for lying on beds of ivory, eating the finest foods, and enjoying the best music.[13] At the frequent banquets given by the wealthy notables of Samaria, the guests reclined on low couches, the legs and backs of which were adorned with carved ivory inlays, comparable to the beds of the Assyrian monarchs.[14] It might be mentioned that the style of the ivory ornaments suggest that they are primarily the products of Phoenician craftsmen. However, the Phoenicians were entrepreneurs, traders, and essentially cosmopolitan. Their art was eclectic and displayed Egyptian and Babylonian motifs. The loot in this palace was probably the plunder that Sargon II brought from Samaria after he destroyed the city in 721 B.C.E.

The ostraca discovered at Samaria described the deliveries of oil and wine to the royal court going back to the days of Jeroboam II. They show the heavy taxes the king exacted from the people to enable him and his court to live in the lap of luxury.[15] Most of the consignments were intended for the king. It is possible to regard these consignments as compulsory taxes to be paid to the king and his officials. Such taxes were collected from different towns and tax districts by tax collectors and forwarded to the king's palace. A certain portion of the tax from each district was set aside for the high officials. Thus, the ostraca shed interesting light on the system of taxation in the days of the kings.

They also show that the art of writing was well developed and practiced, not only for public services but also in private life. The religious state of the people is also revealed by them to a certain extent. Many of the personal names of the ostraca contain the element Baal, which points to either worshiping of the Canaanite deity or syncretism in which YHWH was identified with Baal. These ostraca, though uninteresting themselves, are of significance for the script, spelling, personal names, topography, religion, administrative system, and clan distribution of that period.

The reign of Jeroboam II was the period when Amos and Hosea preached in the Northern Kingdom. These prophets denounced vehemently the false sense of security which prevailed owing to the sudden lull in Assyrian power. They proclaimed that a civilization based on injustice and exploitation of the poor and the needy could not endure. These two prophets shared an unshakable belief in the impending crisis and doom — a belief which was eventually fully justified and proven by historical events. The prosperity of the Northern Kingdom was temporary indeed. Tiglath-pileser III in 733 B.C.E., began his conquest campaign once again, taking Damascus, Gilead, Galilee, and the plain of Sharon, and turning them into six provinces ruled by himself.[16] To stem the tide of the growing power of Assyria, Rezin, king of Damascus, and Pekah, king of Israel, formed an alliance and endeavored to force Judah to join in battle with them against the Assyrian assault. But Ahaz at this juncture, as we shall describe in greater detail later, invoked the aid of Assyria against the advice of Isaiah. It did not take long before Tiglath-pileser laid siege to Samaria, and after three years in which this city held out heroically it fell to Sargon II in 722 B.C.E. According to the Khorsabad annals the king boasted: "I besieged and conquered Samaria, led away as booty 27,290 inhabitants of it. I formed from among them a contingent of 50 chariots and made the remaining inhabitants resume their social position."[17] This report dovetails well with the account in the Book of Kings where it is written: "The king of Assyria deported the Israelites to Assyria and settled them in Halah and on the Habor, the river of Gozan, and cities of Media."[18] The policy of Assyria was wholesale transference of populations. The Assyrians did not obliterate the population of the conquered countries, as this was politically and economically unwise. But by breaking up all indigenous cohesion, they reduced enormously the chances of opposition to their policy. The disorientated new settlers could be relatively pliant to the wishes of their masters. The life of the Northern Kingdom of Israel, which had commenced with Jeroboam I and had experienced moments of glory, as archaeology shows, during the reigns of Omri, Ahab, and Jeroboam II, came to its tragic end at the hands of the Assyrian Sargon II.

In common with his earlier colleagues Amos and Hosea, Isaiah likewise decried the extremes of wealth and poverty which prevailed in 8th century Judah, owing to the short-lived and temporary prosperity brought about by King Uzziah. It was Uzziah who reconquered the land of Edom[19] with its rich copper and iron mines and for the first time subjugated completely the coastal plain of Philistia.[20] Isaiah beheld that greed and covetousness were dividing the nation into classes of possessor and dispossessed. The rich built up large estates, and with the help of corrupt judges added house to house and field to field, while the oppressed and dispossessed peasantry sought in vain for legal redress. The pursuit of commerce encouraged the development of cities and city life; and the extremes of wealth and poverty, which had been impossible in an agricultural society based on the Biblical system of land tenure, were now quickly appearing. Landless farmers flowed into the cities in search of a livelihood where wealth, luxury, and vice dwelt side by side with poverty, misery, and squalor. With the exchange of goods went the exchange of ideas. New religious cults, standards of luxury and splendor, and material gain, which had hitherto been foreign to Israel except perhaps in the days of Solomon, were introduced on a large scale from Assyria and Egypt.

From ancient times Isaiah has been considered the greatest of the Hebrew prophets. He has been called "the eagle among the prophets," and the like. Discoveries of cuneiform inscriptions at the palaces of the Assyrian kings, the Ugaritic texts, and Mari documents have brought to light new facts bearing on the times of Isaiah. The dramatic Dead Sea Scroll discoveries have given us a text of Isaiah that is one thousand years older than our copies of the Masoretic text. This is one of the most important aspects of these finds. Whereas one Isaiah scroll is very fragmentary, the other one is in an excellent state and its text varies only slightly from the Masoretic one. Until this discovery the oldest copy of Isaiah that we possessed dated from about 916 C.E. Thus, these finds give us the oldest manuscripts of the Bible that are available, and are therefore most significant for Bible studies. Fragments of every Biblical book have been found to date, except the Book of Esther.[21]

We must interrupt our discussion on Isaiah to investigate what light if any, the new archaeological finds shed on the phenomenon of prophecy.

Scholars do not yet agree on the problem of the origin of prophetism. We have shown that the multitude of mythological texts from Ugarit have put the Canaanite religion into a clearer focus. Likewise the Mari texts have illuminated the religious and socio-political setting for the Patriarchs, the institution of covenant making, the office of the "Judges." The Mari texts have been studied in order to endeavor to find a parallel to prophecy. When reading these texts one feels that in these documents at Mari there are phenomena which remind us of the ecstasy of groups of prophets as described in I Samuel. The prophet met Saul and said to him: "When you reach the Hill of God, where the Philistine governor resides, you will meet a company of prophets coming down from the hill-shrine, led by lute, harp, fife and drum, and filled with prophetic rapture. Then the spirit of the Lord will suddenly take possession of you, and you too will be rapt like a prophet and become another man."[22] Some scholars hold that this type of ecstatic prophecy was part and parcel of Canaanite cultural life. Divination of this sort was widespread, but this has nothing in common with the true spirit of the great prophets in the Bible like Isaiah, Amos, and others.

There is reason to believe that there existed groups of prophets, the so-called "sons of the prophets," who were perhaps connected with the Canaanite sanctuaries; although it must be stressed that nowhere do we see a clear connection between "the sons of the prophets" and the sanctuaries of Canaan. If such a contact existed, Elijah and Elisha would have had no contact with them. We must assume that groups of ecstatics flourished, and on occasion of sacrificial feasts they worked themselves into a state of rapture more or less in the same manner as the dervishes in the East still do today. The Mari texts offer ample evidence for such type of divination. The diviner-prophets of Mari largely acted as the unsolicited and spontaneous mouthpieces of deities by means of ecstatic trances, dreams and the like. One class of prophet is termed the "apilu," feminine the "apiltu," and plural "apilum," which meant the "one who answers." One letter describing the "Answerer," reads: "Speak to my lord: the message of Nur-Sin, your servant . . . In the future do not rebel against me . . . Let my lord take note. Earlier, when I was staying in a different land, Shall I not write to my lord concerning what I hear and what they say to me? If in the future there is any kind of sin, let not my lord say, as follows, 'Why did you not send me the word which the apilum spoke to you while watching over your threshing floor?' Now I have written to my lord, Let my lord take note."[23] These apilum appear always to bring some message which contained threats and promises and all were contingent upon whether the king gave the desired material gifts to the gods and their temples or not.

The chief concern of these various gods, who were represented by the apilum, was that the king paid more attention to them, to their temples, and to their sacrifices. The texts do not enlighten us as to the manner of inspiration of the apilu.

Apart from male and female laity, imbued with such esoteric attributes, there were cult diviners, usually attached to sanctuaries – for example, the Dagon temple at Terqa, or the temple of the goddess Annunitum at Mari, professionals designated by the Akkadian term "muḫḫum," which meant the "frenzied one," as the apilum means "answerer." The "muḫḫum" were also chiefly concerned to remind the king to offer material gifts to the gods, especially sacrifices.

In contrast with the prophetism of exaltation and ecstasy found at Mari, purely Israelite prophetism is not associated with sacrificial cult and artificial excitement, and is characterized by high ethical standards: a prophetism of the Divine Word as against the prophetism of human emotions. "For the uniqueness of Biblical prophecy lies in its socio-ethical pathos, its religious ideology and its popular level – all of which are missing in the Mari material, where the ruling interests alone are promoted, satisfying local and immediate material demands."[24] When reading the Bible one often gets the impression that some of the true prophets, such as Samuel and Elisha, tried to win over the prophets of emotion, the "sons of the prophets," to their side. Their success was only temporary, and in other parts of Holy Scripture these bands are described as false prophets against whom the true prophets fought bitterly. One has but to think of Micah, who is the only prophet dauntlessly telling Ahab he will fall in battle.[25] The false prophet Zedekiah smote Micah on the face for daring to contradict his words and those of his four hundred dervishes. Jeremiah likewise came into constant conflict with the false prophets who said peace would come, while he foretold doom and exile. He said: "For prophet and priest alike are godless."[26] In the end the whole phenomenon of prophetism was viewed with great suspicion. For Zechariah said: "On that day, says the Lord of Hosts, I will erase the names of the idols from the land, and they shall be remembered no longer; I will also remove the prophets and the spirit of uncleanness from the land. Thereafter, if a man continues to prophesy, his parents, his own father and mother, will say to him, 'You shall live no longer, for you have spoken falsely in the name of the Lord.' His own father and mother will pierce him through because he has prophesied. On that day every prophet shall be ashamed of his vision when he prophesies, nor shall he wear a robe of coarse hair in order to deceive."[27] The mistrust of false prophets and their ecstatic practices is clearly echoed in this verse. From this and from Mari we see that divination was widely indulged in then, as in many places of the East until today. However, as Orlinsky says: "Prophecy is a uniquely Israelite phenomenon and it is divination and not prophecy that finds its parallels in the Mari documents." [28]

The great prophets in Israel, such as Isaiah and many others, were God's charismatic instruments for the interpretation of his intention and action in the history of the time. The essential difference between these two types of prophecy lay not in the form so much as in the faith which animated the preaching prophets.

We now return to the teachings of Isaiah in order to investigate what light archaeology sheds on his message. Isaiah, whose name signifies "help" or "deliverance" of God, tells us that he was married and had at least two children. These facts are brought into the narrative indirectly, as the children carry symbolic names embodying the prophecies of their father. His two sons are respectively called "a remnant shall return" [29] and "the spoil speedeth, the prey hasteneth"; [30] the third child, referred to in the book as "Immanuel'" is regarded by some as also the prophet's offspring, whereas others believe it refers to the child of the king or of some woman living at that time. The name of each child was a symbol indicating the fate that would overcome Damascus, Israel, or Judah.

Isaiah lived during the reigns of the kings Uzziah, Jotham, Ahaz, and Hezekiah. When he embarked on his prophetic mission about 740 B.C.E., Judah was a flourishing state where the rich lived in the lap of luxury while the poor were being sold for a pair of shoes. However, the days of plenty passed very quickly and Judah was subjected to many invasions which caused a depletion in her power and prestige. The first significant threat that appeared on the horizon was the Syro—Ephraimitic invasion in 735 B.C.E. When these two invading armies laid siege to Jerusalem King Ahaz was terrified. As the prophet put it in the exquisite language of the book: "And it was told the house of David saying: 'Aram is confederate with Ephraim.' And his heart was moved, and the heart of his people, as the trees of the forest are moved with the wind." [31] Ahaz immediately wanted to send to the Assyrian giant to come and assist him against these enemies. The prophet Isaiah intervened and tried to halt this action. He assured the panic-stricken king that both Syria and Israel would be destroyed by the Assyrian advance on their respective countries. At the same time Isaiah warned Ahaz against seeking Assyrian protection and urged implicit trust in God's salvation. It was at this juncture that the symbolic names of his children were given to them, in order to encourage faith and hope in God's ultimate salvation. Particularly is this so with the verse which is now in the light of evidence from Ugarit translated in the

New English Bible as follows: "A young woman is with child, and she will bear a son, and will call him Immanuel." It was a subject of constant debate. [32]

The word *almah* used to be rendered as "the virgin." It was claimed that it meant an unmarried woman. However, the Ugaritic texts teach us that the word *almah* means just young woman, and does not indicate if she was a virgin or not. These texts show that *almah* can be a woman who has children. Even the word *betulah* in the Ugaritic did not mean virgin, as it later did in Hebrew. The goddess Anat is called *btlt 'nt* and she is most certainly not a virgin, as the texts show, but was the mistress and sister of Baal. Thus, the word *almah* merely described an adolescent woman of marriageable age. The translation of *almah* as virgin originated with the Septuagint, where the word was rendered as *parthenos*. From this Greek version it crept into the Vulgate, where it is translated as *virgo,* and from here into the medieval and 16th century Bible. The gospel of Matthew i:23 likewise translates *almah* with the Greek word *parthenos.*

Most translations today no longer render the word as "virgin," and do not regard this any longer as a prediction of Mary and Jesus, who lived 700 years later. It is difficult to say with certainty who this young woman was. The fact that this sign was to convince Ahaz of the certain fulfillment of the prophecy makes it feasible that the woman referred to was either the king's wife or the prophet's, or any woman living in Judah at that particular time. The verse in Isaiah is reminiscent of the Ugaritic text where an oracle of birth is announced with the identical words: "Lo the maid will bear a son." [33] Ahaz did not take notice of the prophet's signs of assurance and called in the Assyrian king to help him. Thus, Judah became a satellite state of Assyria. The prophet Isaiah gives a vivid description of the intrigues that took place at the court of the king, one party endeavoring to enlist the favor of Assyria and the other of Egypt. On this occasion Ahaz ignored Isaiah's message, which he regarded as a military and political impracticability, and sent to the king of Assyria, saying: "I am your servant and your son. Come and save me from the king of Aram and the king of Israel who are attacking me." [34] After this event Judah became a vassal state of Assyria and part of the duty of such vassal kings was to recognize the state religion of the overlord. Therefore, we find Ahaz introducing an Assyrian type of altar into Judah, and practicing the Assyrian cult, even passing his children through fire to the gods. [35] Isaiah vehemently opposed the policy of Ahaz, and alliances with either Assyria or Egypt were anathema to him. He said strength lies in faith: "If you will not have faith, surely you shall not be established." [36] Throughout his ministry he contrasted the foolish plans of the Judean politicians with God's purpose and plan in history. Isaiah in the name of God counsels allegiance and loyalty to Assyria once Ahaz accepted his suzerainty. He warns that Egypt will betray and disappoint their trust. Events proved Isaiah correct and Egypt only once came to Hezekiah's assistance at the battle of Eltekeh, in which the Egyptian army was defeated.[37] After that Hezekiah waited for Egyptian help but he was disappointed as were the kings of Samaria. Egypt never again came to their rescue.

However, Jerusalem unlike Samaria was saved from annihilation by Assyria by a mixture of active defense measures and diplomacy. As already stated, part of the duty of a vassal king was to recognize the state religion of his overlord. Hezekiah, perhaps with political reliance on Egypt against which the prophet Isaiah continuously inveighed, gives expression to his repudiation of allegiance to Assyria by eradicating foreign worship in Jerusalem. In II Chronicles we have his inspiring call to Judah and the remnant of Israel to unite once again in pure worship of the Lord, the God of Israel.[38] He recognized that enthusiasm was not enough and that concrete actions had to be taken to achieve this lofty aim.[39] Hezekiah proceeded to eliminate the high places and to destroy the altars, standing stones and related objects associated by the masses with local cults of YHWH; he even went so far as to destroy the copper representation of a snake which had been preserved in the Temple and which was reputed to have been made by Moses. Hezekiah was greatly influenced in his action by having seen the catastrophic collapse of Samaria. He wished by his religious activities to prevent destruction from overtaking Judah. Then he turned to improve his defenses. Hezekiah acted bravely and made good every breach in the city wall and erected towers on it. There is an abundance of archaeological evidence for the Biblical record of some of Hezekiah's measures to defend Jerusalem against the attack of the Assyrians. Archaeology provides ample evidence of Hezekiah's attempt to buy off Sennacherib.[40] Archaeology does not give evidence for the plague which the Biblical record suggests was the ultimate cause of the Assyrian withdrawal.[41] But external material makes it quite clear, as the Bible claims, that the kingdom of Judah and Jerusalem survived and outlived the Assyrian threat.

When Hezekiah beheld the approach of the Assyrian army he took measures to defend his city: "And when Hezekiah saw that he, Sennacherib, had come, and was determined to attack Jerusalem, he consulted his civil and military officers about blocking up the springs outside the city, and they encouraged him. They gathered together a large number of people and blocked up all the springs and the stream which flowed through the land. 'Why,' they said, 'should the Assyrian king come here and find

Figure 25. Inscription found in the rock wall of Hezekiah's tunnel, late 8th century B.C.E. It describes the last moments in the hewing of the conduit, when the two groups of borers were about to meet each other in the middle of the tunnel.

plenty of water?'[42] The Biblical reference is to "springs" in the plural. From the recent evidence there is only one important spring, the Gihon spring; lower in the Kedron Valley there was Job's Well, but this was somewhat south of the southern point of the city and never had the same importance. The Gihon spring must have been the principal object of Hezekiah's attention.

The dramatic discovery of the inscription on the rock wall, which is usually described as the Siloam inscription has thrown a great deal of light on Hezekiah's activities. The tunnel had been cut by two groups of workers from the south and north, and the inscription records the triumphant moment when they met: "When the tunnel was driven through. And this was the way in which it was cut through: while. . . were still. . . axes, each man toward his fellow, and while there were still three cubits to be cut through, there was heard the voice of a man calling to his fellow, for there was an overlap in the rock on the right and on the left. And when the tunnel was driven through, the quarrymen hewed the rock, each man toward his fellow, axe against axe; and the water flowed from the spring toward the reservoir for 1,200 cubits, and the height of the rock above the heads of the quarrymen was 100 cubits."[43] This inscription was accidentally discovered by a young boy in 1880 and is today housed in the Museum of the Ancient Orient at Istanbul. The language is perfect classical Hebrew prose. In summing up Hezekiah's reign the Chronicler was so proud of this achievement that he even made special mention of the measures taken by Hezekiah to secure Jerusalem's water supply.[44] In order to deprive the besieged enemy of water and ensure the inhabitants an adequate water supply, Hezekiah blocked up the spring and an ancient conduit outside the walls, and diverted the waters of the Gihon into the city by a channel cut through the rock. This tunnel should be distinguished from the Jebusite waterworks used in Joab's attack, leading from the fountain directly into the city and the open canal, bringing the water along the slope of the mountain in a roundabout way to Siloam, as mentioned in Isaiah, vii:3. An echo of the acclamation with which Hezekiah's achievement was received can still be heard in the words of Ben Sira: "Hezekiah fortified his city, in that he brought water into it, and he hewed through the rocks with an iron and dammed up the pool with mountains."[45]

Sennacherib appears to have been sufficiently gratified by his exploits at Lachish and the other cities he had conquered to have four carved stone panels placed in his palace at Nineveh in order to commemorate the events that happened in Judah. There is no hint in this picture depicting his victory of any defeat befalling his forces as the Bible claims. However, it is likewise significant that the relief speaks of Lachish and not Jerusalem. Had he conquered the latter, which was the capital, the relief would have portrayed it. In view of the general note of boasting which pervades the incriptions of the Assyrian kings, it is hardly to be expected that he would record a defeat but only harp on the successful side of the campaign. Perhaps the fact that he claims to have shut up Hezekiah in Jerusalem "like a bird in a cage,"[46] but does not claim to have taken the city, is evidence that he did suffer discomfiture there. Incidentally, the Biblical account finds support in the writings of Herodotus. According to this historian, a plague of field mice broke out in Sennacherib's camp at Pelusium in Egypt. In one night the mice gnawed the thongs of his armies' shields as well as their bows and, by depriving them of their main weapons, exposed them to the mercy of their enemies.[47] The mention of mice may well indicate that it was plague which struck Sennacherib's army, since mice are a Greek symbol of pestilence and since rats are carriers of the plague. Perhaps this is the real explanation of the disaster referred to in the Bible as a smiting of the army by an angel of the Lord. The Bible employs in its usual manner religious terminology to describe a physical event. The Biblical statement that Sennacherib when he returned home was murdered by his sons is true, but we know that it took place many years later.[48]

The relief which depicts Sennacherib's victory over Lachish not only offers information about the Assyrians' methods of war and policy of

Figure 26. Hexagonal clay prism of Sennacherib, king of Assyria, bearing a cuneiform inscription describing the military campaigns of Sennacherib against King Hezekiah of Judah and against Philistia, 701 B.C.E. The prism is the most detailed Assyrian description of an episode related to the Bible. It describes Sennacherib's siege and conquest of 46 cities in Judah, and the booty taken from them.

deportation of conquered peoples, but also illustrates the mode and manner of dress of those days. The Israelite soldier in this relief wears a short skirt, T-shirt "girdle" or waistband, and turban. The elders and important men of the city, however, are depicted by the artist as wearing long white dresses of a type that fits closely and could be slipped on and off over the head. They reach the lower part of the leg just above the ankle, and their sleeves cover the upper part of the arm. This dress is the Hebrew *ketonet* or tunic. If an Israelite man did not wear the short skirt, he wore the long *ketonet,* for it was a basic garment. From ancient portrayals we learn that the tunic was made in a much more elaborate fashion depending on the man's means and status in life. The Black Obelisk depicts the Israelites wearing long garments covered with fringed cloaks, pointed soft caps or turbans, and sandals with upturned toes. These were also the apparel of the Syrians on this relief. The fringed garment is probably the Hebrew *me'il*, an outer garment of linen or wool. The clothing worn by women on this Lachish relief is similar to that of the men, except that they did not wear the short skirt and in all probability they could adorn themselves in a greater variety of garments if they possessed the means to purchase them. The basic garments were the tunic and the cloak or robe. The most detailed description of the attire of wealthy women comes from Isaiah's fashion journal in Chapter iii. [49] Some 21 different articles of adornment are mentioned here but, since so many of the words are obscure, it is useless to speculate about them without more detailed archaeological information. The use of jewelry and a variety of cosmetics was as widespread then as it is today. Cosmetic bowls were used to prepare colors for the face, eyebrows, and eyelashes. The coiffure of women was also very elaborate, judging by figures of the goddesses recovered from excavations. All these figurines illustrate the elaborate hairstyles worn by the affluent women in the Ancient Near East. No doubt the Israelite woman followed styles in clothes, as she did in ivory furnishings and musical entertainment, and she was as frivolous as Isaiah and Amos claim. [50]

The tomb of Shebna, containing the third longest monumental inscription in archaic Hebrew, (the longest being the Moabite stone and the second the Siloam tunnel engraving), dates from the days of Isaiah. Shebna was a man of wealth and high position in the court of Hezekiah. He is variously designated minister, "which is over the house," [51] secretary, [52] and treasurer. He was rebuked by the prophet Isaiah for preparing a striking and lavish monumental rock-hewn tomb for himself, emulating the manner of the affluent aristocracy of the Ancient Near East. He also incurred the wrath of Isaiah because the prophet preached a policy of non-involvement, [53] while Shebna sought to influence Hezekiah to revolt against the Assyrian overlord and rely on Egyptian military support. [54] Isaiah foretold the fall of Shebna from his important role of "he who is over the house," and this prophecy was realized, for by the time of Sennacherib's invasion he is only called royal secretary, *sopher,* [55] and Eliakim has been made prime minister, as Isaiah said he would be. [56] In the village of Siloam, at the foot of the Mount of Olives, an epitaph has been discovered in the ancient Hebrew script, engraved in stone above the entrance to an impressive tomb. The name given is Shebna. But this apparently was an abbreviation of "Shebnayahu" according to Avigad. [57] The inscription on the grave which ends with "yahu" has been ascribed to Shebna, since there is no other mention in the Bible of a royal official who was rebuked for building a pretentious sepulcher. The inscription on the grave curses the person who will open it, but this merely indicates how widespread the practice of tomb robbing was. Likewise, neither the statement nor the curse availed, for the tomb has long since been emptied of its contents. The date of the epitaph cannot be long before 700 B.C.E. for the manner in which the letters were formed is very similar to that of the Siloam inscription. It is the first known text of a Hebrew sepulchral inscription from the pre-Exilic period.

Hezekiah, who was one of the most outstanding kings of Judah, famous as we have seen both for his piety and vigorous political activities, became very ill. Traditionally it is believed that Hezekiah's illness occurred three days before the collapse of Sennarcherib's army. On this occasion Isaiah came advising him to prepare for death. However, Hezekiah prayed and received an extension of 15 years more of life. Here Isaiah, following the example of some of the earlier prophets such as Elisha, prepared a cure for the king. He told them to put a cake of dried figs on the boil; it was done, and Hezekiah recovered. It is interesting that the word for fig-cake appears in a veterinarian recipe for a horse plaster in the Ugaritic texts. "When a horse tosses his head and whinnies much, take an aged fig cake and aged raisins and grocer's flour; it is to be injected together."[58] It appears that this must have been part of a medical practice understood and followed in that period. Isaiah likewise used the same adjectives to describe the Leviathan[59] as did the Ugaritic poet six centuries earlier. For the Biblical writers were well acquainted with Canaanite poetical forms, but filled them with new content and meaning. Thus, Isaiah uses the image of Leviathan to symbolize God's creative power and control over the chaos of the world. Ugaritic literature lies closer than any other literature to the Bible. The similarities between the two are strictly literary and not spiritual. Indeed, as shown earlier in this book, the Hebrew Bible is to a great extent a conscious polemic against the Canaanite milieu.[60]

Archaeology has reconstructed the world of Isaiah, one of the greatest of the Hebrew literary prophets. He was far from being a practical down to earth politician, militarist, or statesman; he was concerned solely with morals and religion and preaches a policy based on faith. For him, God is the cause of everything that happens or exists. For Isaiah, Assyria is simply God's tool for meting out punishment to the nations of the world, and particularly Israel and Judah. But in turn Assyria is to be destroyed not by man but by God.[61] He warned against social injustice in all areas of life, for which punishment was inevitable. Isaiah's own faith was vindicated when Sennacherib laid siege to Jerusalem and the city and Temple were saved. By his visions of the Messianic age and of the ideal

Messianic ruler,[62] Isaiah fired the imagination of his own and later generations. The marvelous deliverance of Jerusalem which is confirmed by
external sources led the people to create a dogma of the inviolability of
Zion. This belief constituted a great danger, material and spiritual. It gave
them a false sense of security; surely God will protect His own city and
Temple. Jeremiah was faced with the unenviable task of energetically
combating their superstitious trust in the Temple as a source of deliverance
in time of crisis, and teaching the people that only their own righteous
actions could save them from evil and destruction. To his times and
teachings we now turn.

NOTES

[1]   Is. x:5; vii:20; vii:8.

[2]   Hallo, W.W. "From Qarqar to Carchemish: Assyria and Israel in the
Light of New Discoveries," *Biblical Archaeologist Reader,* 2, 1964,
pp. 152ff.

[3]   Is. x:28; Na. ii, iii.

[4]   Na. iii:2–5.

[5]   *Views of the Biblical World,* Vol. 11, pp. 286–7.

[6]   Luckenbell, D.D. *Ancient Records of Assyria and Babylonia,*
1926–7, Vol.1. paragraphs 443,447. It is interesting to contrast the
cruelty of the Assyrian kings with the magnanimity of Ahab. When
the Arameans lost a battle against him, they said to their King Ben-
hadad: "We have heard that the kings of the house of Israel are
merciful kings; let us, we pray thee, put sackcloth on our loins, and
ropes upon our heads, and go out to the king of Israel; peradventure
he will save thy life." (I Ki. xx:31). Ahab indeed spared the life of
Ben-hadad at this juncture. Translation from *Soncino Bible.*

[7]   This incident of Jehu paying tribute to the Assyrian king is described
in greater detail in Chapter Six of this book.

[8]   II Ki. xv:19.

[9]   II Ki. xvii:5.

[10]   II Ki. xiv:25.

[11]   II Ki. xxv:23ff.

[12]   Albright, W.F. *The Biblical Period from Abraham to Ezra,* 1963, p.
72.

[13]   Am. iv:1ff; vi:4ff.

[14]   *Views of the Biblical World,* Vol. 111, p. 238.

[15]   Dreyer H.J. *Lecture Notes to Classical Hebrew,* University of South
Africa, p. 48.

16   II Ki. xv:29.
17   *ANET*, pp. 284ff.
18   II Ki. xvii:9ff.
19   II Ki. xiv:7.
20   II Ch. xxvi:6ff.
21   For authorship see Harrison, Peake, the *Interpreter's Bible*, and others. Each one of these writers offers a detailed bibliography of the subject.
22   I Sa. x:5ff.
23   Huffmon, H.B. "Prophecy in the Mari Letters", *The Biblical Archaeologist Reader*, 3, 1970, pp. 204ff.
24   Malamat, A. Mari *The Biblical Archaeologist*, 1971, Vol. xxiv, No. 1, pp. 20ff.
25   I Ki. xxii:19ff.
26   Je. viii:10–17; xiv:14–18; xxiii:9–40.
27   Zc. xiii:2ff.
28   Orlinsky, H.M. *Ancient Israel*, 1956, pp. 142ff;
      Heschel, A.J. *The Prophets*, 1962, pp. 351–367; 426–447.
29   Is. vii:2.
30   Is. viii:3.
31   Is. vii:2.
32   Is. vii:14;
      Gordon, C.H. *Ugaritic Textbook*, Text 51:7, 1965, see Glossary No. 1969. The English "virgin" is rendered by *parthenos* ($\pi\alpha\rho\theta\epsilon\nu o\varsigma$) in the Septuagint; see Septuagint in Greek and English, p. 842.
33   Gordon, C.H. *Ugaritic Texts*, Text 77:7, *(hl glmt tld b)*; 1965; *Ugaritic Literature*, 1949, p. 64.
34   II Ki. xvi:7.
35   II Ki. xvi:3, 4, 10–16; II Ch. xxviii:2–4, 23–25.
36   Is. vii:9.
37   *ANET*, p. 288.
38   II Ch. xxix–xxxi.
39   II Ch. xxxii:2ff.
40   II Ki. xviii:14–16; *ANET*, pp. 288ff.
41   Is. xxxvii:36ff; II Ch. xxxii:21.
42   II Ch. xxxii:4.
43   *ANET*, p. 321.
44   II Ch. xxxii; II Ki. xx:20.
45   Ecclesiasticus, xl:17.
46   *ANET*, p. 288.
47   Finegan, J. *Light from the Ancient Past*, 1969, pp. 213ff.
48   *ANET*, p. 288; Gordon, C.H. *An Introduction to the Old Testament*, 1953; p. 231; II Ki. xix:36; Is xxxvii:38.

49   Is. iii:16–24.

50   Is. iii:16–24; Am. iv:2ff;

Heaton, E.W. *Everyday Life in Old Testament Times*, 1956.

51   Is. xxii:15.

52   II Ki. xviii:18; xix:2; Is. xxxvi:3.

53   Is. vii:4.

54   Is. xxxi:1.

55   II Ki. xviii:18.

56   Is. xxii:21–3.

57   The translation of this inscription is given in Chapter Six.

58   The Ugaritic original reads: *dblt ytnt wsmgm ytnm. Ugaritic Textbook*, p. 175, text 55:28. Translation in Gordon's *Ugaritic Literature*, p. 129. The word *dblt* resembles the Hebrew *dvelet* (Is. xxxviii:21), which means a cake of pressed dried figs.

59   Is. xxvii:1.

60   See Chapter Six.

61   Is. x:7ff.

62   Is. ii and xi.

CHAPTER EIGHT

Jeremiah—The Fall of Judah

Manasseh did not follow in the ways of his pious father, but rather in the impious ones of his grandfather Ahaz. His rule was a period of religious retrogression caused by terror of Assyria and a fascination with her cults. This resulted in a syncretism of Baalism, a cult of Astarte at the high places, with spiritism and divination. His long reign was bloody and reactionary, and notorious for the introduction of illegal altars into the Temple courts; and like Ahaz he passed his sons through fire in the valley of the son of Hinnom.[1] His name appears on the Prism of Esarhaddon and on the Prism of Ashurbanipal, among the 22 tributaries of Assyria.[2] The Book of Chronicles narrates his capture and deportation to Babylon, and his subsequent repentance and release.[3] Manasseh's evil work, the introduction of polytheism and its ways, was undone by the great religious revolution inaugurated by Josiah.[4] The climax of his religious activities was reached when "the Book of the Law" was found by Hilkiah, the high priest in the Temple.[5] Many scholars have assumed that the book he found was Deuteronomy. This theory was based on the character of Josiah's reforms, which particularly sought to abolish the "high places," centralize worship in Jerusalem, and reaffirm the covenant between God and Israel. However, an eminent scholar like Gordon writes: "It is often surmised (falsely, I think) that the scroll of the law found in Josiah's reign, and read at his Passover reunion, was only a part of Deuteronomy. It is apparent, that to be appropriate for Passover, it must have included Exodus; and to cement the tribesmen into a nation in accordance with Josiah's program, it should have included the patriarchal narratives. It is much more likely that Josiah's scroll was pretty much like our modern Pentateuch."[6] It is also telling to notice that the word Jerusalem does not occur in this book, though some scholars wish us to believe that centralization of worship in this city is Deuteronomy's salient aim.[7]

Josiah's revival was made possible by the death of Ashurbanipal in 632 B.C.E., and the subsequent decline in Assyrian power. Ashurbanipal was more a scholar than a warrior. He devoted himself to literature and learning, and his library in the palace at Nineveh has enlightened us richly about the past. Among the tablets found in this royal library were the creation and flood stories, and a galaxy of magnificent reliefs which represent the climax of Syrian art.[8] After his demise, decline overtook Assyria and Josiah's reformation was made possible. The Medes and the Babylonians broke up the Assyrian Empire and the Babylonians established themselves as rulers of Syria and Palestine after defeating Necho in 605 B.C.E. The capital of Assyria, Nineveh, fell in 612 and the rejoicing of her foes at the event is echoed in Nahum:

> Your shepherds slumber, O King of Assyria,
> your flock-masters lie down to rest;
> your troops are scattered over the hills,
> and no one rounds them up.
> Your wounds cannot be assuaged, your injury is mortal;
> all who have heard of your fate clap their hands in joy.
> Are there any whom your ceaseless cruelty has not borne down?[9]

But Josiah's brief successes came to a violent end when the Egyptians under Pharaoh Necho tried to take advantage of the weakness of Assyria after the death of Ashurbanipal to reestablish their rule in Palestine and Assyria. Josiah was tragically killed by Necho at Megiddo in 609 B.C.E. In the light of archaeological and Biblical sources, it appears that Josiah was anti-Assyrian, while Egypt wanted a weak Assyria as a buffer against Babylonia.[10] Josiah knew that with Egypt in control of Syria and Palestine his newly erected state of Judah could not survive. His only hope for survival was to delay the forces of Necho by making them deploy for siege, so that the latter would not arrive in time at Harran to help the Assyrians, who were staging their last and desperate stand. Thus, Josiah, Judah's godliest king, met his heroic death in open battle in the pass near Megiddo.[11] Archaeological evidence for the siege near Megiddo, which resulted in Josiah's death, is the destruction of the city at Stratum II. After this battle Megiddo was never again an important place. But the Egyptian interference was itself short-lived.

Jeremiah is probably the most tragic of all the preaching prophets, and also the most self-revealing. The call of Jeremiah came in 625 B.C.E., whereas Josiah's reforms began only in 621 B.C.E., yet the king consulted the prophetess Huldah and not Jeremiah when he found "the Book of the Law."[12] Judah was politically in a very dangerous situation when Jeremiah began to prophesy. His ministry lasted until 586 B.C.E., and thus he prophesied under the last five kings of Judah, namely Josiah, Jehoahaz, Jehoiakim, Jehoiachin, and Zedekiah. While he was preaching, important personalities lived and acted, and events of great moment took place. Empires and kings rose and fell. It was one of the most crucial periods in the history of the Ancient Near East, and it affected Judah's history as well.

Jeremiah's life and times, which fall within this fateful yet all important period in history, are remarkably well documented and the intimacies of his personality are more vividly portrayed than those of Isaiah, Hosea, or Micah, or those of his contemporaries such as Nahum, Habakkuk, and Zephaniah. The latter never revealed to us so much about themselves, their feelings, and emotions as this tragic prophet Jeremiah, who was fated to minister in the period of twilight, decline, and destruction. One admires the boldness with which he pronounces doom and rejects the irrational sense of security of the people, who held onto the belief of the indestructibility of Zion.

Despite the fierce animosity of his family, friends, and the people at large, Jeremiah pronounced doom on the nation that would not better their ways. He mocked their superstitious belief that the Temple could save them, stating: "These are the words of the Lord of Hosts the God of Israel: 'Mend your ways and your doings, that I may let you live in this place.' You keep saying, 'This place is the temple of the Lord, the temple of the Lord, the temple of the Lord.' This catchword is a lie; put no trust in it. Mend your ways and your doings, deal fairly with another, do not oppress the alien, the orphan, and the widow, shed no innocent blood in this place . . . Then I let you live in the place . . . You steal, you murder, you commit adultery and perjury, you burn sacrifices to Baal, you run after other gods whom you have not known; then you come and stand before me in this house which bears my name and say, 'We are safe'; safe, you think, to indulge in all these abominations. Do you think that this His house, this house which bears my name, is a robbers' cave?"[13] Jeremiah continued to warn that if they did not change their evil ways the Temple and Jerusalem would be destroyed like Shiloh had been annihilated in the days of Eli and Samuel.[14]

Jeremiah was very much aware of the catastrophe which had overtaken Shiloh. This is understandable when we remember that he was a scion of a priestly family from Anathoth. He was a descendant of Abiathar, the survivor of the priests of Nob who were killed by Saul after they had assisted David. But Abiathar was eventually banished from officating as a priest in the Temple by Solomon. Jeremiah began to prophesy at an early age, probably before he was twenty. As he describes it in his book: "The word of the Lord came to me: 'Before I formed you in the womb I knew you for my own; before you were born I consecrated you, I appointed you a prophet to the nations.' 'Ah! Lord God,' I answered, 'I do not know how to speak, I am only a child.' But the Lord said, 'Do not call yourself a child; for you shall go to whatever people I send you and say whatever I tell you to say. Fear none of them, for I am with you and will keep you safe.' "[15]

Like Moses before him, Jeremiah was hesitant to accept the call. His reluctance was due to a natural shrinking from so great a task and to his own temperament — timid, sensitive, introspective, and distrustful of his own capabilities. Or perhaps he was aware of the enormity of the task placed upon him, preaching an unpopular message, the doom of a nation. He indeed needed superhuman powers, and therefore God promised him that he would make him strong like a fortified city, a pillar of iron, a wall of bronze, to stand fast against the whole land, and against the kings and princes of Judah.[16] The people could not endure his preaching against their idolatry and apostasy, but the words that truly infuriated them were when he prophesied saying: "I will make this house like Shiloh and this city an object of ridicule to all nations on earth."[17] When the priests and the people heard Jeremiah's words they took hold of him, shouting: "Thou shalt surely die."[18] They regarded his speech as not only daring but blasphemous. Jeremiah was often harassed and hounded, beaten and imprisoned in his life, but on this occasion it was decided to try him for treason and put him to death. The priests at the trial repeated their demand that Jeremiah be put to death for his blasphemy. Undaunted, Jeremiah remained firm and insisted on the legitimacy of his cause. As for himself, Jeremiah warned that if they put him to death, "you will bring innocent blood upon yourselves and upon this city."[19] Jeremiah's heroic words, reminiscent of those of Socrates before the Athenian jury, had an effect on the people and the princes who joined him in remonstrating with the priests and false prophets: "This man ought not to be condemned to death, for he has spoken to us in the name of the Lord our God."[20] Some of the members present at the trial defended the prophet, citing the precedent of the prophet Micah in the days of Hezekiah a century before, who had also predicted destruction of the Temple saying:

> Zion shall become a plowed field
> Jerusalem a heap of ruins,
> and the temple-hill rough heath,

and he had been spared and not put to death by the king. Others, however, put forward the more recent example of Uriah who had prophesied against the city and had fled to Egypt, whence Jehoiakim had him extradited and then executed. Jeremiah was only saved from death on this occasion because of Ahikam ben Shaphan, who interceded on his behalf and hastened the proceedings of the court, so that they complete judgment before the arrival of the cruel and tyrannical King Jehoiakim, who despised the prophet.

Scholars claim that the proceedings against Micah were not cited during Jeremiah's trial. They state that the story was added by Baruch in order to show how real Jeremiah's danger was. They likewise believe that Ahikam played no role in the trial. He protected Jeremiah somewhat later in the days of Micah's death. Though Jeremiah escaped from the vindictive crowd, he knew it was only temporary because his message, which was one invariably of warning, violence, and destruction, engendered hatred and persecution of him. Jeremiah, during his ministry occasionally, was despondent,[21] and on other occasions he was caught up in moments of spiritual exaltation.[22] The nature of his office precluded participation in the more normal activities of human society, including marriage. Jeremiah was forbidden to marry not on account of his prophetic office (other prophets were married) but because it seemed senseless to bring children into a doomed society.[23]

Through periods of persecution and imprisonment Jeremiah maintained his spiritual integrity and never once stooped to an act of compromise in face of danger. But he often reveals that in moments of weakness he wished to escape the heavy burden of prophecy which made him a lonely figure: "A man of strife and contention to the whole earth."[24] The most telling words in this connection are the following:

O Lord thou hast enticed me,
and I was enticed,
Thou has overcome me, and hast prevailed;
I am become a laughing-stock all the day,
Everyone mocketh me.

And if I say: 'I will not make mention of Him,
Nor speak any more in His name,'
Then there is in my heart as it were a burning fire
Shut up in my bones,
And I weary myself to hold it in, but cannot.[25]

In these lines the prophet reveals his innermost secrets to us. He would rather be silent and not suffer. But an overpowering realization of his mission compels him to speak words which he would rather leave unsaid, but they burn within him until he has given utterance to them. The true prophet follows the Divine call in spite of himself. Jeremiah discloses the psychology of the prophet, lays bare the emotion of the man singled out to be the mouthpiece of God. At times he felt fulfilled, but often he feels poignant sorrow, even rebelliousness against the divinely ordained mission. Jeremiah's life, in a nutshell, is the story of the lover of Judah whom Judah maligned.

The political side of life in Judah, which led to the captivity of the Jews to Babylon and which was until recently only known from the Bible and a few references in Josephus and Herodotus, has been further illuminated by new finds. The publication in 1956 by Wiseman of the British Museum of additional tablets of the contemporary Babylonian Chronicle now enables a full picture of the major historical episodes to be taken from this unique source. The Chronicle narrates the fall of Nineveh to the Babylonians and Medes in 612 B.C.E., and continues to trace the relations between Necho II of Egypt and Nabopolassar of Babylon until the Battle of Carchemish in 605 B.C.E. The crown prince at this time was Nebuchadnezzar, and he claimed to have conquered the whole of Syro-Palestine as implied indeed by II Kings xxiv[26] and, immediately after his accession in 605 B.C.E., to have received a tribute from all the kings of Hatti (Syro-Palestine) who came before him. Among the kings who submitted to him at this juncture is Jehoiakim who remained loyal until after the defeat of the Babylonians by the Egyptians in a great battle in 601 B.C.E., known only from this chronicle. The inevitable Babylonian revenge came after raids on the Arabs of Kedar as described in Jeremiah, xlix.[27] The fifth paragraph of the chronicle, which is housed in the British Museum, [number 21946] relates the capture of Jerusalem in 597 B.C.E., the deportation of Jehoiachin and his court, and the appointment of Zedekiah as king of Judah.[28] When the latter revolted later against his Babylonian overlord, he and Jeremiah knew that the consequence would be invasion and destruction for breaking the vassal treaty to which the king had sworn allegiance. The real nature of this final siege of Jerusalem is shown by the utter devastation of Judah which took place at this time. A number of archaeological discoveries illuminate the background to the prophecies of Jeremiah.

King Jehoiakim had little time either for the prophet or his message,[29] for his religious inclinations were idolatrous, and this, combined with his selfishness and personal vanity, contributed to the misfortunes of the Southern Kingdom. He was essentially a political opportunist, as his vacillating policies with regard to Egypt and Babylon clearly indicate. He likewise was a pleasure-seeking king who exploited the poor and the needy and accordingly was rebuked by Jeremiah.[30] Excavations at the tell of Ramat Rahel have shed interesting light on the encounter between prophet and king. Ramat Rahel lies between Bethlehem and Jerusalem. The mound has become one of the most interesting archaeological sites in the vicinity of Jerusalem, not only because of its historic link with Jerusalem, but because, here, for the first time, a royal palace and fortress of one of the Judean kings has been unearthed. Although Ramat Rahel's ancient name is unknown, it is now suggested by archaeologists that it is the ancient Beth-hakerem. Jeremiah mentions the name of this place when he says: "Blow the trumpet in Tekoa and set up a signal in Beth-hakerem."[31] This indicates that Beth-hakerem was a fortified site south of Jerusalem on the road to Tekoa, south of Bethlehem, on a hill from which a beacon would be visible from Jerusalem. No more suitable site for this can be found than the citadel of Ramat Rahel. All factors indicate that one of the Judean kings converted this site into a large fortress, in the center of which he built a magnificent palace. In the light of the archaeological evidence this can only be one of the last kings and a reference to the building of a palace by Jehoiakim, who ruled about 608–587 B.C.E., is preserved in the Book of Jeremiah. The prophet rebuked the king for using forced labor unjustly for the construction of his palace. He said:

> Shame on the man who builds his house by unjust means
> and completes its roof chambers by fraud,
> making his countrymen work without payment,
> giving them no wage for their labor!
>
> Shame on the man who says 'I will build a spacious house
> with airy roof chambers,
> Set windows in it, panel it with cedar
> and paint it with vermilion.'[32]

Jeremiah warned Jehoiakim that he would pay a heavy price for his sins and would die a tragic death.[33] The description of the palace given in Jeremiah resembles that unearthed at Ramat Rahel. It refers to a wide house and large chambers, cut out windows and cedar and painted vermilion. Since the facade of the main building discovered was decorated with conspicuous ornamented windows, it is not surprising that Jeremiah singles them out. The remains of the balustrade indicate that the capitals

Figure 27. Dignitary seated on throne, painted on sherd from Ramat Rahel, c. 600 B.C.E.

supported wooden beams, and on the stone there are still traces of red paint. It would seem that Jeremiah is describing these very windows. Of course, other palaces in Palestine may have been decorated in the same manner, but the palace at Ramat Rahel is essentially like that described by the prophet and as it is difficult to imagine that the Judean kings were extensive builders of this sort of structure, the identification seems fairly certain. Jeremiah once referred to the king's winter house, from which we might deduce that the king also had a summer house. This may well have been the palace discovered at Ramat Rahel. A potsherd with a drawing of a king found at Ramat Rahel probably represents Jehoiakim. Thus, owing to this sherd, we now possess two concrete visualizations of Biblical kings, one in the Northern Kingdom, Jehu, the other in Judah, Jehoiakim. These are our only sources as to what a Biblical personality looked like in those far-off days.

What moved Jehoiakim to build such a pretentious palace in his short reign? The prophet Jeremiah also enlightens us about this when he says: "If your cedar is more splendid, does that prove you a king? Think of your father. He ate and drank, dealt justly and fairly; all went well with him." [34] It would seem from this that Jehoiakim, who was put on the throne by the Egyptians, tried to emulate their building activities and thus alienated his people. This was openly expressed by the daring prophet Jeremiah. Instead of following in the footsteps of his father, and gaining the confidence and support of his people by wise and just deeds, Jehoiakim ruled with a strong arm, securing himself as Herod did later within the walls of this strong fortress. He may have built the citadel overlooking Jerusalem in order to sweep down on the city in case of an uprising. These fortifications could likewise be connected with his unsuccessful revolt against Babylon which brought about the fall of his kingdom. Whatever the case, we see once again that every new archaeological discovery touching on the Bible affects our understanding of it and affords us a much clearer setting for the activities of its heroes. [35]

Another fascinating discovery is the Lachish letters which were found in the debris of the guardroom by the city gate. The first 18 letters were found by Starkey in 1935, and three more were added during a supplementary excavation in 1938. Most of the ostraca were letters or lists of names written in classical Hebrew. However, only a third of these documents are preserved in such a condition as to be reasonably intelligible throughout. Nearly all of the potsherds come from the latest occupation level of Biblical Lachish, and archaeologists generally place them before the beginning of the Chaldean siege of the city in about 589 B.C.E. The letters offer a vivid illustration of the crisis that prevailed in Judah in those distant days. The documents indicate to what an extent the morale of the people had been weakened both by internal dissension and by the threat of invasion.

The letters appear to be correspondence between Hoshaiah, the commander of an outpost on the outskirts of Lachish, and Yaosh, military governor of Lachish. Thus, for instance, in letter iv, Hoshaiah writes:

> And let my Lord know that we are watching for
> the signals of Lachish, according to all the indications
> which my lord hath given, for we cannot see Azekah.[36]

In other words, the writer informs his superior that he and his men are faithfully carrying out the orders given by fire signals from Lachish, but they have lost contact with Azekah.[37] It has been suggested that, at the time of the writing of the letter, Azekah had already been cut off by enemy forces, and may have even fallen, whereas Lachish itself continued to hold out for a little longer. This letter dovetails beautifully with a verse in Jeremiah, where the prophet informs King Zedekiah that the Babylonians were attacking Jerusalem and the remaining cities of Judah, namely Lachish and Azekah. These, the prophets informed him, were the only fortified cities left in Judah.[38] The Lachish letters, as it were, supplement our knowledge of what happened in these last tragic moments of Judah's struggle to survive. We learn that first Azekah, then Lachish, and finally Jerusalem fell to the enemy.

Another informative letter is number vi, where it is stated that the king and his ministers were enraged against certain *sarim* (princes), for "weakening the hands" of the populace. They call for measures to be taken to silence them. It is telling to notice that the charge of "weakening the hands" of the people was, ironically enough, the identical one which was leveled against Jeremiah by the *sarim* in the days of Zedekiah.[39] In another letter (number iii) we read about the mission of a senior officer called Coniah, son of Elnathan, and his men, who went down into Egypt perhaps for the purpose of bringing back the prophet, and about a warning sent to the prophet to keep out of their way. The identity of the prophet in these letters has been a matter of considerable speculation, with some scholars assuming that Jeremiah himself was referred to and others claiming that an unknown contemporary prophet had been spoken of. Torczyner identifies the prophet in these letters with Uriah, whose rash utterances had caused his flight into Egypt from where he was extradited and executed in Jerusalem by King Jehoiakim. He claimed that the name Uriah could also be Uriyahu, and thus fits in well with the ending of the prophet's name in the Lachish letter. The only difficulty is that the story of Uriah takes place during the reign of Jehoiakim, whereas the Lachish letters belong to the rule of Zedekiah. It is quite possible, therefore, that

Figure 28.   Clay tablet inscribed in Babylonian cuneiform with a chronicle of the years 605–595 B.C.E., including an account of the fall of Jerusalem in 597 B.C.E. From Babylon. 6th century B.C.E.

there were actually two different prophets, one in the time of Jehoiakim and the other in the time of Zedekiah, who, like Jeremiah, incurred the

wrath of the king and his ministers. The Lachish letters have a dual
significance: on the one hand they are the only corpus of documents in
classical Hebrew prose, and thus have an unusual philological importance;
and on the other hand they shed fascinating light on the life and times of
Jeremiah.[40]

A number of tablets which were found in an administrative building
at Babylon near the famous Ishtar gate shed new light on the captivity of
Jehoiachin in the land of his exile. This king is actually a rather tragic
figure. At the age of eighteen he became king of Judah, and he remained
under the control of his domineering mother, Nehushta, until the end of
his short reign of three months. During his brief reign the country lay at
the mercy of the Babylonians, against whose King Nebuchadnezzar,
Jehoiachin's father had rebelled. The latter apparently met a tragic
death, probably in a palace revolt, since his body was thrown outside
the gates of the city and left to lie there like the carcass of an ass.[41] Soon
afterward the prospect for Judah seemed so bad that the king, his mother,
and all the principal officials surrendered and were carried off as captives
to Babylonia, along with thousands of other people, the flower of the
land. Jehoiachin never returned to his native land but died in exile.
According to the Book of Kings, 37 years after his surrender to the
Babylonians he was released from prison by Nebuchadnezzar's son, Evil-
merodach, and was given preferential treatment: "He showed favor to
Jehoiachin, king of Judah. He brought him out of prison, treated him
kindly and gave him a seat at the table above the kings with him in
Babylon. So Jehoiachin discarded his prison clothes and lived as a
pensioner of the king for the rest of his life. For his maintenance, a regular
daily allowance was given by the king as long as he lived."[42]

The first external evidence about Jehoiachin appeared when Albright
unearthed a broken jar handle stamped with a beautifully carved seal
inscribed: "Belonging to Eliakim, steward of Yaukin." Excavating near the
Ishtar gate, archaeologists discovered lists of payment of rations in oil and
barley to captives and skilled workmen from many nations. Among those
mentioned were Yaukin, king of Judah, and five royal princes as well as
numerous other men of Judah. Almost as significant as the mention of
Jehoiachin himself is the reference to his five sons, who are mentioned
three times immediately after his name. These five princes doubtless
included several who lived long enough to be included in the list of
Jehoiachin's seven sons given by the Chronicler.[43] The names of the seven
sons of Jehoiachin born while he was a captive are known; the oldest of
them was Shealtiel, father of Zerubbabel. This discovery about
Jehoiachin's rations of food is striking indeed, for these texts fill out the

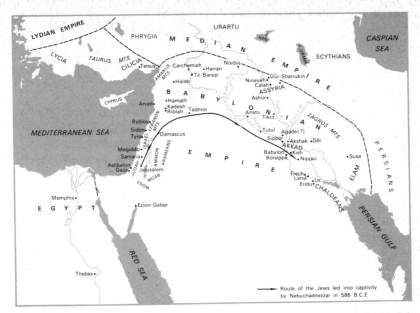

Figure 29. The Empire of Nebuchadnezzar II (604–562 B.C.E.). Based on M.A. Beek, *Atlas of Mesopotamia*. Nelson, London, 1962.

Bible narrative by actually specifying the exact amount of rations dealt out to the king, who is mentioned by name in the text, and his sons and fellow prisoners. Such direct points of contact between archaeology and the Bible are, it may be stated, exceptional indeed, and when they do occur they are all the more fascinating and valuable.[44] The archaeological finds vividly illustrate the upheavals and crises that characterized Jeremiah's age.

The Babylonians appointed Gedaliah to be governor in Judah, and for a while it looked as if he would be successful in organizing the government for the surviving Jews. Unfortunately Ishmael, a descendant of the royal house of Judah, murdered him. At this juncture the people, fearing the vengeance of Nebuchadnezzar, asked Jeremiah to inquire of God whether they should flee to Egypt. Jeremiah urged them to stay in the land and not to fear the king of Babylon. They refused to heed his counsel and, forcing the prophet to join them, they all went down into Egypt. Here the Jews, and especially the women, began to worhip the heathen idols again. Jeremiah warned them against these practices, but they replied that as long as they had served the "queen of heaven" it had been well with them and that they would continue to worship her. Jeremiah, as he had done so often during the previous 40 years, predicted their destruction and announced that Pharaoh Hophra would suffer a defeat at the hands of his enemies. This is the last we hear of Jeremiah.

In conclusion, it might be stated that Jeremiah is not only a prophet of doom and destruction but also a spokesman of hope and happiness. As a dramatic symbol of his faith in the future restoration of Judah he bought a tract of land, though the fields lay fallow and the Babylonians were attacking. His signing a deed was an act of trust that "fields and vineyards will yet be planted in this land."[45] When destruction came and the groups of captives began their long trek to Babylon, Jeremiah urged them to set up markers and observe the road carefully so that they could find their way back. He wrote a letter to the Jews in Babylon telling them how to live and behave in exile, and promising them that they would eventually return to the land of Judah.[46]

His message of faith to his people was:

I will build you up again, O virgin Israel,
and you shall be rebuilt
Again you shall adorn yourself with jingles,
and go forth with the merry throng of dances
Again you shall plant vineyards on the hills of Samaria.
For a day will come when the watchmen on Ephraim's hills cry out,
Come, let us go up to Zion, to the Lord our God.[47]

NOTES

[1]   II Ki. xxi:1ff; II Ch. xxxiii:1ff.

[2]   *ANET*, p. 291ff.

[3]   II Ch. xxxiii:10−13.

[4]   II Ki. xxii:7. Here Hilkiah finds the Book of Law which leads to the reforms of King Josiah described in these chapters. See also II Ch. xxxiv:14, 15.

[5]   *Ibid.*

[6]   Gordon, C.H. *Before the Bible,* 1962, p. 293.

[7]   The name Jerusalem does not occur in the Pentateuch. Only in Genesis xiv:18 is the city referred to when it describes Melchizedek as being the king of Salem.

[8]   Finegan, J. *Light From the Ancient Past,* 1969, pp. 215ff.

[9]   Na. iii:18ff; Zp. xii:13.

[10]   Rowton, M.B. "Jeremiah and the Death of Josiah," *Journal of Near*

Eastern Studies, 1951, Vol. x, pp. 128–130.

11   II Ki. xxiii:25ff.

12   II Ki. xxii:14. The Rabbinic sages claimed that the king consulted a prophetess as she would be more tenderhearted and would pray on behalf of the people who sinned in ignorance. (See *Megillah* 14b).

13   Jer. vii:3ff.

14   Isa. iii:10–15.

15   Je. i:2–8.

16   Je. i:18.

17   Je. xxvi:6.

18   Je. xxvi:8.

19   Je. xxvi:15. The article, "Jeremiah before His Judges," by S.D. Goitein in *Bible Studies,* 1957, offers an interesting analysis of the respective trials of Jeremiah, Socrates, and Jesus. (pp. 130ff, Hebrew).

20   Je. xxvi:16. The Bible often describes the quarrels between the true and false prophets. See I Ki. xxii:24ff for the conflict between the prophet Micah and the false seer Zedekiah; Mi. iii:5. In Jeremiah we find him constantly coming into conflict with the false prophets as in chapters ii, v, vi, xiv, xxvi, xxvii, xxviii, xxix. In this connection, it is fascinating to read the clash in chapter xxviii between the false prophet Hananiah and Jeremiah. The latter walked with a yoke on his neck symbolizing the doom that was coming. This prophecy of defeat was an offence and provocation to the people of Jerusalem and especially to the war party. Hananiah breaks the yoke off Jeremiah's neck and foretells the return from Babylon of the exiles within two years. These words of Hananiah receive an enthusiastic reception and even Jeremiah at first says "amen." But then he returns and repudiates Hananiah's words, foretells destruction of Judah by Babylon, and utters a condemnation of Hananiah and judgment on all he stood for.

21   Je. xv:10; xx:14ff; xx:7.

22   Je. ii:13; xv:16; xx:11.

23   Je. xvi:1ff.

24   Je. xv:10.

25   Je. xx:7–11. The translation comes from the *Soncino Bible.*

26   II Ki. xxiv:7.

27   Je. xlix:28–33.

28   II Ki. xxiv:8ff.

29   Je. xxvi:20; ix:26.

30   Je. xxii:18ff.

31   Je. vi:1.

32   Je. xxii:13ff.

33   Je. xxii:19.

34 Je. xxii: 15ff.

35 Aharoni, Y. "The Citadel Of Ramat Rahel," in *Archaeological Discoveries in the Holy Land*, 1967, pp. 77ff.

36 *ANET*, p. 322.

37 Jer. vi: 1. Here the word for fire signals is the Hebrew *massuoth* and the same term is used in the Lachish letters.

38 Je. xxxiv:7.

39 Je. xxxviii:4.

40 *ANET*, p. 322.
Torczyner, H. *Lachish I, Lachish Letters*, 1938, *BASOR*, No. 70, p. 11; No. 73, p. 16. These letters are open to many different interpretations owing to the many lacunae in the texts. For instance, there is no definite indication that the mission of Coniah ben Elnathan concerned the capture of the prophet. The warning "take heed" could be read as being uttered by the prophet and not to the prophet.

41 Je. xxii: 18; xxxvi:30.

42 II Ki. xxv:27.

43 I Ch. iii: 17-18.

44 Albright, W.F. King Jehoachin in Exile, *The Biblical Archaeologist Reader*, 1,1961, pp. 106ff.

45 Je. xxxii.

46 Je. xxix; xxx; xxxi.

47 Je. xxxi:4ff.

CHAPTER NINE

Nehemiah—The Restoration of Judah

The fact that the Jewish people did not disappear as a nation after destruction and exile overtook them and their country was due primarily to the work of the great prophets Jeremiah and Ezekiel, and after them to Nehemiah and Ezra. The Babylonian exile was the supreme test of Judah's vitality. The Judeans were the only people in ancient times known to have been taken wholesale into captivity and still to have retained their religious and social identity. As Albright writes, "No other phenomenon in history is quite so extraordinary as the unique event represented by the Restoration of Israel in the fifth and sixth century B.C.E. At no other time in world history, so far as is known, has a people been destroyed, and then come back after a lapse of time and reestablished itself."[1] That Israel did not disappear after this overwhelming disaster was due to the philosophy of the prophets. For the exile could be interpreted in two ways. According to some people, God was Israel's infallible protector; but in the contact with Babylonian deities, he was obviously defeated. There were others, however, who believed also on covenantal grounds that the Lord had visited destruction on Judah as a punishment for its wickedness; it was this idea which was championed by the prophetic movement and which enabled Judah, unlike Israel, to survive even the catastrophe of destruction and deportation to a foreign land.

This period of Exile in Babylon and the return has been regarded by scholars as one of the most obscure periods in Jewish history. However, many important discoveries help to dispel the darkness today.

The devastation in Judah was thorough.[2] The Temple and the central religious organization were totally destroyed. The first factor to remember is that the Book of Kings tells us that the intellectuals, the leaders and the worthies of the nation were exiled to Babylon. Only the poorest and humblest of the people were left behind in Judah to be wine-dressers and husbandmen.[3] With no spiritual leaders left to guide them, this remnant of rustics gradually amalgamated and intermarried with the neighboring peoples, namely the Samaritans and the Edomites, who occupied the deserted areas of Judah. The bleak picture represented was one of a general tendency toward social and intellectual deterioration, assimilation, and syncretism. Finally, Judah, much reduced in territory, came under the control of a governor who resided in Samaria.

Though Judah presents us with a dismal picture, the Jews who went into Babylon fared well in their new environment. The Judean exiles were treated no differently from the other captive people. The common folk were generally enslaved outright, and those of higher status were given limited freedom to earn a living and choose their abode. Information about their way of life has come from archaeological sources. It appears that very quickly they learnt to sing the song of Zion on foreign soil. Being practical people, they recognized that life went on in any case, made up their minds to learn to adjust to Babylonian ways and customs, and heeded the advice of Jeremiah's letter sent to them, saying: "These are the words of the Lord of Hosts, the God of Israel: to all the exiles whom I have carried off from Jerusalem to Babylon: build houses and live in them; plant gardens and eat their produce. Marry wives and beget sons and daughters; take wives for your sons and give your daughters to husbands, so that they may bear sons and daughters and you may increase there and not dwindle away. Seek the welfare of any city to which I have carried you off, and pray to the Lord for it; on its welfare your welfare will depend."[4] It should be noted in passing that the verses exemplify the philosophy of Jeremiah discussed above. Like Ezekiel, he placed no blame on the Babylonians for having subdued Judah. The Lord, having condemned Judah, delivered her people to Babylon to serve out their sentence of exile. According to Jeremiah, the only thing to do was to suffer the captivity and build up a record of good behavior until the Lord remembered his people and restored them to Zion. Ezekiel labored tirelessly to remind the people in Babylon of their origin, their faith, and their mission. He taught them the teachings of Moses and the other prophets, and found in them not only the explanation of Judah's defeat and exile but also a program for national and spiritual regeneration. The Book of Ezekiel can be divided into almost two equal sections. The first part, namely chapters i-xiv, deals with the approaching destruction and dissolution of the nation. Ezekiel, it must be remembered, was exiled with Jehoiachin in 597 B.C.E., and he either started to prophesy in Judah and continued in Babylon, or started, as the book claims, in Babylon.[5] But the moment the prophet heard of the fall of Jerusalem his tone changed completely and he concentrated only on prophesying about the restoration of the religious life of the community in the land of their origin.

There are numerous problems involved with this book, as with that of other prophetical books. Already in the Talmud we hear echoes of this difficulty. The School of Shammai repudiated the prophecy, holding it to be apocryphal, on the grounds that the first ten chapters appeared to be theosophical in character, and that the book conflicted at certain important points with the Torah, which for them was the norm of canonical Scripture. The Torah prescribed for instance two bullocks, seven lambs, and one ram as the new moon offering.[6] Ezekiel prescribed only one unblemished bullock, six lambs, and one ram.[7] According to Talmudic tradition Hananiah ben Hezekiah, head of the School of Shammai, burned the midnight oil to the extent of 300 jars before he was able to justify the admission of the exilic work into the Scriptural canon.[8] Modern scholars have followed this up with a whole school of criticism and problems connected with the Book of Ezekiel. It is interesting that archaeology has shed some light on the life of the prophet and only this aspect will concern us in this book.

The prophet tells us that he lived and prophesied in the Jewish community in the land of the Chaldeans, by the River Kebar.[9] The River Kebar is now known from the cuneiform records to be the Babylonian canal, Kabar in central Babylonia, running between the capital Babylon and the city of Nippur sixty miles to the southeast. Nippur, excavated by an American expedition under Peters, Haynes, and Hilprecht between 1880 and 1900, yielded several thousand clay tablets, including a Sumerian account of the flood. It is not known how close to Nippur the colonies of the deported Jews to whom Ezekiel ministered were located. But Ezekiel's residence, Tel-abib[10] is now known to be Babylonian Tilabubi, "mound of the deluge," a term used in Akkadian cuneiform to designate the low mounds scattered throughout Mesopotamia.[11] The captives were settled in and near Nippur and were afforded many opportunities to live comfortably and enrich themselves by many commercial enterprises.

Torrey was one of the critics who questioned the authenticity of the Book of Ezekiel. Now archaeology affords a few important references which make this prophecy stand out in bold authenticity. One of Torrey's chief arguments agains the genuineness of Ezekiel's prophecy is the dating of events by King Jehoiachin's captivity. Since this king ruled only three months and was carried off to Babylon such a procedure is truly unusual. However, archaeology has shed fascinating light on this matter. That

Jehoiachin was considered king of Judah by the Babylonians themselves was vividly illustrated by the list of rations mentioned in the previous chapter, discovered by the archaeologist Weidner near the gate of Ishtar. Likewise the jar handles with the inscriptions "Eliakim, steward of Yaukin" also show that this man was in charge of crown property, and that the exiled monarch was still recognized as the rightful sovereign by the people of Judah and by the Babylonian authorities.

Torrey likewise claimed that Ezekiel painted the material situation of the exiles in too glowing colors. He mentions that Ezekiel claims that he lived in a house, possessed an iron pan, and could eat wheat, barley, beans, lentils, millet, and spelt. The rations allocated to prisoners and those eating at the king's table in the Bible included such food, which one might add was not too lavish.

The documents also refer to the fact that some Jews were skilled craftsmen, for the rations mention that they are for skilled laborers. Thus, Torrey's claim that the Jews in exile were not farmers nor craftsmen is contradicted by these tablets. They indicate that the word "gardener" occurs, and likewise that skilled artisans were in great demand and received good wages and working conditions.[12]

A final case in favor of Ezekiel's authenticity is the reference to the country Persia in very early sources. Torrey claimed that Ezekiel could not make mention of this nation, for it had not yet appeared on the stage of history. Archaeology has likewise provided an answer to this question.[13] Albright mentions that the land of Persia and its king, Cyrus I, were mentioned on recently discovered inscriptions at Ashurbanipal (Biblical Asenappar) of Assyria, dating from about 640 B.C.E. Now he shows that there are several Persians mentioned by name on one of the new tablets; they are said to come from the land of Parsuwash, the regular form of the name of Persia in older documents. Thus, the discoveries of Weidner have an importance far beyond the mere mention of the rations of King Jehoiachin. They supply interesting background to the prophecies of Ezekiel, indicating that the name Persia, the professions followed by the Hebrews, the food eaten, and the luxuries enjoyed were very much part of the civilization in which he lived.[14]

Further evidence of the presence of Jews in Babylon has been furnished by the discovery of the archives of a family of Babylonian businessmen known as Murashu.[15] These finds are of interest to us only in so far as they again offer proof of the presence of Jews in Babylonia. These bankers recorded a variety of names in their receipts and contracts. Among the unearthed tablets were names of many Jews who seem to have been free citizens in that country and had heeded the advice of Jeremiah, settling and prospering in the land of their exile. Many of the names in the Murashu records contain the word "Yah" in them, such as Gedaliah, Pedaiah, and others. It appears that the name Mordecai was very widespread. This might then be the right moment to leave the Jews of Babylon and see what life was like in other parts of the Persian Empire, before we describe the rise of Cyrus. The reason for this is, that we are observing the life of the Jews in exile, which remained a permanent feature even after the restoration of Judah. It is well known that the majority of Jews remained in the Diaspora and only the idealistic minority returned to the land of their fathers.

The Book of Esther affords us some meager information about the life of the Jews in Persia at this juncture in history. It is known that very few scholars accepted the historicity of the Book of Esther. But archaeology once again has shed some light on the background of this book. Firstly, it is well to note that there is an absence of Hellenistic coloring in the Book of Esther which would suggest a date at least before the late fourth century. The Book shows some familiarity with the administration of the Persian kings and especially of the construction of a palace at Shushan. [16] It is now well known from excavations that Shushan, the palace referred to in the Book of Esther, hints at the Acropolis of the Elamite city of Susa, on the site of which magnificent ruins remain from the splendor of the Persian kings. French excavators between 1880 and 1890 uncovered Xerxes' splendid royal residence covering two and a half acres. The finds of this palace were so gratifying that the Louvre in Paris devoted large rooms to the exhibition of these treasures. In fact there is no event described in the Hebrew Bible whose structural surroundings can be so vividly and accurately restored from actual excavations as "Shushan the Palace." [17]

The name Mordecai, as mentioned, occurred frequently and is derived no doubt from the name of the god Marduk. However, the names Vashti and Esther have not yet been found in contemporary sources. Especially striking is the light these discoveries at Susa shed on Haman's method for fixing the date for the destruction of the Jews by casting dice. [18] The excavator at Susa actually recovered one of these quadrangular prisms on which were engraved the numbers one, two, five and six. The word for "dice" at Susa at this time was "pur," now known to be derived from the Assyrian "puru" with the same meaning.

In the Book of Esther it is written they cast "pur" – that is, the lot. It is an explanation added for the Jews to indicate that the ceremony at Susa corresponded to the practice of casting the lot among them. [19]

Whereas the Nippur colony in Babylonia was an agricultural and commercial one, the Elephantine community (Elephantine is the Greek name for the Egyptian Yeb) was primarily a military and administrative post. A large collection of documents was acquired by archaeologists which made it clear that there was an Aramaic-speaking Jewish colony at Elephantine, Egypt, in the days of the Persian kings.[20] Owing to the dry climate in Egypt, these documents were well preserved and they clearly describe the life of these Jews at Yeb. All transactions carried out by this community were safeguarded by agreements, and contracts were drawn up in proper manner attested by witnesses, and then rolled and sealed. This procedure is reminiscent of the manner in which Jeremiah purchased his land and preserved his document.[21] The manuscripts are basically transactions dealing with business and daily life, but especially numerous marriage contracts were found. These incidentally indicate that the status of women in this community was very high indeed. It was possible for the woman to sue for divorce, just like the man. In the case of a husband who used his wife's money, he had to write out a promissory note to repay within a month. Real estate transactions are numerous among the papyri as well. The Jews could buy and sell houses and make legal transfer of gifts of houses and lands. Once again it is interesting to note that daughters seem to have been specially favored as the recipients of houses, but more particularly on the occasion of marriage.

The religious life of this community is attested by the fact that they built a temple and seemed to have worshiped YHWH. They observed the Jewish festivals, as it was the custom of the Persian kings to allow and encourage, as we shall see, their subjects to adhere to their own faith.[22] Nevertheless they appear to have worshiped other deities as well. They invoked the names of gods as 'Anatyahu and Herem-Bethel when taking oaths. It is not certain whether this colony possessed copies of Scripture. Nevertheless, one literary piece that we do know for certain that they had was the story of Ahiqar, the ancient wise man who had various exciting adventures and acquired a good deal of sound knowledge which he passed on to his son.[23] In the temple sacrifices were offered. This we learn from a letter sent to the governor of Judah requesting assistance in the rebuilding of the temple at Yeb. This manuscript informs us that anti-Jewish feeling had broken out and their temple had been destroyed c. 410 B.C.E. They appealed to the rulers in Jerusalem to help them rebuild the temple and and reinstitute the sacrificial worship. The Jewish leaders ignored their request. Thus the Elephantine Jews approached the Persian political leaders Bagoas and Sanballat. Bagoas agreed to their request but with certain restrictions. The letter to Bagoas states:

To our Lord Bagoas, governor of Judah, your servants Yedoniah and
his colleagues, the priests who are in the fortress of Elephantine.
May the God of Heaven seek after the welfare of our Lord exceedingly at all times and the nobles a thousand times more than now.
May you be happy and healthy at all times. . . [24]

These spokesmen of the Elephantine community then continue to
narrate that the priests of the god Khnub, together with the commander-
in-chief Vidaranag, who were at a fortress in Elephantine, destroyed the
temple of Yahu. They point out that their forebears built this sanctuary
and that Cambyses allowed it to stand when he conquered Egypt and
destroyed the other temples.[25]

Bagoas advised them to rebuild the temple, but to offer no animal
sacrifices there – only meal and drink offerings. The letter sent by the
Elephantine authorities to the Persian ones appear to imply such a situation.
The letter reads:

If your lordship is favorable, and the temple of our God Yahu is
rebuilt in the fortress of Elephantine, as it was formerly built, and
no sheep, ox or goat are offered there as burnt offering, but only
incense, meal-offering, and drink-offering, and if your lordship gives
orders to that effect, then we shall pay into your lordship's house
the sum of. . . and a thousand ardabs of barley.[26]

However, these Aramaic papyri assist us in arriving at a definite date
at least for Nehemiah, and shed some meager light on Ezra as well.

Now that we have seen what life was like for the Jews in the lands of
their exile, namely Babylon and Egypt, let us turn back to describe the
conquest of Babylon by Cyrus. Under Nebuchadnezzar's rule Babylon, the
capital, reached its greatest expansion and highest prosperity. Nebuchadnezzar embellished this city and turned its hanging gardens into one of the
seven wonders of the world. Nebuchadnezzar died in 561 B.C.E. and was
succeeded by his son, Evil-merodach who showed mercy to Jehoiachin.
Little is known of his brief reign and those of his successors, a brother-in-
law and a nephew. The lack of an energetic ruler led to the Empire's rapid
decline. The last king of the Neo-Babylonian Empire was Nabonidus, a
priest who was more interested in prayer and theology than in politics. He
was blind to the dangers which threatened Babylonia from the rise of
Persia, which under the leadership of Cyrus had already caused the downfall of Media. For years Nabonidus lived in northern Arabia and during

that time his son, Belshazzar, mentioned in Daniel,[27] acted as his viceroy. But the day of reckoning came upon the great Babylonian Empire. The fall of this great giant reminds us of the words of Isaiah:

> Babylon fairest of Kingdoms
> proud beauty of the Chaldeans,
> shalt be like Sodom and Gomorrah
> when God overthrew them.
> Never again shall she be inhabited,
> no man shall dwell in her through all the ages;
> Her time draws very near,
> and her days have not long to run.[28]

Or as Jeremiah put it:

> I will plead your cause, I will avenge you,
> I will dry up her sea and make her waters fail
> and Babylon shall become a heap of ruins, a haunt of wolves
> a scene of horror and a derision, with no inhabitants.[29]

The last days of Babylon were indeed heralded by the dramatic rise to power of Cyrus, king of Anshan, a vassal of Astyages, king of Media. Cyrus revolted against his suzerain and defeated Croesus of Lydia, thereby gaining control of Asia Minor. In 539 B.C.E. he attacked Babylon. The Babylonian records depict his peaceful conquest of the city as follows:

> Without any battle, he Marduk made him enter his town Babylon, sparing Babylon any calamity. He delivered into his [Cyrus'] hand Nabonidus, the king who did not worship him [Marduk]. All the inhabitants of Babylon as well as the entire country of Sumer and Akkad, princes and governors [included], bowed to him [Cyrus] and kissed his feet, jubilant that he had received the kingship, and with shining faces. Happily they greeted him as a master through whose help they had come again to life from death and had been spared damage and disaster and they worshiped his very name. . . When I entered Babylon as a friend and when I established the seat of government in the place of the ruler under jubilation and rejoicing, Marduk, the great lord, induced the magnanimous inhabitants of Babylon to love me and I was daily endeavoring to worship him. My numerous troops walked in Babylon in peace, I did not allow anybody to terrorize any place of the country of Sumer and Akkad.[30]

Thus Cyrus brought peace and prosperity to the countries he conquered and did not inflict any suffering upon them. He reversed the cruel policies of the Assyrians and Babylonians and did not transfer the inhabitants from their native lands to other remote places. On the contrary, he allowed those inhabitants who wished to do so to return to their original home-land. The Judeans were the people who immediately availed themselves of his magnanimity. The book of Ezra contains two proclamations, one in Hebrew and the other in Aramaic, which Cyrus issued allowing the Jews to return to their mother country, Zion. The first one reads as follows:

> This is the word of Cyrus King of Persia: the Lord the God of
> heaven has given me all the kingdoms of the earth, and he himself
> has charged me to build him a house at Jerusalem in Judah. To every
> man of his people now among you I say, God be with you, and let
> him go up to Jerusalem in Judah, and rebuild the house of the Lord,
> the God of Israel, the God whose city is Jerusalem. And every
> remaining Jew, wherever he may be living, may claim aid from his
> neighbors in that place, silver and gold, goods and cattle, in addition
> to the voluntary offerings for the house of God in Jerusalem. [31]

The second of the two decrees in the Book of Ezra written in Aramaic, [32] rather than the one quoted above written in Hebrew was held by scholars to be the more authentic one. However, when compared with other Ancient Near East royal decrees, particularly those of the Persian period, both documents appear to be substantially accurate and authentic. The first was a characteristic royal proclamation framed for verbal utterance in the language of the people addressed, while the second was not for public use but was reserved for filing in the archives of the king. Quite clearly there is every reason to regard the Biblical accounts as authentic. As Albright writes: "The substantial historicity of the edict of Cyrus in 538 has been confirmed by archaeological discoveries." [33]

The returning exiles were led by the descendants of the Davidic house. The most prominent among them were Sheshbazzar and Zerubbabel. [34] By 516 B.C.E. the Temple was rebuilt, owing to the efforts of Haggai and Zechariah. Then for a long period of time we know nothing about the events in Judah till we come to the period of Nehemiah and Ezra. Here the Aramaic papyri and other sources help to pierce through the darkness. Scholars have vied with each other in their endeavor to find convincing evidence as to who came first, Ezra or Nehemiah. To this question we now turn.

The history of Israel presents few problems more perplexing and difficult of certain solution than the one concerning Ezra and Nehemiah. Scholars have offered three suggestions for solving this complex issue. Some accept the position, seemingly supported by Scripture, that Ezra came in the seventh year of Artaxerxes I (458 B.C.E.), in other words, placing him 14 years before Nehemiah's arrival in Jerusalem.[35] Other scholars regard the seventh year as the seventh year of Artaxerxes II (398 B.C.E.) and place Ezra's coming after Nehemiah had completed his work and passed completely from the scene. The third opinion places Ezra's arrival after Nehemiah's in 428 B.C.E., but before the latter's activity had been finished. The supporters of this third point of view regard "the seventh year" as a scribal error for some other year — perhaps the thirty-seventh year of the reign of Artaxerxes I. The real difficulty revolves around the date of Ezra's arrival in Jerusalem. The date of Nehemiah's career is now certain, having been independently confirmed by evidence from the Elephantine texts as we shall show.

In these manuscripts, already discussed above, we find the name of a high priest, Johanan, who according to Nehemiah xi:22, was the second high priest after Eliashib, the priest referred to in the days of Nehemiah. Again in Nehemiah xii:10, 11, we have a list which places Johanan after Eliashib. Another important reference is to be found in Josephus, who speaks of an officer of the Persians, Bagoas, and a high priest John, which is Johanan.[36] According to this reference, Bagoas, living in the days of Johanan, must have ruled after Nehemiah. Bagoas is the governor referred to in the Aramaic letter which the Jews of Elephantine addressed to him and the other leaders of Judah, asking them for assistance in rebuilding their destroyed temple to Yahu. The Sanballat referred to in this same letter is the notorious enemy of Nehemiah who endeavored to hinder his work of rebuilding the wall and conspired unsuccessfully to have him done away with. We are thus led to the conclusion that Nehemiah lived before 407 B.C.E. Since he went to Jerusalem in the twentieth year of King Artaxerxes, we look for a king by this name who ruled prior to 407 B.C.E. This is, of course, Artaxerxes I, who reigned from 465 to 425 B.C.E. — which means that Nehemiah's arrival in Jerusalem is to be dated at about 444 B.C.E. Thus, in a most striking manner the discovery of an Aramaic papyrus in Egypt, hundreds of miles away from the Land of the Bible, enables us to give an exact date as to the existence of an important Biblical personality.[37]

The Aramaic papyri discovered by the Ta'amireh Bedouin in a cave of the Wadi Dâliyeh in 1962 have shed more fascinating light on the figure of Sanballat, who features so prominently in the Book of Nehemiah. The ardent Judean reformer, Nehemiah found his most vehement opponent in the man called Sanballat. The discovered papyri reads ". . . Yahu, son of Sanballat, governor of Samaria." [38] The appearance of the name Sanballat, who flourished in Samaria in the first half of the 4th century, gives an unexpected answer to a question debated for generations by students of the history of the Jews and the Samaritans in the post-exilic era.

Sanballat is mentioned very frequently in the canonical book of Nehemiah. [39] Sanballat is also mentioned, as we have shown, in the Elephantine papyri and now in the newly discovered Dâliyeh manuscript. Sanballat was governor of Samaria when Nehemiah arrived in Jerusalem and by 407 B.C.E., he was already an old man whose son Delaiah acted in his name. This governor of Samaria gained notoriety for his strong opposition to the restoration of the walls of Jerusalem and for plotting against the life of Nehemiah in league with Tobiah, the governor of Ammon, and Geshem, king of the Kedarite League, whose territory extended from northern Arabia into southern Palestine. Nehemiah, however, proved to be a very powerful opponent. He outwitted his enemies and succeeded in rebuilding the wall and fortifying it. It should be mentioned here that Kenyon, who excavated in Jerusalem claimed to have found Nehemiah's wall, and includes a picture of the relics of this edifice in her book. She writes: "The wall in the background was built by Nehemiah, who was the Governor of Jerusalem from 446 to 434 B.C.E. The walls of Jerusalem destroyed by Nebuchadnezzar in 586 B.C.E. had remained in ruins until the time of Nehemiah. In the Book of Nehemiah, a description is given of how he rebuilt the walls in the remarkably short period of fifty-two days. This has been always taken to mean that substantial remnants of the earlier walls survived and that Nehemiah had only to repair them. The 1961–7 excavations have shown that the walls, low on the eastern slope, were in fact not repaired. Nehemiah, when he made his survey of the state of the walls, found the eastern slope of the hill in chaos as the result of the collapse of the terraces. . . He therefore decided to abandon this whole area, and to build his wall on the crest of the eastern ridge." [40] She continues: "The archaeological evidence is not only clear that the eastern slope was abandoned, but has also enabled Nehemiah's wall to be identified. . . An excavation against the foot of this scarp showed that midden rubbish tipped over the wall, accumulating against the scarp belonged to the fifth–fourth centuries B.C. The wall could therefore be dated to the time of Nehemiah. It was solidly built, c. 2.75 meters thick, but its finish was rough, as might be expected in work executed so rapidly." [41]

Now to return to our story of Sanballat as it emerges from the evidence of the new papyri. The Book of Nehemiah, in short, tells the story of Nehemiah's life and work from the time he obtained the permission of the Persian king to go to Judah, institute the building of the wall, increase the population of the city, remove the social evils that prevailed, and together with Ezra, reorganize the religious life of the nation. After a governorship of 12 years, Nehemiah returned to the Persian court. In his absence his work suffered and the old evils reappeared. He therefore revisited Jerusalem and instituted resolute measures for their eradication. He was a powerful personality who impressed himself strongly on his contemporaries.

At the close of his memoirs, recounting the details of his reforms in Judah, Nehemiah relates an episode in which Sanballat plays an important role. Nehemiah discovered that the son of Joiada the Zadokite high priest and the daughter of Sanballat the Horonite had been joined in a diplomatic marriage uniting the two great families of Judah and Samaria.[42] Nehemiah was furious when he heard about this, and in righteous indignation chased the young man out of Jerusalem. Unfortunately the name of Sanballat's son-in-law is not given in the verse. Josephus tells us that when Johanan son of Joiada became high priest he killed his brother Jesus in the temple. The Persian governor was infuriated by this action, entered the temple by force, defiled it, and imposed a heavy tax on the Jews for seven years.[43] Jesus had apparently laid claim to the high priesthood with the aid of Bagoas, the Persian governor of Judah. It would not be suprising if Jesus were the elder brother, son-in-law of Sanballat, who had proper claims to the diadem.[44]

However, Josephus tells a similar story with similar names, only the plot is laid in a different period of history, in the era of Darius III and Alexander the Great. Sanballat, appointed governor of Samaria by Darius III, arranged a marriage between his daughter and a certain Manasseh identified as the brother of Johanan the high priest. Manasseh was expelled from the altar and returned to Samaria. This, according to Josephus, angered Sanballat and he built a temple for his son-in-law on Mt. Gerizim with the blessing of Alexander the Great.[45]

Most scholars viewed these two stories with great skepticism, and regarded the account of Josephus as a reflection of the stories of the Biblical Sanballat and of the intermarriage of the 5th century. Cowley wrote: "The view that there were two Sanballats, each governor of Samaria and each with a daughter who married a brother of a High Priest at Jerusalem, is a solution too desperate to be entertained."[46] Though this scholar and others thought it improbable that there were two Sanballats, the most striking information emerges from the papyri of Dâliyeh. This new manuscript appears to indicate that there were probably not only two men by this name but three. As Cross writes: "Once the existence of a second Sanballat, father of governors of Samaria, is firmly established, paradoxically it becomes far easier to accept a third Sanballat in the age of Alexander. That is to say, with the appearance of Sanballat II in the Dâliyeh Papyri, most if not all objections to a Sanballat III melt away. The point is this. We know well that it was a regular practice in the Achaemenid empire for high offices, that of satrap or governor, to become hereditary. It is evident that the Sanballatids held the governorship of Samaria for several generations, as did the Tobiads of Ammon. Moreover, we know that the practice of paponymy (naming a child for its grand-father) was much in vogue among the Jews and surrounding nations precisely in this era. One may refer to the Tobiads, where paponymy is documented for about nine generations. The high priests of Judah in the Hellenistic era present almost as striking a picture. The Oniads alternate with the names Onias and Simon over five generations."[47]

Thus, with the help of the newly discovered papyri, one can reconstruct the sequence of governors at Samaria in the 5th and 4th centuries. Sanballat the Horonite is evidently the founder of this line of governors. He was a mature man when Nehemiah arrived to alter the state of affairs in Judah. His son Delaiah acted for his aged father as early as 407 B.C.E. The grandson of Sanballat, Sanballat II, evidently inherited the governorship early in the 4th century, to be succeeded by an elder son, Yeshua, and later by another son, Hananiah. Hananiah was governor by 354 B.C.E., and his son, or his brother's son, Sanballat III, succeeded to the governorship in the time of Darius III and Alexander the Great.[48] The Dâliyeh papyri, together with the Elephantine, help date and give an excellent background for the work of Nehemiah, and the men with whom he was in contact.

The problem with dating Ezra is somewhat more difficult, and we do not have as much archaeological evidence as for Nehemiah. The date in which Ezra carried out his activities is not clearly indicated in the Bible, where it merely says that it was in the seventh year of Artaxerxes the King.[49] The question immediately arises as to whether this was the first or the second king by the name Artaxerxes. If it was the first, the date would be 458 B.C.E., but if it was the second it would be 398 B.C.E. The Bible certainly gives the impression, as already mentioned, that Ezra arrived in Jerusalem before Nehemiah. There is little in the way of archaeological evidence to help solve this problem conclusively. However, one discovered papyrus which indicates King Darius' concern for the religious observance

Figure 30. A portion of an Aramaic papyrus dated to the 5th century B.C.E. In it a father in Yeb (Elephantine), makes a gift of a house to his daughter.

of his Jewish subjects might shed some light on Ezra and his activities and place him before the the arrival of Nehemiah. One document reads as follows:

To my brethren Yedoniah and his colleagues in the Jewish garrison, your brother Hananiah. The welfare of my brothers may God seek at all times. Now, this year, the fifth year of King Darius, word was sent from the king to Arsames saying, "Authorize a festival of unleavened bread for the Jewish garrison." So do you count fourteen days of the month for Nisan and observe the Passover, and from the 15th to the 21st of Nisan observe the festival of unleavened bread. Be ritually clean and take heed. Do no work on the 15th or the 21st day nor drink beer, nor eat anything in which there is leaven from the 14th at sundown until the 21st of Nisan. For seven days it shall not be seen among you. Do not bring it into your dwellings but seal it up between these dates. By order of King Darius to my brethren Yedoniah and the Jewish garrison, your brother Hananiah.[50]

Artaxerxes in his seventh year, following the practice of other Persian kings, could have decided to investigate the religious situation of the Jews in Judah. Such an interest taken by a Persian king in the affairs of his subjects, as the above quoted papyri indicates, was not unique or unusual. Ezra, a Jew living in Persia, who probably had a reputation as an expert in Jewish law was thus selected by the king and commissioned to go to Judah and investigate the state of religious affairs there. He was to take free-will offerings from the Jews in his own land and have access to the government funds if he needed extra money. After investigating the situation there he was to teach the ignorant and then enforce the law with penalties.[51] Meanwhile illegal measures were taking place to rebuild the wall around Jerusalem and fortify the city. This apparently was against the wishes of the king, and the next thing we know is that he forbade the building of the wall and the work of Ezra was cut short.[52] At this juncture Ezra may have fallen into disfavor and gone into retirement, and only resumed his activities with the arrival of Nehemiah. If this theory could be accepted as a true picture of events, then Ezra preceded Nehemiah and later they worked hand in hand as the book indicates.[53] The truth is however, that we do not have enough external evidence in the case of Ezra to solve this thorny problem.

Nevertheless, let us conclude by stating that it was due to these two men that, in the third quarter of the 5th century B.C.E., a thorough-going reorganization took place of the Jewish community in Judah which clarified its status and saved it from disintegration. It was Nehemiah who gave the community political status and administrative reform, while Ezra organized and reformed its spiritual life. The discovered archaeological material, especially relating to Nehemiah but also to the whole period in general, makes this picture of his activity most acceptable. In Judaism, Ezra is acknowledged as having been one of its outstanding personalities. The Talmud says: "When the Torah was forgotten in Israel, Ezra came up from Babylon and established it."[54] Nehemiah and Ezra appear by temperament and action to have been completely different kinds of persons. Nevertheless Nehemiah was a most powerful personality who left his imprint on his age. The esteem in which he was held can perhaps be seen from the words of Ben Sira, who, singing the praises of the famous men of Israel, includes Nehemiah as one whose "memorial" is great; who raised up for us the walls that were fallen, and set up the gates and bars, and raised up our homes again.[55]

NOTES

[1] Albright, W.F. "Israel — Prophetic Vision and Historical Fulfilment" in Davis, M. *Israel: its Role in Civilization,* 1956, pp. 31ff.

[2] Burrows, M. *What Mean These Stones?* , 1960, pp. 107.

[3] II Ki. xxv:12.

[4] Je. xxix:4ff.

[5] Mo'ed Katan 25a; also Rashi *ad loc.; Mechilta Bo i;* Targum to Ezk. i:3.

[6] Nu. xxviii:11.

[7] Ezk. xlvi:6.

[8] *Shabbat* 14b; *Menahoth* 45a; *Hagigah* 13a.

[9] Ezk. i:1, 2.

[10] Ezk. iii:15.

[11] Albright, W.F.*Old Testament Commentary,* 1954, p. 105.

[12] Albright, W.F. "King Joiachin in Exile," in *The Biblical Archaeologist Reader,* 1961, 1, pp. 111ff.

[13] Ezk. xxvii:10; xxxviii:5.

[14] *Ibid.,* note [12] .

[15] Olmstead, A.T. *History of the Persian Empire,* 1948, pp. 299, 356—358.

[16] Bentzen, A. *Introduction to the Old Testament,* 1948, Vol. 11, p. 192.

[17] Price, I. *The Monuments of the Old Testament,* 1925, p. 408.

[18] *Ibid,* also Est. iii:7;

[19] *Ibid.*

[20] Kraeling, E.G. Light on the Elephantine Colony, in *The Biblical Archaeologist Reader,* 1961, 1, pp. 128ff.

21   Je. xxxii:14.
22   *ANET*, p. 491.
23   *ANET*, p. 427–430.
24   *Ibid.*
25   *Ibid.*
26   *ANET*, p. 492.
27   Dn. V:1ff.
28   Is. xiii:19ff.
29   Je. Li:36ff.
30   *ANET*, pp. 315–316.
31   Ezr. vi:3ff.
32   Ezr. vi:3ff.
33   Albright, W.F. *The Biblical Period from Abraham to Ezra,* 1963, p. 87.
34   Zc. iv:3.
35   Ezr. vii:7.
36   Josephus, F. *Antiquities of the Jews,* Book xi, 7, 1.
37   *ANET,* p. 491.
38   Cross, F.M. "Papyri of the Fourth Century B.C. from Dâliyeh," in *New Directions in Biblical Archaeology,* edited by Freedman, D.N. and Greenfield, J.C., 1971, pp. 45ff.
39   Ne. ii:10, 19; iii:33; iv:1, 2, 5, 12, 14; xii:28.
40   Kenyon, K.M. *Jerusalem,* 1967, p. 122, note to figure [54]
41   *Ibid.*
42   Ne. xiii:28.
43   Josephus, F. *Antiquities of the Jews,* Book xi, vii, 1.
44   *Ibid.*
45   *Ibid.* Book xi, viii, 2,3, 4.
46   Cowley, A. *Aramaic Papyri of the Fifth Century B.C.,* Oxford University Press, 1923, p. 110.
47   Cross, F.M. "Papyri of the Fourth Century B.C. from Dâliyeh," in *New Directions in Biblical Archaeology,* edited by Freedman, D.N. and Greenfield J.C., 1971, pp. 61ff.
48   *Ibid.*
49   Ezr. vii:7.
50   *ANET,* p. 491.
51   Ezr. vii:11ff.
52   Ezr. iv:11ff.
53   Ezr. vii-x; Ne. ii:11 – vii.: 73; Ne. 1–8, xii:36; viii.
54   *Succoth,* 20a.
55   Ecclesiasticus, xlix:13.

Bibliography

BIBLICAL TEXTS, TRANSLATIONS AND COMMENTARIES

The New English Bible, The Old Testament, 1970.
Cambridge Bible for Schools and Colleges (different dates and authors for the various books).
Artom, E.S.
   Commentary to the Hebrew Bible, 1961.
Cohen, A.
   Soncino Bible (different dates for the various books).
Friedlander, M.
   Hebrew Bible with English Translation, 1953.
Gordon, S.L.
   Commentary to the Hebrew Bible, 1954.
Hertz, J.H.
   Pentateuch and Haftorahs, 1952.
   International Critical Commentary to the O.T. (different dates for different books).
Kittel, R.
   Biblia Hebraica, 1937.
   Mikra'ot Gedolot – The Bible with 32 Commentaries, 1951.
   The New Testament, Cambridge University Press.

BIBLE DICTIONARIES

Butterick, G.A.
   The Interpreter's Dictionary of the Bible, 1965 (4 volumes).
Davis, J.D.
   The Westminster Dictionary of the Bible, 1944.
Douglas, J.D.
   The New Bible Dictionary, 1962.
Hamburger, J.
   Real Encyclopädie des Judentums, Neustrelitz, 1896.
Hastings, J.
   Dictionary of the Bible, 1954[13] in one volume.

Hastings, J.
   Dictionary of the Bible, 1951 [13] in five volumes.
Sukenik, E.L. and Cassuto, M.D.
   Encyclopedia mikra'it, 1955ff.

ENCYCLOPEDIAS

Landman, I. (editor).
   The Universal Jewish Encyclopedia, 1948 (10 volumes).
Roth, C. and Wigoder, G. (editors)
   Encyclopaedia Judaica, 1970 (16 volumes).
Singer, I. (editor)
   The Jewish Encyclopedia, 1905.

DICTIONARIES

Jastrow, M.
   *A Dictionary of the Targumim, The Talmud Babli and Yerushalmi, and
   The Midrashic Literature,* 1943.
Ben-Jehudah, Eliezer
   Thesaurus Totius Hebraitatis, 1940.
Koehler-Baumgartner.
   Lexicon in Veteris Testamenti Libros, 1958.
   Supplementum ad Lexicon in Veteris Testamenti Libros, 1958.
Mandelkern S.
   Veteris Testamenti Concordantiae Hebraicae atque Chaldaicae,
   1917.

TALMUDIC REFERENCES

   Babylonian Talmud (according to usual editions).
Epstein, I. (editor).
   Babylonian Talmud (English transl.) Soncino Edition, 1952.
Maimonides
   The Guide of the Perplexed, 1881 (trans. M. Friedlander).
   Mishneh Torah (usual editions).

GENERAL

Aharoni, Y.
   The Land of the Bible, 1962, 1967.
Albright, W.F.
   The Archaeology of Palestine, 1956.
   Archaeology and the Bible, 1932.

Archaeology and the Religion of Israel, 1946.
From the Stone Age to Christianity, 1957.
The Biblical Period from Abraham to Ezra, 1963.
Allen, H.C. and Flack, E.E.
Old Testament Commentary, 1957.
Amiran, R.
Ancient Pottery of the Holy Land, 1969.
Anderson, B.W.
The Living World of the Old Testament, 1958.
Barnett, R.D.
Illustrations of Old Testament History, 1968.
Barthélemy D. and Milik J.T.
Discoveries in the Judean Desert, 1955.
Bentzen, A.
Introduction to the Old Testament, 1948.
Breasted, J.H.
A History of Egypt, 1959.
Bright, J.
History of Israel, 1964.
Bronner, L.
The Stories of Elijah and Elisha, 1968.
Sects and Separatism during the Second Jewish Commonwealth, 1967.
Burrows, M.
What Mean These Stones? , 1957.
The Dead Sea Scrolls, 1956.
More Light on the Dead Sea Scrolls, 1958.
Campbell, Jr. E.F.
The Biblical Archaeologist Reader, 2, 1964; 3, 1970.
Cassuto, U.
The Documentary Hypothesis and the Composition of the Pentateuch, 1961 (translated from Hebrew by I. Abrahams).
Charles, R.H.
Eschatology, The Doctrine of a Future Life, 1963.
Chiera, E.
They Wrote on Clay, 1939.
Cornill, C.H.
The Prophets of Israel, 1910.
Cowley, A.
Aramaic Papyri of the Fifth Century B.C., 1923.
Crowell Company Publication
Archaeological Discoveries in the Holy Land, 1967.
Curtis, E.L. and Madsen, A.A.
A Critical and Exegetical Commentary to the Book of Chronicles, 1952.

De Vaux, R.
    Ancient Israel: Its Life and Institutions, 1961 (translated from
    French by J. McHugh).
Engnell, I.
    Gamla Testamentet I, 1945.
Epstein, I.
    The Faith of Judaism, 1954.
Ewald, H.
    History of Israel, 1878.
Eybers, I. (editor)
    De Fructu Oris Sui, Essays in Honour of Adrianus van Selms, 1971.
Finegan J.
    Light from the Ancient Past, 1969.
Flack, E.E. and Alleman, H.C.
    Old Testament Commentary, 1957.
Fohrer, G.
    Elia, 1957.
Freedman, D.N. and Greenfield, J.C. (editors)
    *New Directions in Biblical Archaeology,*1971.
Freedman, D.N. and Wright, G.E. (editors)
    Biblical Archaeologist Reader, 1, 1961; 2,1964; 3, 1970.
Freud, S.
    Moses and Monotheism, 1959.
Garstang, J.
    Joshua – Judges, 1931.
Glueck, N.
    Rivers in the Desert, 1959.
    Other Side of the Jordan, 1945.
Gordon, C.H.
    *Ugaritic Textbook Grammar, Texts in Transliteration, Cuneiform
    Selections, Glossary, Indices,* 1965.
    Ugaritic Literature, 1949.
    The Ancient Near East, Revised Edition of *An Introduction to Old
    Testament Times,* 1953.
    The World of the Old Testament, 1958, 1964.
    Before the Bible, 1962.
    Forgotten Scripts, 1968.
Gunkel, H.
    Elias, Jahve und Baal, 1906.
Harrison, R.K.
    An Introduction to the Old Testament, 1970.
Heaton, E.W.
    Everyday Life in Old Testament Times, 1956.
Heidel, A.
    The Babylonian Genesis, 1969.

Herford, R.T.
    The Pharisees, 1962.
Hertz, J.H.
    The Pentateuch and Haftorahs, 1962.
Heschel, A.J.
    The Prophets, 1962.
James, F.
    Personalities of the Old Testament, 1963.
James, O.E.
    The Old Testament in the Light of Anthropology, 1934.
Josephus, F.
    The Life and Works of Flavius Josephus, translated by Whiston, W., no date given.
Kaufmann, Y.
    Toledoth HaEmunah HaYisraelith, 1955.
    (*The Religion of Israel*, 1960.)
Kenyon, K.M.
    Beginning in Archaeology, 1957.
    Digging up Jericho, 1957.
    Archaeology in the Holy Land, 1970.
    Jerusalem, 1967.
    Royal Cities of the Old Testament, 1971.
Kierkegaard, S.
    Fear and Trembling, 1958.
Kitchen, K.A.
    Ancient Orient and Old Testament, 1966.
Kittel, R.
    History of the Hebrews, 1896.
Klausner, J.
    The Messianic Idea in Israel, 1955.
Kraeling, E.G.
    The Brooklyn Museum Aramaic Papyri, 1953.
Kramer, S.N.
    History Begins at Sumer, 1956.
Lapp, P.W.
    Biblical Archaeology and History, 1969.
Luckenbell, D.D.
    Ancient Records of Assyria and Babylonia, 1926.
Madsen, A.A. and Curtis, E.L.
    A Critical and Exegetical Commentary to the Book of Chronicles, 1952.
Maybaum, I.
    The Sacrifice of Isaac, 1958.
Mazar, B. (editor)
    Views of the Biblical World, 1961.

McHardy, W.D.
  Hebrew and Semitic Studies, 1963.
Meek, T.J.
  Hebrew Origins, 1936.
Mendenhall, G.E.
  Law and Covenant in Israel and the Ancient Near East, 1955
Montet, P.
  Le drame d'Avaris, 1940.
Nielsen, E.
  Oral Tradition, 1954.
Olmstead, A.T.
  History of the Persian Empire, 1948.
Orlinsky, H.M.
  Ancient Israel, 1956.
Owen, G.F.
  Archaeology and the Bible, 1961.
Parrot, A.
  Abraham and His Times, English translation, 1971.
Pfeiffer, R.H.
  An Introduction to the Old Testament, 1941.
Piggott, S.
  Approach to Archaeology, 1959.
Price, I.
  The Monuments of the Old Testament, 1925.
Pritchard, J.H.
  Ancient Near Eastern Texts (ANET), 1955.
  The Ancient Near East in Pictures (ANEP), 1954.
  Archaeology and the Old Testament, 1958.
Reik, T.
  Temptation, 1958.
Robinson, H.W.
  Corporate Personality in Ancient Israel, 1964.
Rowley, H.H.
  From Joseph to Joshua, 1948.
  The Servant of the Lord and other Essays on the Old Testament, 1965.
  The Old Testament and Modern Study, 1956.
  The Growth of the Old Testament, 1969.
  Peake's Commentary on the Bible (together with Black, M.), 1962.
Russell, B.
  History of Western Philosophy, 1957.
Sanders, J.A.
  Near Eastern Archaeology in the Twentieth Century, Essays in Honour of Nelson Glueck, 1970.

Sarna, N.M.
>   *Understanding Genesis*, 1967.
Schaeffer, C.F.A.
>   *Cuneiform Texts of Ras Shamra-Ugaritic Texts*, 1949.
Segal, M.H.
>   *The Pentateuch,* 1967.
>   *Mevo HaMikra*, 1957.
Sellin, E. and Watzinger, C.
>   *Jericho*, 1913.
Smith, G.A.
>   *Historical Geography of the Holy Land*, 1894.
Smith, W.R.
>   *The Religion of the Semites*, 1959.
Snaith, N.H.
>   *Distinctive Ideas of the Old Testament*, 1946.
Speiser, E.A.
>   *Genesis*, Anchor Bible Series, 1964.
van Selms, A.
>   *Marriage and Family Life in Ugaritic Literature*, 1954.
van Zyl, A.H.
>   *The Moabites*, 1960.
Watzinger, C. and Sellin, E.
>   *Jericho*, 1913.
Wellhausen, J.
>   *Prologomena to the History of Israel*, English edition, 1961.
Wiseman, D.J.
>   *Illustrations from Biblical Archaeology*, 1966.
Winton Thomas, D.
>   *Archaeology and the Old Testament Study*, 1967.
Woolley, C.L.
>   *Excavations at Ur*, 1954.
Wright, G.E.
>   *Biblical Archaeology*, 1957.
>   *The Westminster Historical Atlas to Bible*, 1957.
>   *The Old Testament against its Environment*, 1950.
>   *Biblical Archaeologist Reader*, 1, 1961.
>   *The Bible and the Ancient Near East*, 1961.
Yadin, Y.
>   *The Message of the Scrolls*, 1957.
>   *The Scroll of the War of the Sons of Light Against the Sons of Darkness*, 1962.
>   *Masada*, 1966.
>   *Bar-Kokhba*, 1971.

PERIODICALS, PAPERS, AND OTHER PUBLICATIONS

Archiv für Orientforschung
Weidner, E.F., "Der Vertrag Asarhaddons mit Ba'al von Tyrus," p. 29.

Archiv Orientalni
van Selms, A., "The Goring Ox in Babylonian and Biblical Law," 1960, pp 321ff.

BASOR — *Bulletin of the American Schools of Oriental Research*
Mendelsohn, I.,"Samuel's Denunciation of Kingship in Light of Akkadian document from Ugarit," 1966, No. 143, pp 17ff.

CNW — *Christian News from Israel*
Flusser, D., "Melchizedek and the New Testament," 1966, pp. 23—29

Handelingen van het zeventiende Vlaamse Filologen Congres
De Langhe, R., "Jahweh, de wolkenrijder," 1948, p. 96.

Hebrew Union College Annual
Glueck, N., "Some Biblical Sites in the Jordan Valley," 1950-1951, p. 111.

Hervormde Teologiese Studies
van Selms, A., "Die Uitdrukking 'Man van God' in die Bybel," 1959, xv, pp. 133-149.

IEJ — *Israel Exploration Journal*
Aharoni, Y., "Excavations at Arad," 1967, Vol. 17, No. 4.
Avigad, N., "The Epitaph of a Royal Steward from Siloam Village," 1953, Vol. 3, No. 3.

JAOS — *Journal of the American Oriental Society*
Montgomery, J.A., "Ras Shamra Notes," III, 1935, pp. 55, 89ff.

JQR — *Jewish Quarterly Review*
Segal, M., "The Religion of Israel before Sinai," 1961, pp. 52, 41—48.

JBL — *Journal of Biblical Literature*
Greenberg, M., "Another Look at Rachel's Theft of the Teraphim, " pp. 239ff.

NTS — *New Testament Studies*
De Jonge, M. and Van der Woude, A.S. "11Q Melchizedik and the New Testament," 1966, No. 4, Vol. 12, pp. 301ff.

TSF — *Journal for Theological Students*
Kitchen, K.A., Bulletin no. 59, 60, 61, 62.

List of Abbreviations

Gn.	Genesis	La.	Lamentations
Ex.	Exodus	Ezk.	Ezekiel
Lv.	Leviticus	Dn.	Daniel
Nu.	Numbers	Ho.	Hosea
Dt.	Deuteronomy	Joel	Joel
Jos.	Joshua	Am.	Amos
Jdg.	Judges	Ob.	Obadiah
Ru.	Ruth	Jon.	Jonah
Sa.	Samuel	Mi.	Micah
Ki.	Kings	Na.	Nahum
Ch.	Chronicles	Hab.	Habakkuk
Ezr.	Ezra	Zp.	Zephaniah
Ne.	Nehemiah	Hg.	Haggai
Est.	Esther	Zc.	Zechariah
Jb.	Job	Mal.	Malachi
Ps.	Psalms	D.S.S.	The Dead Sea Scrolls
Pr.	Proverbs	O.T.	Old Testament
Ec.	Ecclesiastes	No.	Number
Ct.	Canticles	B.C.E.	Before the Common Era (=B.C.)
Is.	Isaiah		
Je.	Jeremiah	C.E.	Common Era (=A.D.)

Index

Illustration Credits

Figs. 1, 3: *Encyclopaedia Judaica,* Jerusalem, 1971, Vol. XVI; Vol. II.

Fig. 2: By courtesy of the Ashmolean Museum, Oxford, England.

Fig. 4: E. Unger, *Babylon, die Heilige Stadt, W. De Gruyter,* Berlin, 1931.

Figs. 5, 10: C.R. Lepsius, *Denkmaeler aus Aegypten und Aethiopien,* Berlin 1849.

Fig. 6: L.H. Grollenberg, *Atlas of the Bible,* Nelson, London, 1957.

Figs. 7, 8: *Qadmoniot, Quarterly for the Antiquities of Eretz-Israel and Biblical Lands,* Israel Exploration Society, Jerusalem. Vol. IV, No. 4 (16), 1971.

Figs, 9, 24: London, The Trustees of the British Museum.

Fig. 12: Jerusalem, Israel Museum, Israel Department of Antiquities collection.

Fig. 13: Paris, Louvre, Ao 15775.

Fig. 14: Ch. Virolleaud, *La Déesse 'Anat,* P. Guethner, Paris, 1938.

Figs. 15, 21: Department of Antiquities and Museums, Jerusalem.

Figs. 17, 18 photo: David Eisenberg, Jerusalem.

Fig. 19: Jerusalem, Israel Museum.

Fig. 20: By courtesy of Y. Yadin, Jerusalem.

Figs. 22, 25: Replicas in Israel Museum, Jerusalem.

Fig. 23: Aleppo, Syria, National Museum.

Fig. 26: Baghdad Museum.

Fig. 27: Y. Aharoni, Tel-Aviv University, Institute of Archaeology.

Fig. 28: J.B. Pritchard, *The Ancient Near East, Texts and Pictures Relating to the Old Testament* (Supplementary), Princeton University Press, New Jersey, 1969.

Fig. 29: M.A. Beek, *Atlas of Mesopotamia,* Nelson, London, 1962.

Fig. 30: By courtesy of the Brooklyn Museum, New York.

Cover: London, The Trustees of the British Museum.